By the Light of the Moon

By the Light of the Moon

Candrakīrti's Prāsaṅgika Madhyamaka

JAY L. GARFIELD AND SONAM THAKCHÖE

OXFORD UNIVERSITY PRESS

OXFORD
UNIVERSITY PRESS

Oxford University Press is a department of the University of Oxford. It furthers the University's objective of excellence in research, scholarship, and education by publishing worldwide. Oxford is a registered trade mark of Oxford University Press in the UK and certain other countries.

Published in the United States of America by Oxford University Press
198 Madison Avenue, New York, NY 10016, United States of America.

CIP data is on file at the Library of Congress

ISBN 978–0–19–783075–8 (pbk.)
ISBN 978–0–19–783074–1 (hbk.)

DOI: 10.1093/oso/9780197830741.001.0001

Paperback printed by Integrated Books International, United States of America
Hardback printed by Lightning Source, Inc., United States of America

The manufacturer's authorized representative in the EU for product safety is Oxford University Press España S.A., Parque Empresarial San Fernando de Henares, Avenida de Castilla, 2 – 28830 Madrid (www.oup.es/en or product.safety@oup.com). OUP España S.A. also acts as importer into Spain of products made by the manufacturer.

For Blaine and Tenzin,
whose steady wisdom provides the cool moonlight that
illuminates our lives

and for the most ven. Samdhong Rinpoche,
the ven. Geshe Ngawang Samten,
the ven. Dr. Wangchuk Dorje Negi,
and to the memory of the ven. Lobsang Norbu Shastri,
whose generous and wise leadership of the Central Institute of
Higher Tibetan Studies
has made our work possible

Contents

Preface

This book is a study of Candrakīrti's (c. 600–660 CE) philosophy and of his place in the history of the Madhyamaka, or Middle Way, school of Buddhist philosophy as it has developed in India, in Tibet, and in modernity. We do not pretend to address every aspect of Candrakīrti's thought, every text he composed, or every controversy regarding how to interpret his thought. Instead, we will sketch how the structure of Candrakīrti's epistemology, ontology, and ethical theory hang together. We will do so with attention to how his thought might inform contemporary philosophical debates. As Wilfrid Sellars (1963) wrote, "The aim of philosophy, abstractly formulated, is to understand how things in the broadest possible sense of the term hang together in the broadest possible sense of the term" (1). We want to understand how Candrakīrti takes things to hang together, and how the various projects he undertakes themselves hang together to the extent that he offers us a single, coherent Madhyamaka vision.

Much of Candrakīrti commentary and scholarship—whether canonical or contemporary—has been concerned with the question of whether Candrakīrti is a radical nihilist who denies the possibility of any knowledge, and who denies the reality both of the external world and of the mind. Eminent Tibetan exegetes Taktsang Sherab Rinchen Lotsawa (sTag tsang lo tsa ba shes rab rin chen, 1405–1477) and Gorampa Sonam Senge (Go rams pa bSod nams Seng ge, 1429–1489) have argued that Candrakīrti does deny the reality of the world and the possibility of any knowledge of conventional reality, that this is the correct understanding of Madhyamaka itself, and that Madhyamaka so understood is the correct philosophical position. Contemporary scholars such as Anne MacDonald (2009) and Tom Tillemans (1990, 2003, 2009; Newland and Tillemans 2011; Priest, Siderits, and Tillemans 2011) are less sanguine regarding the cogency of the position they ascribe to Candrakīrti, but they read him explicitly as an ontological and epistemological nihilist. Tillemans has famously referred to the situation in which he argues that Candrakīrti leaves us as "the dismal slough" in which there is no distinction between truth and falsity, no possibility of knowledge, and nothing that counts as real (Tillemans 2011: 152).

We will argue, following the lead of Tsongkhapa Lobsang Drakpa (Tsong kha pa bLo bzang grags pa, 1357–1419) and his successors in the Geluk tradition, that this is the wrong way to understand Candrakīrti. We will show that rather than leading us into the slough, Candrakīrti develops a sophisticated understanding of knowledge in the context of massive delusion, of reality in the world of conventional truth, and of ethics in the domain of human life. We will see that in doing so, he develops a plausible, constructive understanding of Nāgārjuna's (c. second century CE) Madhyamaka analysis of the two truths and its implications for epistemology, ontology, and ethics. This analysis reconciles the claim that all phenomena are empty—that they lack any intrinsic existence or identity—with a moderate realism about the conventional world.

This realism is *moderate* because Candrakīrti insists that there is no determinate way the world is independent of subjectivity and convention. His position is *realistic* because he reconstructs empirical reality, the difference between truth and falsity regarding the conventional world, and the possibility of knowledge within that framework. So, while it would appear that panfictionalism or illusionism with regard to conventional reality and realism with regard to it are diametrically opposed, Candrakīrti achieves a synthesis of these positions, a synthesis that constitutes a unique and important contribution to epistemology and metaphysics.[1] He achieves this synthesis through an account of reality in terms of thoroughgoing interdependence (*pratītyasamutpāda*).

Richard Rorty developed a similar position with regard to reality. He called it *pan-relationalism*, and he characterized this view as "thinking of things as being what they are by virtue of their relations to other things" by "shaking off the influence of the metaphysical dualisms"

[1] Panfictionalism is the thesis that everything we encounter is fictional, or an artifact of human construction. Illusionism regard to a phenomenon or domain is the thesis that that phenomenon or the phenomena in that domain do not exist as they appear to exist, or that we are in persistent error regarding their true nature.

such as the essence/accident, substance/property, and appearance/reality distinctions inherited from the Greeks and by replacing "these oppositions with a flux of continually changing relations, relations whose terms are themselves dissoluble into a nexus of further relations" (2021: 85). On our view, Candrakīrti is an ancestor of Rorty: he is an early booster of pragmatism, coherentism, and supervenience theory, and his argument that it allows us to synthesize fictionalism and realism demonstrates its importance.[2] We therefore see him not only as one of the most creative philosophers of the medieval Indian Buddhist world, but also as an important dialogue partner for contemporary philosophy.

Our method is one familiar to historians of philosophy: that of rational reconstruction. We are working not *on* Candrakīrti, but *with* Candrakīrti. We are engaged not in an *empirical* or purely *philological* enterprise attempting to discover what was in the mind of a long-gone Indian scholar but in a *hermeneutical* enterprise in which we attempt to make the best philosophical sense of the complex corpus attributed to that scholar. Philological evidence drawn from these texts and careful reading are necessary, but not sufficient for this task; we must also ask—with attention to Candrakīrti's antecedents, interlocutors, and commentators, and with a concern to provide a unitary interpretation of his corpus—what he *must have meant*, or at least, *what it makes the most sense to us to attribute to him*. And this requires that we supplement philology with philosophy, asking what positions make sense, what the most charitable reading of his texts would be, which

[2] Coherentism in epistemology is the thesis that justification does not reflect dependence on a self-justifying foundation of truths or methods, but that justification emerges from the coherence of a practice or thesis with other practices or theses taken to be justified and justificatory, and that there are no privileged foundations of knowledge.

Supervenience is global determination that need not be reductive. A domain of phenomena (the supervenient domain) supervenes on another (the base domain) if, and only if, any two worlds identical with respect to the base domain are identical with respect to base domain are identical with respect to the supervening domain. This is possible even if the entities in the supervenient domain are not reducible to those of the base domain. For instance, to say that economics is supervenient on physics would be to say that any two physically identical worlds would also be identical economically. This is highly plausible. But it does not follow from this that the laws of economics can be reduced to the laws of physics, or every type of economic event corresponds to a type of physical event; there need be nothing physical shared by all purchases of shares in AT&T, for instance.

claims are best taken as the fixed points around which others are read, and which are subject to interpretation in light of those fixed points.

Such hermeneutical work is always tentative, always subject to the prejudices that constitute the horizon of interpretation that we bring to the text. It follows that no interpretation can claim finality. Others might have addressed the same texts with the same concerns and have come to very different conclusions, and we expect that future readers of Candrakīrti will find reason to disagree with our approach. We therefore write with genuine respect, admiration, and gratitude for those with whom we disagree, recognizing both that their insights and research inform and enable our work, and that there are good arguments in favor of their readings as well as in favor of ours. We only hope that our reading gives one more reason to take Candrakīrti seriously, both in the context of the history of Indo-Tibetan Buddhist thought and as a historical interlocutor for contemporary philosophers.

As the two of us think together and as we write, we each recall the kindness of our teachers who introduced us to his work, who have nourished our engagement with his texts and thought, and who have enabled us to pass these thoughts on to our readership. We are forever grateful to them. We note especially the ven. Prof. Geshe Yeshes Thabkhas, the ven. Prof. Geshe Ngawang Samten, the ven. Geshe Lobzang Gytaso, the ven. Prof. Geshe Tenzin Nyima, and the ven. Prof. Dr. Tashi Tsering, all of the Central Institute of Higher Tibetan Studies, an institution that has supported much of our research. We also gratefully acknowledge our other colleagues in the Cowherds and the Yakherds, from whom we have learned so much over the years: José Cabezón, Amber Carpenter, Ryan Conlon, Georges Dreyfus, Thomas Doctor, Douglas Duckworth, Bronwyn Finnegan, Jed Forman, Charles Goodman, Steve Jenkins, Guy Newland, John Powers, Graham Priest, Mark Siderits, Koji Tanaka, Tom Tillemans, and Jan Westerhoff. We are grateful to Anne MacDonald, Tisha Mathura, and Kevin Vose for useful conversations and for their recent work on Candrakīrti. Thanks to Eyal Aviv, Dan Arnold, Tenzin Bhuchung, José Cabezón, Douglas Duckworth, Stephen Harris, Pierre-Julien Harter, Maria Heim, Bryce Huebner, Guy Newland, John Powers, and Jan Westerhoff for very helpful comments on an earlier draft of this book.

We also thank the members of the Five College Buddhist Studies Faculty Seminar who read an earlier draft of this manuscript and whose critique has improved it: Laura Guerrero, Maria Heim, Steve Jenkins, Doug Krem, Dan Lusthaus, Sara McClintock, Susanne Mrozik, Chris Rahlwes, Andy Rotman, Ajay Sinha, Mei Ying, and two anonymous readers.

We thank the Fonds Elisabeth De Boer, Australian Research Council, and the Singapore Ministry of Education for support that contributed to the success of this research. Jay Garfield thanks Smith College for sabbatical leave and for additional research support. Sonam Thakchöe thanks the University of Tasmania for continued research support. And we thank Jade Mosley and Regina Hu for invaluable research and editorial assistance.

The order of authors is entirely alphabetical; we worked side by side on this project, and we share responsibility for all errors that remain.

Introduction

Candrakīrti's Place in Buddhist Philosophy

Candrakīrti is well known to modern students of Buddhist philosophy as a Mādhyamika, follower of the "middle Way" school, a school inaugurated by the *Perfection of Wisdom* sūtras (Conze 1993, 1975, 1973) and the work of Nāgārjuna.[1] He is generally regarded as the principal progenitor of the Prāsaṅgika Madhyamaka (*reductio-wielding*, or perhaps better, *skeptical* Madhyamaka school), but we know little about his life.[2] Tibetan sources provide only hagiography; Chinese sources do not even mention his name. All we really know about Candrakīrti—besides his approximate dates of birth and death, that he is from South India, and that he taught at Nālandā University—is what we can glean from his philosophical corpus.[3] Candrakīrti was a prolific scholar. His principal texts include four commentaries on earlier Madhyamaka texts and two independent

[1] *Madhyamaka* is the Sanskrit name of the Middle Way school; a *Mādhyamika* is a follower of that school.

[2] When we used the term *skeptical*, we intend it to refer to *Pyrrhonian* skepticism. For a discussion of the structure of Pyrrhonian skepticism and its connections to the Prāsaṅgika tradition, see Dreyfus (2011); Dreyfus and Garfield (2011); and Garfield (1990). See also Beckwith (2015); Kuzminski (2008); and McEvilly (2012).

[3] Based on Candrakīrti's refutation of Bhāviveka's interpretation of Nāgārjuna's *Fundamental Verses on the Middle Way*, Candrakīrti is generally dated almost thirty years after Bhāviveka. Nonetheless, if the text attributed to Bhāviveka, *Lamp for the Jewel of the Middle Way School* (*Madhyamaka-ratna-pradīpa*; Tib. dBu ma rin po che sgron me; dBu ma, tsha: 259b–289a) is genuine, it casts doubt on this theory. Interestingly, the text mentions Bhāviveka as its author and also states that he wrote *Blaze of Reasoning* (*Tarka-jvālā*). This text makes clear references to Candrakīrti. These statements are supported by Bhāviveka's own words, which say: "For the detailed meaning of [the atomic theory,] see *Explanation of the Five Aggregates in the Middle Way School* (*Madhyamaka-pañca-skandha-[prakaraṇa]*; dbu ma, ya: 239b–266b), composed by Ācārya Candrakīrti; my own composition (Blaze of Reasoning, dBu ma, dza: 1b–40b); and similar works" (dBu ma, tsha: 266b). See Ruegg (1981) for a more extended discussion. Loizzo (2001) offers a speculative reconstruction of Candrakīrti's biography.

By the Light of the Moon. Jay L. Garfield and Sonam Thakchöe, Oxford University Press.
 DOI: 10.1093/oso/9780197830741.003.0001

treatises. The commentaries are *Clear Words* (*Prasannapadā*), which is his commentary on Nāgārjuna's *Fundamental Verses on the Middle Way* (*Mūlamadhyamakakārikā*); *Commentary on Nāgārjuna's Sixty Stanzas of Reasoning* (*Yuktiśaṣṭikavṛtti*); *Commentary on Nāgārjuna's Seventy Stanzas on Emptiness* (*Śūnyatasatativṛtti*); and *Commentary on Āryadeva's Four Hundred Verses* (*Catuḥśatakaṭīkā*). His two autonomous treatises are *Introduction to the Middle Way and Its Commentary* (*Madhyamakāvatāra-bhāṣya*) and *Explanation of the Five Psychophysical Clusters* (*Pañcaskandhaprakaraṇa*). In this study, we draw on all of Candrakīrti's texts, in order to develop a comprehensive understanding of his Madhyamaka philosophy.

This book is inspired by a medieval Tibetan debate—explored in detail by the Yakherds (2021)—regarding how to interpret Candrakīrti. The Yakherds show that Tibetan exegetes, despite agreeing that Candrakīrti provides the definitive account of Madhyamaka philosophy, disagree deeply among themselves about what that definitive account is (2021: 4). The debate is crystallized by Taktsang's (1405–1477) critique of Tsongkhapa's (1357–1419) account of Candrakīrti's position and of Madhyamaka epistemology. While Tsongkhapa defends the reality of the conventional world and the possibility of a normative epistemology within the bounds of the conventional, Taktsang denies that there is any sense in which the conventional is true—despite the fact that we can say what those who take the conventional to be real *say* that some things are true—and argues that there can be no epistemology in the context of massive illusion.

Each, however, cites Candrakīrti as their authority, and the debate they initiate regarding metaphysics and epistemology is largely framed as a hermeneutical debate in Candrakīrti exegesis. Our goal is to defend a moderately realistic reading of Candrakīrti, one that takes the reality of the conventional seriously in the context of its ultimate emptiness, and one that eschews the claim that the ultimate emptiness of phenomena undermines causal efficacy, moral normativity, and our ability to know the conventional world. We will attend not only to his metaphysics and epistemology, but also to his ethical thought.

Candrakīrti is variously described as a global error theorist, an epistemic eliminativist, and an epistemological coherentist; as a nihilist and as a pragmatic realist; as a critic of the very enterprise of philosophy; and as a highly destructive philosopher. One might legitimately conclude that his corpus constitutes nothing more than a philosophical set of Rorschach blots.[4] We think that this pessimistic conclusion is unwarranted, and that if we read carefully, we can reconstruct a plausible account of Candrakīrti's overall philosophical program as constituting a coherent (and indeed *coherentist*) philosophical view.

Candrakīrti's ethical thought is an important part of this picture, although recent scholarship has paid little attention to it.[5] Candrakīrti is a Mahāyāna philosopher writing about the bodhisattva path, and the bodhisattva path is defined by the cultivation of *bodhicitta*—the aspiration to awaken, or to attain buddhahood in order to be able to assist other sentient beings to escape the suffering of samsara. That is both an ethical and a soteriological aspiration: the greater part of the path involves the attainment of ethical perfections (*pāramitās*), and the goal is awakening so as to be an agent for the liberation of all beings from suffering. Not only is Candrakīrti's best-known autonomous philosophical work—*Introduction to the Middle Way*—organized by the bodhisattva path, but he composed an extensive commentary on Āryadeva's *Four Hundred Stanzas*, which is a principal source for Mahāyāna ethical thought.

So, while Candrakīrti is often studied only for his epistemology and metaphysics, if one fails to see that these are in the service of an ethical program, one fails to understand the basic framework of his project. That project is one of attaining moral perfection. Candrakīrti therefore cannot undermine the cogency of moral distinctions, the reality of sentient beings who are the object of the bodhisattva's concern, or the possibility of action itself, despite the global illusionism that constitutes the context of Madhyamaka thought. In what follows, we will show how he establishes a realism that provides a basis for his moral theory, and then articulates that moral theory, without abandoning the thesis that nothing exists ultimately, and that even ethical theory can only be articulated in the domain of conventional truth.

[4] Tuck (1990) offers a similar assessment of Nāgārjuna.

[5] The exception is Lang 2003, but while that is a fine translation, there is little attention to the structure or content of the ethical theory, per se.

There is so much attention on Candrakīrti in contemporary Madhyamaka studies, and he figures so prominently in Tibetan Mādhyamika literature, that it is easy to think that he was always an influential figure in the development of Madhyamaka thought. But this is not so. When we look for Candrakīrti's influence in India, it is rather scant. He is rarely cited, and few philosophers adopt his arguments. There are important exceptions, though. Śāntideva (eighth century CE) follows Candrakīrti very closely, structuring his *magnum opus How to Lead an Awakened Life* (*BodhicāryāvatāraI* in part around the classification of kinds of attitudes of care (*karuṇā*) that Candrakīrti distinguishes in *Introduction to the Middle Way* (*Madhyamakāvat āra*).[6] In chapter 9 of that text, Śāntideva returns to arguments regarding the nature of the self and the person that Candrakīrti advances in *Introduction to the Middle Way*. Śāntideva's commentator *Prajñākaramati* (950–1030) also refers to Candrakīrti's arguments and notes that Śāntideva follows Candrakīrti closely (Arnold forthcoming: 248). And Ratnakīrti (late tenth/early eleventh century CE) is also clearly influenced by Candrakīrti (MacDonald 2015b: 5). Finally, *Introduction to the Middle Way* is discussed by Ratnākaraśānti (eleventh century) and is cited extensively in Buddhaśrījñāna's (twelfth century CE) *Introduction to the Buddha's Path* (*Jinamārgāvatāra*).[7]

In India, that seems to be the extent of Candrakīrti's influence. Candrakīrti's works were not translated into Chinese, and so he is unknown in the East Asian Buddhist traditions. They were, however, translated into Tibetan, and, as in India, he seems to have been a minor figure in early Tibetan philosophical history. Nonetheless, following developments in the twelfth century, his influence in Tibet waxed considerably. Candrakīrti's texts became the principal focus for Tibetan studies of Madhyamaka thought and generated vast philosophical and hermeneutical disagreements among medieval Tibetan commentators and contemporary academics alike, leading to vastly different accounts of Candrakīrti's epistemology (Vose 2009; Yakherds 2021).

[6] See Jenkins (2015) for a discussion of the role of the three objects (*ālambana*) of care that Candrakīrti identifies in structuring Śāntideva's text.

[7] See Cabezón forthcoming for a translation of this text.

The dramatic rise in his position, influence, and perceived stature in Tibet is due to the influence of Atiśa (c. 982–1054), who brought Madhyamaka to Tibet, and to the work of Jayānanda (c. 1000–1100) and his student and translation colleague Patsab Nyima Drak (Pa tshab nyi ma grags pa, 1055–1145). Together, they re-translated *Introduction to the Middle Way* and distinguished for the first time two subschools of Madhymaka in India: *those who advance their own positions* (*rang rgyud pa/Svātantrika*), and *those who use reductio arguments* (*thal 'gyur pa/Prāsaṅgika*). These doxographic categories became normative for Tibetan philosophers and are largely taken for granted as a rubric for systematizing medieval Indian Madhyamaka thought by scholars in contemporary Buddhist studies (although, there is considerable disagreement about how to draw this distinction and what its significance is).[8]

Atiśa introduced Candrakīrti's interpretation of Madhyamaka philosophy to Tibet. In his *Introduction to the Two Truths* (*Satyadvayāvatāra*), Atiśa speaks highly of Candrakīrti, describing him as an authentic Mādhyamika, the disciple of Nāgārjuna whom the Tathāgata prophesied, and as "the one who sees the truth as it is" (V.14–15, 20 dBu ma, a: 72b). Atiśa's disciple Naktso (Nag 'tsho Tshul khrims rgyal ba, 1011–1064) was the first to translate *Introduction to the Middle Way* into Tibetan. His translation, unfortunately, is now lost and was not included in any version of Tibetan canon. There are explicit references to this translation in Rendawa's (Red mda' ba gZhon nu blo gros, 1349–1412) and Tsongkhapa's commentaries on Candrakīrti's *Introduction to the Middle Way.*

Jayānanda is perhaps the most important figure in the early development of Tibetan Madhyamaka, particularly in the shaping of Tibetan understandings of the Prāsaṅgika school of interpretation. His *Commentary on Introduction to The Middle Way* (*Madhyamakāvatāra-ṭīkā; Tib. dBu ma la 'jug pa'i 'grel bshad*) is a word-by-word exegesis of the *Introduction* and—besides Candrakīrti's autocommentary—is the only known Indian commentary on the text (although it was composed in Tibet, it was originally written

[8] See Dreyfus and McClintock (2003) for a set of fine studies of this distinction and its history.

in Sanskrit). His *Hammer of Debate* (*Tarka-mudgara/rTog ge tho ba*) is a concise text on the Madhyamaka critique of Dignāga's and Dharmakīrti's Pramāṇavāda logic and epistemology, an approach to epistemology that dominated medieval Indian Buddhist philosophy, and that was taken very seriously in Tibet. Even though Jayānanda's interpretation of Candrakīrti's Madhyamaka is controversial among the Tibetan exegetes, no one disputes the critical contributions he made in its propagation. Kevin Vose puts the point this way: "While we may debate Jayānanda's fidelity to Candrakīrti's views, his text is of undeniable importance for understanding how Candrakīrti's ideas gained prominence in the twelfth century" (2009: 23).

Patsab argued that Candrakīrti's Prāsaṅgika interpretation was the most sophisticated version of Madhyamaka, and few Tibetan scholars since have disagreed—once again despite intense disagreement regarding just what that interpretation is.[9] From that time to the present many Tibetan scholars have composed commentaries on Candrakīrti's principal texts and independent treatises on Madhyamaka inspired by his views. Among those are Rendawa Shönyo Lodrö (1348/9–1412), Tsongkhapa, Rongtön Sheja Kunrig (1367–1449), Taktsang, Shakya Chogden (1428–1509), Gorampa Sonam Sengye (1429–1489), Karmapa Mikyö Dorje (1507–1554), 'Ju Mipham Rinpoche ('Ju mi pham rgya mtsho, 1846–1912), and many others. Current interest in Candrakīrti beyond Tibet is largely due to the impact of that extensive Tibetan literature on more recent scholarship.

In this volume, we provide a broad but comprehensive overview of Candrakīrti's philosophical system, demonstrating that it constitutes a unitary vision of reality, with his views on metaphysics, epistemology, and ethics each contributing to that systematic unity. We will argue that Candrakīrti introduced a radical communitarian conventionalism into Indian Buddhist philosophy, arguing that ontology and epistemology are constituted by the conventions of communities. That communitarian conventionalism, in turn, underpins a robust realism about the ordinary world in the context of a doctrine of universal emptiness of intrinsic identity.

[9] See Yakherds (2021) for a history of part of that debate.

We will thereby show that Candrakīrti is a welcome partner in contemporary philosophical conversations: he is talking about the questions that occupy us, working from a perspective that is close enough to those deployed in our recent literature, but distinct enough—particularly in its commitment to global illusionism—to provide unique insights that can move those conversations in promising directions. For that reason, we will sometimes juxtapose Candrakīrti's arguments with those of recent Western philosophers. In each case, the goal is not simply to *compare*, but also to show that introducing Candrakīrti into our conversations is worthwhile. We will also from time to time use insights or formulations from recent Western philosophy to illuminate Candrakīrti's arguments, showing that what might look very foreign is actually very familiar.

We organize our treatment topically, rather than providing a detailed study of or commentary on any single treatise. While we draw upon canonical texts that provide context for Candrakīrti's thought—including both texts on which he reflects as well as canonical and recent commentaries on his own work—our purpose is not to study those texts, or to present a history of Madhyamaka, but to focus squarely on Candrakīrti's corpus to understand his views. Because many of his readers, canonical and recent, have misread Candrakīrti as a global nihilist—an interpretation that would make him interesting, but only a curio—we begin by considering and rebutting that interpretation before turning to a positive account of his system.

1
The Dismal Slough
Is Candrakīrti a Nihilist?

Into the Slough

This enigmatic statement from the *Heap of Jewel of Sūtra* (*Ratnakūṭa-sūtra*) is often quoted in canonical Madhyamaka texts as well as in recent scholarship:

> The world (*loka*) argues with me. I do not argue with the world. Whatever that the world agrees (*saṃmata*) exists, I also take to exist. I also agree that whatever the world agrees to be nonexistent does not exist. (dBu ma, ʻa:118b)[1]

[1] loko māyā sārdhaṃ vivadati nāhaṃ lokena sārdhaṃ vivadāmi | yal loke ʻsti saṃmataṃ tan mamāpy asti saṃmatam | yal loke nāsti saṃmataṃ mamāpi tan nāsti saṃmatam | *Ārya-mahāratnakūṭa-dharmaparyāya-śatasāhasrika-granthe* | *trisaṃvara-nirdeśa-parivarta-nāma-mahāyāna-sūtra*
(Lhasa (lha sa): (H 45) dkon brtsegs, ka 1b1-68b3 (vol. 35). *The Trisaṃvaranirdeśaparivarta (chapter 1) of the Ratnakūṭasūtra* (Degé folio 9b; Lhasa [H 45]), folio 14a: ngas ʻdi skad du ʻjig rten ni nga la rgol gyi | nga ni ʻjig rten dang mi rtsod do zhes gsungs so| (I have said that the world argues with me, but that I do not argue with the world). The Tibetan version cites only the first half: de la byis pa'i rang bzhin can la la zhig grib ma de'i ldem po ngag dam pa de ma shes pa de ni de bzhin gshegs pa la rgol te| de la nges ʻde skad du ʻjig rten ni nga la rgol gyi| nga ni ʻjig rten dang mi rtsod do zhes gsungs so| In the Pāli canon in *Saṃyutta Nikāya* III: 138 (ed. Léon Feer), we find an almost identical passage, with the important exception that *the Saṃyutta Nikāya* speaks about "the wise (paṇḍitānam) in the world (loke)" and "Of that which the wise in the world agree upon as not existing, I too say that it does not exist. And of that which the wise in the world agree upon as existing, I too say that it exists." nāham bhikkhave lokena vivadāmi loko ca mayā vivadati || na bhikkhave dhammavādī kenaci lokasmiṃ vivadati || yam bhikkhave natthi sammataṃ loke paṇḍitānam aham pi tam natthīti vadāmi || yam bhikkhave atthi sammataṃ loke paṇḍitānam aham pi tam atthīti vadāmi || ("Bhikkhus, I do not dispute with the world; rather, it is the world that disputes with me. A proponent of the Dhamma does not dispute with anyone in the world. Of that which the wise in the world agree upon as not existing, I too say that it does not exist. And of that which the wise in the world agree upon as existing, I too say that it exists") (Bhikkhu Bodhi 2000: 949).

By the Light of the Moon. Jay L. Garfield and Sonam Thakchöe, Oxford University Press.
 DOI: 10.1093/oso/9780197830741.003.0002

Citing this passage, as well as Candrakīrti's own citations of this passage, both in *Clear Words* in the commentary to Nāgārjuna's verse 18.8 (dBu ma, 'a: 118b, 2003: 323) and in his *Commentary to the Introduction to the Middle Way* in the commentary on verse 6.81 (dBu ma, 'a: 267a, 1992: 168), Tom Tillemans distinguishes between two radically different ways to interpret Candrakīrti's Madhyamaka (Tillemans 2011: 151–165; 2019: 642). On the one hand, it could be read as enlightened deflationism, advocating "full-fledged truths" for both the ordinary persons and for the exalted (*āryas*) warranted by "full-fledged *pramāṇas*" (epistemic warrants), but truths understood only as that which one is warranted in accepting, not as having any real purchase on reality.

On the other hand, Candrakīrti's Madhyamaka could be read as an error theory or as panfictionalism. On this reading, truth is not even in the picture; the Buddha is merely asserting that he is not interested in disputes, that when asked how things are, he just says, "whatever." Tillemans ascribes the first approach to Tsongkhapa, but he denies that it is an accurate representation of Candrakīrti's position, calling it an "atypical Prāsaṅgika" reading (2011: 151–165; 2019: 642). Tillemans argues that to follow this reading is to read Candrakīrti as both an epistemological inflationist and an ontological deflationist. That is, Tillemans argues, Tsongkhapa's Candrakīrti treats epistemic warrants very seriously as the guide to truth but regards the empirical world as inadequate to serve as a truthmaker; instead, on this reading, Candrakīrti holds that truth has to be understood as emerging from an ontology in which we and our epistemic practices are implicated, and not as a relation to a pre-given reality. Tillemans argues that on Tsongkhapa's reading, Candrakīrti is a decent pragmatist philosopher. But Tillemans also argues that Tsongkhapa was an incompetent philologist, imposing his own views on Candrakīrti, which, while philosophically plausible, are very different from those Candrakīrti actually advanced.

Tillemans defends the accuracy of what he calls the "typical reading" as an interpretation of Candrakīrti. He attributes this reading to Jayānanda and to Taktsang (Tillemans 2011: 151–165; 2019: 642). On this reading, Tillemans argues, Candrakīrti emerges as a hopeless philosopher—an epistemological nihilist, error theorist and global fictionalist—who argues that we are all stuck in what Tillemans calls a "dismal slough" (2016: 4; 2019: 640). He argues that Candrakīrti regards mundane truth as simply whatever ordinary people think (*lokaprasiddha*), and that what we call knowledge of the conventional is nothing more than knowing what they think.

Tillemans characterizes Candrakīrti's account of truth variously as a "dismal position," "duplication," a "trivialization of the idea of truth," "dumbed-down truth," "easy-easy truth," and "hopelessly dismal" truth (2016: 47). He writes that Candrakīrti shuns "any and all deeper questions about what there actually is" and finds satisfaction in whatever the world of deluded beings provides (5). He therefore claims that Candrakīrti has no interest in "constructive philosophizing," and that he has "nothing constructive to offer as a theory of universals, particulars, negative facts, perception, memory, reflexive awareness, and the like" (6). He concludes that Candrakīrti "fails the basic standards of a rational, intellectual approach—he is not judicious (*pretkṣāvat*), as he only copies the world and eschews sources of knowledge (*pramāṇa*) that confirm or correct the world's beliefs" (60).

Tillemans argues that this dismal position regarding truth leads Candrakīrti to epistemological nihilism. He characterizes Candrakīrti as a destructive global skeptic who argues that whatever we encounter in ordinary experience is a false appearance, completely unreal, and existent only from the perspective of "mistaken minds" (*blo 'khrul ba'i ngor yod pa*) (4). On this reading, Candrakīrti is a global error theorist, or a panfictionalist according to whom conventional "truth" is not truth at all, but only fiction or error (*bhrānta/'khrul ba*) (5). He therefore takes Candrakīrti to eschew any belief in the reality of the conventional world or any difference between truth and falsehood in the conventional domain (52). This reading suggests that Candrakīrti takes there to be no "genuine sources of knowledge" (*pramāṇa/tshad ma*), or epistemic resources whatsoever.[2]

[2] We emphasize that, while we take Tom Tillemans as a *pūrvapakṣa* in this volume, we do so only with regard to one aspect of his scholarship on Madhyamaka, namely his reading of Candrakīrti. Tillemans is one of the giants of recent Madhyamaka scholarship, for whom we have enormous respect and to whom we have enormous gratitude. His philosophical exposition of the Madhyamaka system, of Pramāṇavāda, and of the work of Tibetan Madhyamaka in particular is definitive. We only disagree with regard to how to understand Candrakīrti's understanding of conventional truth.

Following Tillemans, Mark Siderits also argues that:

> On the Prāsaṅgika view, conventional truth is a set of brutely given practices which must be taken at face value. To seek to analyze these practices is to introduce the standards of philosophical rationality, standards which the Mādhyamika believes to be thoroughly discredited. If the only truth is that which accords with conventional practices, then we must resist all temptation to analyze and explain these practices. (2016: 32–33)

Nurboo (2023) offers a slightly more nuanced view in the same vicinity. He agrees with Tillemans that Tsongkhapa's reading is unfaithful to Candrakīrti, and that Candrakīrti takes conventional reality to be entirely non-existent and so takes conventional truth not to be a genuine truth. But he argues that Candrakīrti does assign conventional truth a normative status as that which must be accepted provisionally in order to progress on the path to awakening. Despite this normative status, though, Nurboo—although providing a somewhat more charitable and cogent reading of Candrakīrti—argues that Candrakīrti takes conventional truth to be rejected as entirely false at the stage of awakening, and so that its status is merely provisional, and might be better conceived as a *quasi-truth*.

Anne MacDonald also argues that Candrakīrti is an epistemic and ontological nihilist, and she does so with philological rigor. Her introduction to *Clear Words* suggests that Candrakīrti's primary aim is to respond to Dignāga's construction of a "more refined" account of conventional reality (2015a: 8). She argues that while Dignāga sees epistemic conventions as grounding a robust sense of conventional truth, Candrakīrti rejects that program, asserting that conventional reality is nothing but illusion. She argues that even when Candrakīrti anticipates and attempts to refute accusations of nihilism in chapter 1 of *Clear Words*, he affirms that conventional reality is a product of ignorance, and that the Mādhyamika's aim is to detach from the falsehoods of convention (2015b: 174). On MacDonald's view, Candrakīrti finds no truth in the conventional world: not only is there nothing that would constitute knowledge of the conventional world; it is literally nonexistent.[3]

Kevin Vose defends a related interpretation. He argues that Candrakīrti's Prāsaṅgika view is a form of "transcendent nihilism: minds and appearances cease while Buddhahood emerges" (2024: ms p. 16). Vose argues that Candrakīrti, both in *Clear Words* and in *Introduction to the Middle Way*, explicitly rejects the reality of the conventional and the probative value of conventional epistemic instruments. He writes, "Do Mādhyamikas aim to be content with a 'worldly' understanding and with the mutually dependent world? Can they let the world be? The answer to these questions, as to most questions in Madhyamaka, is No" (4). Vose quotes Patsab Nyima drak's assertion that "conventional truths are 'nonexistent, not true, false appearances, like the appearance of floating hairs to one with eye disease,' nothing more than a 'concealing conventional'" (5). Vose takes Patsab's reading as evidence that while *Clear Words* might lend aid and comfort to a more realistic reading of conventional truth, Candrakīrti is univocal in *Introduction to the Middle Way* in asserting that the primary meaning of *saṃvṛti* is *concealing*, and that "Candrakīrti identifies *lokavyāvahāra*, our ways of thinking and speaking, with conceptual proliferation, the very problem that emptiness is meant to overcome" (5–6). He concludes that "verdical in the world just means conceived to be true by a 'worldly, mistaken concealer'" (6).

Vose argues for this interpretation in part on epistemological grounds. He quotes Candrakīrti's commentary in *Clear Words* on verse 24.8 of Nāgārjuna's *Fundamental Verses on the Middle Way*, in

[3] Westerhoff (2016) might appear to be in at least partial agreement with this nihilistic reading of Candrakīrti, when he writes that "Candrakīrti [says that] what the nihilists and the Mādhyamikas are saying is fundamentally the same, even though the status of their assertions is vastly different" (351). But context makes it clear that Westerhoff does not in fact read Candrakīrti as a nihilist at all. Westerhoff does *not* take him to deny the reality of the world of or value *tout court*; he only means to say that Candrakīrti affirms that he agrees with the nihilists in a very specific respect: Candrakīrti agrees that such things as moral values (and for that matter, the external world) do not exist *ultimately*. This is not nihilism because, as Westerhoff points out later in this discussion, Candrakīrti also explicitly distinguishes his position from that of the nihilists: a nihilist, Candrakīrti asserts, denies the ultimate existence of things *on the grounds that they do not exist at all*; the Mādhyamika denies their ultimate existence on the grounds that they exist, but exist only *conventionally*. It is the Mādhyamika's insistence on conventional reality that distinguishes them from nihilism, a fact that Westerhoff properly emphasizes.

which Nāgārjuna asserts that the Buddha teaches two truths and that one must understand the conventional in order to understand the ultimate. The Buddha

> expounded conventional truth in accordance with conformity to the appearances to the awareness of ordinary beings; he expounded ultimate truth in conformity with appearances to the wisdom of *āryas*. (24.8; dBu ma, 'a: 163a; 2003: 440, quoted at 7)

Vose quotes Patsab's citation of Candrakīrti *Madhyamakāvatāra*:

> If the world were valid cognition/authoritative (*pramāṇa*),[4] that very world would see reality; what point would there be for the others, the *āryas*? It is not reasonable for foolishness to be called valid cognition. Since the world is not in any way valid cognition/authoritative, the world does not invalidate on the topic of reality. (6.30, dBu ma 'a: 256a; 2005: 111; quoted at 2024: 7)

Vose follows Patsab in concluding that Candrakīrti rejects the authority of all conventional epistemic practices, effectively denying that there can be any knowledge of conventional truth. This is the dismal slough. And it gets even more dismal! Vose cites Jayānanda in support of the view that nothing whatever appears to awakened beings, and so, because their epistemic status is privileged, the fact that nothing appears to them means that nothing at all really exists:

> [Candrakīrti's] assertion that the movement of mind and mental factors has utterly ceased, since awakening is by way of a complete lack of knowing, is an assertion that all activities of mind and mental factors—feeling and so forth—characterized by experiencing, cease their engagement. Saying "mind and mental factors do not engage" is to say, "therefore, there are no appearances at all," as conceptuality has ceased. (11.17; dBu ma, ra: 333a, quoted at 2024: 12)

4 We will turn to a discussion of the meaning and importance of *pramāṇa* in this debate in the next section of this chapter.

This gets us to the ontological version of the dismal slough: not only is there no knowledge, but there is nothing in conventional reality that could be known! Vose confirms this reading in his discussion of Candrakīrti's commentary in *Clear Words* on the final line in 24.18, where Nāgārjuna says that to see that emptiness is dependent origination, and to see that that is a dependent designation is the middle way:

> The very emptiness characterized as nonarising by intrinsic nature is posited to be the middle path. For that which does not arise by intrinsic nature has no existence; and since there is no cessation of that which is nonarisen by intrinsic nature, it has no nonexistence. Thus, since it is devoid of the two extremes of being and nonbeing, emptiness characterized by the nonarising by the intrinsic nature of all is said to be the middle path. (24.18, dBu ma, 'a: 167b; 2003: 450–451, quoted at 2024: 14)[5]

Vose reads this passage as the explicit denial that anything exists, and so as the assertion that to be empty is to be nonexistent. He concludes, "In brief, for Candrakīrti and his followers, nothing is" (16). Despite the fact that Vose agrees that Candrakīrti—like all Mādhyamikas—is concerned to avoid the extreme of nihilism, and to make sense of the importance of action and the path, the position he ends up ascribing to Candrakīrti is effectively nihilistic, or at least *transcendentally* nihilistic, as he puts it.

We have seen that Vose mobilizes four principal lines of argument for the claim that according to Candrakīrti there is no conventional truth: first, a buddha is authoritative and nothing appears to a buddha; second, there are no genuine epistemic warrants for ordinary people, as they are entirely deluded; third, to be dependently arisen is to be *nonarisen*, and to be empty is to be nonexistent, so to be conventionally

[5] rang bzhin gyis ms skyes pa'i mtshan nyid can gyi stong pa nyid de nyid ni dbu ma'i lam yin zhes bya bar rnam par gzhag te| 'di ltar gang zhig rang bzhin gyis ma skyes pa de la ni| yod pa nyid med la| ran bzhin gyis ma skyes pa la 'jig pa med pas med nyid med pa de'i phyir| yod pa dang med pa'i mtha' gnyis dang bral ba de'i phyir rang bzhin gyis ma skyes pa'i mtshan nyid can gyi stong pa nyid de nyid ni dbu ma'i lam ste|

real, or dependently arisen, is to be nonexistent. Finally, the principal meaning of *samvṛti* is *concealing*, and so to say that something is conventionally true (*samvṛti-satya*) is to say that is entirely false, or nonexistent, not that it is true in any sense. We will return to these arguments in the next chapter.

These readings of Candrakīrti are not without support. We have already seen a good deal of *prima facie* textual evidence adduced for them, and we concede that there are even more passages in which Candrakīrti does seem to reject all truth in conventional reality. For example, here he appears to reject the possibility of ascertainment.

> If something called ascertainment existed for us, it would either stem from valid cognition or not stem from valid cognition. But [it] does not exist. Why [not]? According to our system (*iha*), if non-ascertainment (*aniścaya*) were possible, there might be its counterpart (*pratipakṣa*), [i.e.,] the ascertainment which relies on that [non-ascertainment]. Yet when, first of all, [that] very non-ascertainment does not exist for us, then how could there be its opposite. (1.9; dBu ma, 'a: 19a; 2003: 41; trans. MacDonald 2015b: 207–209)

Candrakīrti seems to argue that conventional cognition can never serve as an epistemic warrant, and that it can never be veridical. We will return to this passage later, offering a different reading, but we can see how one could cite this as confirmation of the reading of Candrakīrti as an epistemic nihilist. In *Introduction to the Middle Way*, Candrakīrti provides additional grounds for this reading. He writes:

> If ordinary people were authoritative, then ordinary people
>   would perceive reality;
> And if that were the case, of what use would be the states achieved
>   by the noble ones?
> What would the point be of the noble path?
> It makes no sense to say that fools are epistemic warrants. (6.30)
> Ordinary people are not at all authoritative
> With respect to reality, and so cannot undermine it. (6.31ab)

And he cites the *King of Meditation Sūtra* (*Samādhirājasūtra*):

> The eye, ear, and nose are not epistemic warrants.
> Neither are the tongue, body or mind.
> If those senses were accurate,
> What would be the point of the noble path?
> But these sensory faculties are not epistemic instruments;
> They are material and are essentially neutral.
> Therefore, those who aspire to the path of nirvana
> Must follow the noble path. (*Samādhirājasūtra* vv. 9.30–31 Toh 127 sDe dge Kangyur, mDo sde, da: 26b; 1992: 107–108)

In this passage, Candrakīrti appears to deny categorically that knowledge of any kind is possible for any ordinary epistemic agent. In *Commentary on Āryadeva's Four Hundred Verses*, Candrakīrti again apparently argues against accepting sensory cognitions as epistemic warrants:

> Therefore, to ascribe the status of perception to sensory cognitions and to think that those cognitions function as epistemic warrants for their objects is utterly indefensible. From a mundane perspective, an epistemic warrant is regarded as a nondeceptive cognition. The Blessed One has taught that cognition is a conditioned phenomenon, and therefore is false and deceptive, just like an illusion. Being false, deceptive, and illusory, it cannot be nondeceptive, because things appear to it in a way that is different from the way they actually are. Therefore, it is not reasonable to regard such a cognition as an epistemic warrant because then all cognitions would end up being epistemic warrants. (*Catuḥśatakaṭīkā* 13.1; dBu ma, *ya:* 197b; 2019: 350)[6]

[6] mi bslu b'i shes pa ni 'jig rten na tshad ma nyid du mthong na rnam par shes pa yang bcom ldan 'ads kyis 'dus byas yin pa'i phyir brdzun pa bslu b'i chos can dang sgyu ma lta bur gsungs so| |gang zhig brdzun pa bslu b'i chos can dang sgyu ma lta bu yin pa de ni mi bslu ba ma yin te| rnam pa gzhan du gans pa'i dngos po la rnam pa gzhan du snang b'i phyir ro| |de lta bur gyur pa ni tshad ma nyid du brtag par rigs pa ma yin te| rnam par shes pa thams cad kyang tshad ma nyid du thal bar 'gyur b'i phyir ro| | See Suzuki (1994) for the extant Sanskrit fragments of this text.

Tillemans and MacDonald assert that in these statements, Candrakīrti denies any possibility of reliable conventional epistemic warrant. Norboo and Vose would surely agree. These scholars are not the first to read Candrakīrti in this fashion, nor is this reading an invention of contemporary critical Buddhist studies. Six centuries ago, Taktsang and his followers presented a very similar interpretation, but in a very different register, claiming not that Candrakīrti was a nihilist or purely historical interest, but that he was a profound *transcendentalist* (*spros bral smra ba*), according to whom there can be no knowledge of the conventional world and according to whom the emptiness of the world is the object of a transcendent, inexpressible gnosis of a reality that exceeds anything that we suppose that we know or that we take to be real. But despite the difference in register, Takstang's approving reading and Tillemans' disparaging reading agree in hermeneutical substance: they each read Candrakīrti as denying the possibility of knowledge and as denying the reality of the empirical world.

The Importance of Pramāṇa

In order to appreciate why this interpretation is plausible, as well as why that of its critics is also plausible, we need to understand some of the Indian epistemological context in which Candrakīrti was writing and against which debates about how to understand him were framed, and that requires attention to the important technical term *pramāṇa*. *Pramāṇa* is notoriously difficult to translate because of its rich semantic range. In epistemology, it can, depending on context, be translated as *warranted cognition*, *non-deceptive cognition*, *epistemic warrant*, *source of knowledge*, *evidence*, or *epistemic instrument*.

We can see from this list that it sometimes denotes the presence of justification, sometimes a justificatory instrument, and sometimes the knowledge we gain through using such an instrument. In ethics, it denotes a trustworthy, dependable person, and in soteriology, one on whom one can rely to guide one toward awakening.[7] This term can

[7] Just as in English, *truth* and *trust* are cognate, in Sanskrit, *sat* and *satya* denote both the truth of sentences and something in which we can place our trust—something *real*.

also refer to authoritative texts, or to an authoritative person. In law, and jurisprudence, it means warrant, proof, and evidence. There is no single English term that captures all these meanings. In the context of epistemology, we will use *epistemic instrument* when referring to a cognitive process or state, *epistemic warrant* when referring to justificatory status, and *knowledge* to refer to the results of the successful application of epistemic instruments. But in reading the English, it is important to bear in mind that in Sanskrit or Tibetan these feel like instances of the same kind.

In any Indian philosophical system, including the Buddhist systems, *pramāṇa* is theorized as a necessary condition of knowledge and of the accomplishment of human purposes (*puruṣārtha*), including mundane purposes such as finding food and practicing a trade and transcendent purposes such as the achievement of liberation. Philosophical schools are often distinguished based on the particular epistemic warrants they recognize. For instance, the Nyāya school recognizes four warrants: perception, inference, testimony, and analogy or inductive reasoning. While Buddhism is often regarded as the "two '*pramāṇa* school," we will see that Candrakīrti in fact endorses all of the Nyāya warrants, and leaves the door open to even more. We begin this discussion with attention to Taktsang's argument to the effect that a Mādhyamika cannot accept *any pramāṇas*. Only once that argument is disarmed can we spell out Candrakīrti's positive account.

Taktsang's Three Contexts

Taktsang's interpretation of Candrakīrti in his *Commentary on the Treatise Freedom from Extremes Accomplished through Comprehensive Knowledge of Philosophy* (*Grub mtha' kun shes nas mtha' 'bral sgrub pa zhes bya ba'i bstan bcos rnam par bshad pa legs bshad kyi rgya mtsho* 2007; Yakherds 2021) depends in part on his insistence that no

And just as historically, the use of locutions such as a *true friend*, or a *true coin* precede those like *true sentence*, with trustworthiness capturing the central idea in both cases, in Sanskrit it is *things*, not *sentences*, that are primarily *sat*. So, since a *pramāṇa* is an instrument that delivers *satya* or the result of such an instrument, the core idea in *pramāṇa* is that of something in which we can trust to mediate our relations with the world.

Prāsaṅgika Mādhyamika can accept the validity of *any pramāṇa*. His argument for this claim rests on his hermeneutic framework of three contexts (*skab*) of analysis. The first context—that of *no* analysis (*ma brtag ma dpyad pa'i skab*) —is that of ordinary agents in the everyday world. The second—that of *slight* analysis (*cung zad dpyad pa'i skab*)—is that inhabited by sophisticated Mādhyamikas. The third—the context of *thorough* analysis (*legs par dpyad pa'i skab*)—is reserved for highly realized beings. It is useful to keep this framework in mind, as it provides the groundwork for one of the strongest cases for the nihilistic or transcendentalist understanding of Candrakīrti and for reconciling Candrakīrti's *prima facie* realistic statements and his apparent endorsement of epistemic practices and philosophical argument with this nihilistic reading. Tibetan defenders of the moderate realism that we attribute to Candrakīrti took this position seriously and sought to refute it.[8] Taktsang not only defends this tripartite framework as the only way to understand Prāsaṅgika Madhyamaka; he takes it to animate Candrakīrti's position, and to be essential to understanding that position.

Taktsang asserts that in the first context—that of *no analysis*—existence, truth, knowledge, and philosophical reflection make sense. But, he argues, they make sense only because in that context we don't do any critical philosophy, we don't look too closely at what existence, truth, or knowledge entail; any analytic examination of these concepts, he argues, shows them to be incoherent. Taktsang takes this context to contain, among other things, the distinction between truth and falsity and the epistemic conventions adopted by ordinary deluded beings, including canons of inference, accounts of when perception is reliable, inductive practices, and analogical reasoning.

In this context, it makes sense to say that there are tables and chairs, that they are constituted by atoms, that there are subjects and objects, and that our senses deliver knowledge of those objects. We can talk in this context about the reality of the Buddhist path and about actions and their results. Moreover, in this context we can distinguish the water

[8] We return to this debate briefly in Chapter 6. See Yakherds (2021) for a translation of Taktsang's text and for an extensive discussion of his interpretation and of the debates it inspired.

in my glass from the non-existent water in a mirage, the reflection of the moon in a pond from the moon in the sky, sound from unsound inferences, right from wrong, and soon. And we do so by adhering to the conventional practices of ordinary people in the ordinary world, or at least to those to which they give deference.

This might sound like at least a qualified realism from the Prāsaṅgika standpoint, but it is not: this context does not enable any *knowledge*, and there is nothing about it that is *true*; at best, we can say *in that context* what those in that context *take to be true*. But this is not genuine truth: when we subject these practices and views to any serious analysis, we find out that they are incoherent. Mutually contradictory beliefs often each have warrant; epistemic conventions are self-undermining. Conventions conflict with one another. And there are no Archimedean points from which to adjudicate disagreements. The objects we take to exist dissolve into emptiness under analysis, and subject-object duality is seen to be a mere appearance, eliminating both subjects and objects. Taktsang argues that knowledge and reality, if these terms are to mean anything at all, demand more than these castles of sand that are swept away by the first analytical waves to wash over them.

This first context—that of no analysis—Taktsang argues, conforms to the mundane relative truth that is accepted by or that is acceptable to ordinary people. In this context, Taktsang argues, nonanalytical epistemic warrant is the criterion of existence of things and persons, but this is only true from the perspective of the way things appear to the deluded, non-analytical epistemic instruments of common folk. This is because the things that are taken to be true or real by these deluded subjects are entirely false; they neither exist nor contain a grain of truth from the perspectives of Prāsaṅgika Mādhyamikas, or any awakened beings. To take them to be real in any sense or to take there to be any truths about them, Taktsang argues, would be like taking the appearances in a dream to be real, or to take there to be a fact of the matter regarding the objects about which one dreamed. He asserts that what passes for truth in this context is "established without inquiry or analysis by *the minds of ordinary beings* whose error with respect to seeming reality has not yet been crushed by its remedy" (Yakherds 2021: 58).

On Taktsang's view, those who take this to be truth uncritically endorse naïve realism, the assumption that things and persons are substantially real just as they naïvely appear to the senses. That is, they take the reality of the world they experience for granted due to the force of innate confusion (Taktsang 2007: 296; see Yakherds 2021: 58). The conventional world exists, therefore, only as a construction guided by the confusion of the ordinary beings. For this reason, according to Taktsang, Candrakīrti argues that even though conventional reality is taken to be a truth by ordinary beings, it is entirely false, and no access to it can count as knowledge.

Epistemic objects, epistemic subjects, perception, inference, analogy, testimony, justification, warrants, truth, and falsity all turn out to be constructions born from delusion, and thus have a place only as a feature of delusion. These fabrications may be provisionally necessary as ladders that take us to an accurate, non-conceptual, and inexpressible view of reality, but once we achieve that view, even those ladders disappear. In developing and defending this account of Candrakīrti's position, Taktsang follows the lead of Patsab Nyima Drak, who proposed arguments for this conclusion resembling the modes of Aenesidemus articulated by Sextus Empiricus in the Outlines of Pyrrhonism (Cowherds 2011: ch. 6).

Buddhas, bodhisattvas, and sophisticated Mādhyamikas, Taktsang argues, do not take the first context of analysis seriously—it does not yield the world as they see it. At most, they acknowledge its role when—in order to understand the deluded minds of sentient beings—they adopt what we might think of as the perspective of anthropologists on folk epistemology, folk metaphysics, folk ethics, and folk distinctions between truth and falsity. And they do so in order better to interact with those who are deluded, just as an anthropologist might adopt the perspective of those whose culture she is studying when engaged in participant observation, or as a psychotherapist might adopt the perspective of a client in order to help them transcend that very perspective.

This anthropology tells them—and, to the extent that we as Mādhyamika philosophers can work our way into it, can tell us—something about how ignorant beings see things. But it has nothing to do with epistemology, any more than an account of people's beliefs about demonic possession tells us anything about epilepsy, or an account of divination on the entrails of chickens tells us anything about the best way to predict the future. On Taktsang's view, Candrakīrti takes this context to have nothing whatsoever to do with Madhyamaka philosophy, either; it is simply the domain of ignorance, and is not to be taken seriously, or to be the subject of evaluation: while we might say that *they* distinguish between reality and unreality in the conventional, or between warrant and its absence, *we* recognize that that is just child's play.

Buddhist practice is meant to take us beyond that, and Buddhist philosophy—to the extent that it is cogent at all—is of use only as an indicator to point us in that direction. Philosophy, after all, is discursive, and hence inadequate to express reality; only a transcendent, inexpressible gnosis, a state beyond knowledge, could be adequate to the world as it is. This work begins in the second context.

The second context Taktsang distinguishes is that of *slight analysis*. Taktsang explains: "Next, from the perspective of the framework of slight rational analysis, masters of the Great Madhyamaka refute the object of negation, viz., the twofold self, and thus they posit nonarising, emptiness, and the ultimate truth" (Yakherds 2021: 58). In this context, Taktsang argues, Madhyamaka analysis eliminates the objects of negation—the self of persons and the self of phenomena—or to put it another way, the true existence or intrinsic reality of anything that might be understood as a subject or an object. This analysis reveals the deceptive nature of conventional truth, and eliminates any confidence in its reality, demonstrating the epistemic poverty and ontological bankruptcy of the first context.

Taktsang claims that whereas nothing that people do in the first context can be taken seriously as a warrant at all—at least by any Prāsaṅgika—Candrakīrti takes Madhyamaka analysis in the second context to demonstrate conclusively that everything that appears to be real in the first context dissolves into emptiness. Since in this context Candrakīrti demonstrates that nothing can withstand Madhyamaka analysis, epistemology, ethics, metaphysics, and even soteriology are all revealed to be empty of any force and their putative objects are shown to be utterly unreal. Even causal efficacy is undermined in this context, and any probative link between premises and conclusion.

In the second context, the Madhyamaka analysis therefore becomes a powerful sink, draining reality from everything that appears to us, and leaving nothing behind. Thus, while Taktsang takes Candrakīrti to acknowledge that ordinary people draw a distinction between truth and falsity and are committed to epistemic and ethical norms in the first context, he also argues that Candrakīrti, while recognizing the reality of these practices in the first context, takes them to be utterly mistaken. Candrakīrti's position is therefore that Madhyamaka soteriology, ethics, metaphysics, and epistemology—in virtue of being completely detached from reasoning and analysis—are nothing more than the fabrications of nonanalytical deluded minds of the ordinary beings.

This is what Tillemans thinks takes us directly into the dismal slough, and what Taktsang thinks leads us to reject the apparent world in favor of an inconceivable ultimate reality: on this account of the second context, there is no sense in which conventional truth constitutes a truth, and no sense in which knowledge of the conventional is possible. This is because analysis in the second context tells us that nothing that appeared in the first context exists as it appears, and so that all of it is false. For that reason, since knowledge requires truth, knowledge that appears in the conventional world makes no sense whatsoever. Thus, Candrakīrti cannot take any positive stance, or advance any constructive claim about anything, because nothing withstands Madhyamaka analysis, which is the only criterion for existence and reality.

Taktsang's third context is that of *thorough analysis*, the direct route to the mystical intuition of the transcendent and ineffable ultimate. In this context, Taktsang explains:

> the explicit teaching of the Mother of the Victors completely denies that things exist, that they do not exist; that they are permanent or impermanent; or that they are empty or nonempty, and that there is anything to be apprehended in any way at all. (Yakherds 2021: 59)

This context doubles down on the incompatibility between analysis and reality (Thakchöe 2024: 120–125). We learned in the second context that reality is nondual, ineffable, empty of any characteristics, and beyond the domain of thought. The mismatch between that reality and the dualistic appearances that show up as intrinsically existent and as characterized by describable properties delivered accurately by our senses is what constitutes the falsity of the conventional and so its unsuitability as an object of knowledge. But even this apparent knowledge of that falsity—given that we have expressed it conceptually and through language—must be transcended. It cannot be an accurate representation of an ineffable reality, and so cannot itself constitute knowledge.

This is why Taktsang claims that a Prāsaṅgika Mādhyamika can know the transcendent and ineffable ultimate only in this context. At this stage, which—despite the ineffability of its content—arises as a consequence of completing the Madhyamaka analysis in the second context, it is impossible even to assert emptiness and selflessness, and the entire epistemological framework of knower and known is abandoned (Yakherds 2021: 6). Nothing can be said about it; not even this.[9] So, on Taktsang's interpretation, since Candrakīrti asserts that this is the only ultimately correct context in which to understand reality, Candrakīrti denies that the content of Buddhist philosophy itself is any more than the deluded speculation of cowherds: there are no epistemic distinctions worth drawing in the first two contexts, and none can be drawn in the third, the only one in which truth and knowledge might make sense at all.

So, according to Taktsang, attention to the three contexts shows that Candrakīrti is a thoroughgoing transcendentalist who attributes no reality to the apparent world and sees only a provisional utility to analytic thought. On this view, Madhyamaka analysis is entirely destructive, dissolving all commitment to reality and to knowledge. Analysis in the second and third contexts shows that all epistemological systems are philosophically incoherent and inconsistent with the nonfoundationalist metaphysics of Madhyamaka. This rules out any constructive Madhyamaka program: if this reading is right,

[9] See the ninth Karmapa Wangchuk Dorjé's (dBang phyug rdo rje nam mkha' rgyal po, 1556–1603) *Concise Compendium of the Middle Way* for a particularly robust defense of the claim that Mādhyamikas do not say anything at all, not even that they do not say anything at all (Yakherds 2021: vol. 2, 272–276).

Candrakīrti holds that no Mādhyamika can subscribe to any kind of metaphysical, epistemological, ethical, or soteriological view. We can see here the ancestry of Vose's description of Candrakīrti as a "transcendental nihilist" (2024).

From an ontological standpoint, Taktsang argues that Candrakīrti rejects the existence of everything, including the causal regularities of dependent origination. For if anything were real, apprehension of them would constitute a foundation for knowledge, and there would be conventional truth. Instead, on this reading, Candrakīrti claims that a true Prāsaṅgika Mādhyamika, when talking about conventional truth, simply reports on the conventions of naïve realism and common-sense intuitions of ordinary beings without engaging in any critical philosophical work. And since the ultimate truth is ineffable, a Mādhyamika cannot talk about that at all. And as we have seen, many contemporary scholars have followed them down this path. This position is that to which Tillemans refers as "the dismal slough."

The only difference between the position of Taktsang and his Tibetan followers and that of contemporary exegetes such as McDonald, Tillemans, and Vose is that the former regard this radical anti-realism as a salutary transcendentalism, and the latter as an incoherent nihilism or transcendental nihilism. They agree that Candrakīrti is a radical anti-realist both in the domain of epistemology and in the domain of metaphysics. We also note that each of these sophisticated readers of Candrakīrti have focused exclusively on his distinction between the nondeceptive character of the ultimate truth and the deceptive character of conventional truth. To see how this hermeneutical strategy underpins their readings requires attention to yet another important Sanskrit term of art.

What Is Conventional Truth? Reflections on *samvṛti*

The term most often translated as *conventional truth* (*samvṛti-satya*)—as Candrakīrti himself notes in *Clear Words*—is ambiguous. First, it can mean *by agreement*, *nominal*, *everyday*, or *interdependent*. In this sense, it is taken as synonymous with *lokavyāvahāra* (*truth in the ordinary world*, or *transactional truth*); so, to say that something is conventionally true is to say that it is true according to the standards of ordinary epistemic agents, that it is a part of the causal order, that it is verified by our ordinary epistemic practices. But *saṃvṛti* is not only broad in meaning, but *ambiguous*, with a second, distinct semantic range, following a different etymology: it can also mean *concealing* (LVP 492.10–12; Cowherds 2011: ch. 1; Arnold forthcoming: 261–266; Li 2019; Vose 2024). In this sense, to say that something is conventionally true is to say that it masquerades as truth, concealing its true nature.

This ambiguity is not just a source of confusion, however. It also facilitates a philosophically useful Sanskrit pun, one that informs a good deal of Madhyamaka philosophy. Putting these two meanings together suggests that since the conventional truth conceals its merely conventional status, as long as we are apprehending it, we fail to see reality, and so fail to have knowledge. If we lean only on this second meaning of *saṃvṛti*, there is something to be said for the radically anti-realistic interpretations of Candrakīrti we have been exploring. Truth (*satya*) is always glossed in Indian philosophical literature as *non-deceptiveness*, and to be false is always understood as to be deceptive (like a false friend, or a false dollar note). And on any understanding, conventional truth is deceptive and so, in some sense, false. To the extent that knowledge requires truth, this would seem to make the idea of knowledge of the conventional sound like nonsense.

These considerations, however, are not conclusive. To be deceptive in *some* respect is not to be deceptive in *all* respects. A false friend may be a true knave; a counterfeit dollar may be true evidence in a forgery trial. A witness might convince a jury that he now speaks the truth when he says that he lied earlier—as did Michael Cohen in Donald Trump's hush-money trial. We will return to this issue in Chapter 2. And *saṃvṛti*—as Candrakīrti also notes—can mean *by agreement*, or *nominal*. So, to say that since *saṃvṛti-satya* is *saṃvṛti* does not immediately entail that it cannot be known, or that it contains no truth at all.

Divergent readings of Candrakīrti can reflect divergent choices regarding which of these semantic ranges is primary in Candrakīrti's account of *saṃvṛti-satya*. Those who would read Candrakīrti realistically privilege the first; those who read him transcendentally or nihilistically privilege the second.[10] To adjudicate this question will require us to attend not only to the passages where this term occurs, but to his corpus as a whole, and to judge which reading allows us to preserve the cogency of Candrakīrti's system as a whole.

The radically anti-realistic interpretations of Candrakīrti's view—whether read positively as transcendentalist or negatively as nihilistic—we will show, despite being motivated by some of Candrakīrti's words, do not survive a complete survey of his corpus. That larger context, as interpreters including Tsongkhapa and his followers in the Geluk tradition show, requires us to see Candrakīrti's global anti-realism or fictionalism—his commitment to emptiness as the ultimate truth—as tempered by a moderate but robust realism with respect to dependent origination. That moderate realism, we will argue, represents a coherent middle path between the radical anti-realism we have been exploring and a naïve realism that is the principal target of critical analysis in both the Madhyamaka and Yogācāra schools.

This approach, we will argue, allows Candrakīrti to assert the reality of the conventional world and supports an optimistic theory regarding the prospects for human knowledge based on dependent origination. Our reading shows that Candrakīrti provides a deep explanation of Nāgārjuna's insistence on the identity both of the two truths and of their difference; Candrakīrti demonstrates that the emptiness of emptiness amounts to the empirical reality of dependent origination. This moderate realism about conventional truth in turn allows him to make sense of ethical motivation, action, and perfection, and so of the path of a bodhisattva. Candrakīrti and his contemporaries would have viewed this realism as essential principally in the context of the soteriological project of the pursuit of awakening, or buddhahood, in order to make oneself an effective instrument for the welfare of others. This is the content of the *bodhicitta*, the altruistic aspiration for awakening that defines the bodhisattva path: without a world of sentient beings,

[10] It is also worth noting that the Pāli *sammuti*, which is an antecedent for *saṃvṛti* in Sanskrit Buddhist literature, does not share this ambiguity: it only connotes *by agreement*, *nominal*, or *everyday*. So, to take this as the primary meaning of *saṃvṛti* is also to see more continuity between the Pāli and Sanskrit traditions in thinking about the two truths than there would be if *concealing* is taken as the primary meaning.

and without the suffering that this word entails, *bodhicitta* makes no sense at all.

Contemporary readers can understand the centrality of this realism to Candrakīrti's project in more explicitly metaethical terms: it is hard to make sense of ethics without being realistic with regard to persons, their predicaments, and their welfare, and it is hard to make sense of persons without taking the normative dimensions of personhood seriously. Seen this way, Candrakīrti is committed to realism with regard to both the descriptive and the normative dimensions of the world, because that is the only way to take ethics seriously, as seriously as anything else.[11] It is this realism and optimism that enable Candrakīrti to conceive of the possibility of cognitive, ethical, and spiritual progress, and so of liberation. On our reading, Candrakīrti—like his fellow Mādhyamikas—takes the domain of the real to be the domain of the knowable. He therefore takes the theory of epistemic warrant and the account of how we come to acquire that warrant to be the guide to ontology.

Pramāṇa, Conventional Truth, and Foundationalism

Since to be real is to be knowable, to come to know what—if anything—is real, we need to know just what can in principle be known, and this brings us back to the question of the status of *pramāṇa* in the Madhyamaka system. All Indian and Tibetan Mādhyamikas agree that epistemology is the guide to ontology, and this common ground is the basis for the debate in Tibet regarding how to read Candrakīrti. The difference between Taktsang and his followers on the one hand and those who read Candrakīrti realistically on the other is the difference between *modus tollens* and *modus ponens*. Taktsang argues that the fact that we can't know anything shows that the conventional is entirely unreal; Tsongkhapa and other moderately realistic commentators argue that since we can make sense of conventional epistemic practices, we

[11] For more on the distinction between persons and selves, and on Candrakīrti's realism about persons in the context of his denial of even the conventional reality of the self, see Garfield (2022c: chs. 1, 2, 8) and Arnold (forthcoming: 273–275).

can take reality seriously. Let us therefore turn to a brief consideration of the nature of *pramāṇa* as understood in the epistemological framework that dominated the Buddhist philosophical world when Candrakīrti flourished, a framework of which he himself was critical.

The Pramāṇavāda system initiated by Dignāga and adumbrated by Dharmakīrti recognized only two epistemic warrants: perception and inference; in this framework, what look like additional warrants—including testimony and the use of analogy—reduce to these two. These are distinguished on the basis of their respective objects: Dignāga and Dharmakīrti argue that perception engages with particulars and that inference engages with universals. Since this is an exhaustive distinction, they argue, only two *pramāṇas* are necessary. They argue that by using these two warrants, we can achieve our goals through epistemically correct modes of engagement with the world. In his *Analysis of Knowledge* (*Pramāṇaviniścaya*), Dharmakīrti writes: "There are two epistemic warrants: perception and inference. These two are veridical because, when we act upon having determined an object through one or both of these two, we are not deceived with regard to that object's function" (ch. 1.1, Tshad ma, ce: 152b; 2015: 189).

Dharmakīrti's point here is that what makes these two processes warrants is the fact that they are nondeceptive, a point that is critical to bear in mind in the context of Indian epistemology: recall, *truth* is always defined as *nondeceptiveness*, *falsehood* as *deceptiveness*, and this applies equally to people, methods, objects, and sentences. Derivatively, to be a warrant is to be a nondeceptive mode of access to reality, or a reliable guide to achieving our goals. In this system, a *pramāṇa* is both a *means* for acquiring knowledge, or for making contact with the world, and that to which we can appeal in *justifying* a claim. To claim that a cognitive state is one of knowledge is to claim that it accurately takes the measure of the world, and that it does so using the appropriate instrument.[12]

On the Pramāṇavāda view, the fact that perception and inference are—and are the *only*—nondeceptive modes of access to the world issues in a kind of epistemic foundationalism in this school of Buddhist epistemology. That is a methodological foundationalism, not an

[12] The root of *pramāṇa* is *mā*, meaning *to measure*.

objective foundationalism. According to objective foundationalism, the foundations of knowledge are immediately known objects of knowledge; according to methodological foundationalism, the foundations are to be found in a *way* of knowing, as opposed what is known. We find each of these kinds of foundationalism defended in early modern European philosophy. Berkeley defended an objective foundationalism by arguing for the givenness of our knowledge of sensory qualities; Descartes defended a methodological foundationalism according to which the method of clear and distinct perception is the ground of knowledge: whatever it delivers can be taken to be known.

In the Pramāṇavāda system, the two warrants are taken as self-certified and indubitable, and all other knowledge is based upon them. To be sure, there is a kind of pragmatic dimension in their explanation of these warrants in terms of their utility in facilitating the pursuit of human purposes. But the ascertainment of this facility is in turn vindicated by—and only by—these instruments themselves. They thus effectively serve the same kind of foundational role, vindicated by the same kind of putative virtuous spiral, that clear and distinct perception plays in Descartes' epistemology.[13] This is a classic example of methodological foundationalism.

This is important because, as we shall see, the primary question that divides Candrakīrti's commentators is this: is Candrakīrti's anti-foundationalist Prāsaṅgika Mādhyamika consistent with the acceptance of epistemic warrants, and so with the possibility of knowledge? This question in turn raises a second, more fundamental question in Buddhist epistemology: Are warrants necessarily foundational? Is there a non-foundationalist sense of epistemic warrant available to

[13] In the first of the *Meditations on First Philosophy*, Descartes announces that his task is to provide "a firm foundation for the sciences." In the second and third meditations, he argues that what he calls "clear and distinct perception" always yields truth (or, as an Indian epistemologist would have put it, is a *pramāṇa*), and so that the method of clear and distinct perception—of careful reasoned analysis—is the self-justifying foundation of the sciences, and that all other knowledge is justified because it is achieved through this method (Frankfurt 2009). This is a different kind of foundationalism from the content-foundationalism of Berkeley, who argues in the *Principles of Knowledge* that our immediate sensory experience constitutes the foundation of all of our knowledge, that judgments about its character and content are self-justifying, and that all other knowledge is derived from that foundation, a foundationalism resurrected in twentieth-century sense datum theory (Garfield 2012).

Buddhists? To accept that there is a non-foundationalist alternative is to be on the road to a realistic reading of Candrakīrti, since it opens the possibility of making sense of warrant in the context of a Madhyamaka rejection of foundationalism, and so of the reality of a world revealed by those warrants; to deny that there is any such alternative is to move in the direction either of the dismal slough or of a transcendentalism according to which the only truth is cognitively inaccessible and ineffable.

Taktsang and his contemporary followers take the second path. This is in part because Taktsang takes the only sense of *pramāṇa* to be that in which it is used by the Pramāṇavādins: to be a warrant on his view is, by definition, to be foundational. Taktsang writes in his *Freedom from Extremes*, "not being foundational (*tshugs su thub pa*) contradicts being epistemically warranted, for to be epistemically warranted means to be nondeceptive, and being nondeceptive means nothing more than being foundational" (Yakherds 2021: vol. 2, 25).

This is not a crazy view. Taktsang is rehearsing the standard argument for foundationalism in epistemology. If to be justified is to be grounded in a justificatory statement, and if every justificatory statement must itself be justified, then the only way to avoid either an infinite regress or a vicious circle, this argument goes, is for the justificatory regress to ground out in basic, intrinsically justified statements. Descartes argued that these were statements about method; twentieth-century positivists thought that they were claims about sense data, or so-called protocol sentences. In medieval India, Dignāga and Dharmakīrti argued—at least as they are understood by the parties to this debate about how to read Candrakīrti—that the foundations of knowledge were found in perceptual contact with particulars, or dharmas, and that this justification was transmitted to higher-level sentences through inference. Hence the two *pramāṇas*: perception and inference.

Taktsang argues that Dignāga's and Dharmakīrti's Pramāṇavāda account provides the only cogent analysis of genuine knowledge or justification. Nonetheless, he also acknowledges that the consequence of this account is that from the standpoint of the Madhyamaka system, there can be no genuine knowledge of the conventional world. This consequence follows from two premises: first, no Mādhyamika can maintain that anything exists foundationally or autonomously, since everything is dependently originated and since all of conventional reality is dependent upon conceptual designation (Yakherds 2021: vol. 2, 25). Second, to be conventionally real is to be *deceptive*, and indeed that is one of the principal meanings of *saṃvṛti*. Every dependent phenomenon appears as though it exists intrinsically, but none do. Since to be a warrant is to be non-deceptive, and since any apprehension of any conventional phenomenon is deceptive, no apprehension of anything conventional can be warranted.

According to Taktsang, Candrakīrti shares this view. As a Prāsaṅgika Mādhyamika, Candrakīrti cannot accept ontological or epistemological foundations; we agree. As a Buddhist, Taktsang argues, Candrakīrti must accept the Pramāṇavādins' definition of epistemic warrant, which is foundationalist. It follows that from Candrakīrti's view, there is no truth about the conventional, there is no knowledge about the conventional, and everything we say about conventional phenomena is simply erroneous. Candrakīrti, thus, takes us straight into radical anti-realism and does so with his eyes wide open.

This reading, we have seen, has justification, and it is adopted by many contemporary scholars. Nonetheless, we will argue that it is wrong. Following Tsongkhapa, we will show that Candrakīrti can reject foundationalism but retain a robust sense of epistemic warrant, and so of the reality of the conventional world revealed by our epistemic instruments, thereby opening the path to ethical cultivation and so to liberation. In the next chapter, we will explain how Candrakīrti takes us out of the slough and back to firm epistemic ground.

2
Escaping the Slough
Candrakīrti's Positive Epistemology

In the previous chapter, we saw why Candrakīrti might plausibly be read as denying that it is possible to distinguish between truth and falsity within the conventional, and so why it is also plausible to read him as asserting there can be no knowledge of the conventional, and in the end, no reason to take conventional phenomena to be real. The path from semantics to epistemology to ontology—and the descent into the dismal slough of nihilism—begins with the idea that all conventional phenomena are deceptive, and hence illusory—existing in one way, but appearing in another. They are illusory because these interdependent appearances seem to our perceptual and conceptual faculties to be independent and substantial. That is standard Buddhist fare.

The second step on this descent is to note that to be deceptive is to be *false*, something upon which one cannot rely. So, all conventional phenomena are false; only their emptiness is true. But since to know something requires that that thing is *true*—that it exists as it appears—there can be no knowledge of conventional phenomena, no epistemic instrument that accesses the conventional can ever deliver truth. Moreover, only when there is a difference between being right and wrong about something can we say that that thing is real. So, since there is no difference between truth and falsity regarding the conventional—since everything we could ever say about it would be false—the conventional world is entirely unreal. As we have seen, there is a reason to ascribe every one of these premises to Candrakīrti and to think that he would endorse these inferences—and, as we have seen, many eminent scholars in classical Tibet and in contemporary Buddhist studies have read him this way.

In this chapter we will show that this initially plausible reading is wrong, and that the more positive epistemological and ontological

By the Light of the Moon. Jay L. Garfield and Sonam Thakchöe, Oxford University Press.
 DOI: 10.1093/oso/9780197830741.003.0003

reading articulated by Tsongkhapa is both more plausible as a reading of Candrakīrti and a more fruitful way to understand the two truths and the enterprise of inquiry in the context they constitute. We will concede that Candrakīrti takes all conventional phenomena to be deceptive—as any Mādhyamika must—and that this position is correct. But we will then show that to be deceptive in one sense is not to be deceptive in *all senses*. This is because there is a big difference between understanding the truth that things are deceptive—and therefore not being deceived by them—and failing to understand that things are deceptive, and therefore being deceived by them. As we have seen, from a Madhyamaka perspective what conventional phenomena conceal is the very fact that they are merely conventional, and the mechanism of that concealment is our own superimposition of intrinsic existence on that which lacks it. Candrakīrti puts it this way in his autocommentary on verse 6.28 of *Introduction to the Middle Way*:

> This means that sentient beings are confused with regard to the mode of existence of things; this is why they are deluded. Because of primal ignorance they superimpose a non-existent intrinsic reality onto things. Their perception of this intrinsic nature obscures reality, and so is concealing. (dBu ma, 'a: 254b; 1992: 102)[1]

But to be confused with regard to the ultimate mode of existence of things is not to be confused with regard to their conventional reality. Consider the following example: we might, in virtue of being colorblind, get the color of an apple wrong, but still know that it is an apple, and that it tastes good. So, even if we take the apple to exist intrinsically, although it only exists conventionally, we could be correct that it is nourishing. Thus, it does at least make sense to speak of truth and falsity with respect to deceptive phenomena; the fact that they are deceptive in one respect, and therefore false, does not mean that they are not non-deceptive in another, and therefore also true.[2]

[1] de la 'dis sems can rnams ji ltar gnas ba'i dngos po lta ba la rmongs par byed pas na gti mug ste| ma rig pa dang dngos po'i rang gi ngo bo yod pa ma yin pa sgo 'dog par byed pa rang bshin mthong ba la sgrib pa'i bdag nyid can ni kun rdzob bo||

[2] Once again, if we follow Gold's lead (2024), this gives us a way of understanding the unity of the two truths: even that which is false, or deceptive in one respect, may be true,

We will show that Candrakīrti correctly sees epistemic activity as engagement in practices of epistemic inquiry, practices governed by norms reflecting the nature and purposes of epistemic agents. Employing the practices successfully can provide us with knowledge of the conventional world, knowledge we must achieve if we are to know the ultimate, and which we presuppose in presenting any argument at all, even the nihilistic argument wrongly attributed to Candrakīrti.

The Problem of Foundationalism

The fulcrum of the debate between those who read Candrakīrti as a moderate realist and those who read him as a nihilist is an account of epistemic warrant and an account of what it is to endorse mundane conventions regarding inquiry and warrant. An epistemological consequence of the thesis of universal emptiness that defines Madhyamaka is that there are no convention-independent facts that ground conventions; instead, conventions determine what is real. Therefore, to the extent to which one thinks that warrant requires grounding in foundations, one will think that knowledge of the conventional is impossible, since the conventional is ungrounded. To the extent to which one thinks that warrant instead accrues when one has successfully engaged in a conventional practice, one will think that knowledge of the conventional may be possible. This is because knowledge so conceived presupposes no grounding, only successful participation in conventional epistemic practices.[3]

One might think of Wittgenstein's account of epistemology in *On Certainty* (1969) as a recent European venture into this terrain. In that text, Wittgenstein attends closely to the distinction between certainty and knowledge. The former, he points out, is a psychological attitude

or non-deceptive, in another respect. When one sees one's face in the mirror, one can rely on it as a reflection, but not as an interlocutor.

[3] Jayānanda, quoting Nāgārjuna's *Replies to Objections*, makes much the same point when he argues that to require each item of knowledge to be justified by appeal to another item of knowledge, instead of by mundane conventions leads to a vicious regress of justification (2012: vol. 2, 66–67).

toward a statement, a high degree of subjective confidence in its truth. But one may be certain about that which one does not know, and indeed may know something about which one is not certain. This is why to rely on one's certainty as warrant is dangerous. To know is *not* to be in a subjective psychological state. Instead, it is to be correct and to be *justified*, and justification is a social practice: the practice of seeking and giving reasons. Even when we reflect individually on our reasons for a belief or a course of action, that reflection only amounts to justification to the extent that it accords with our collective epistemic standards. Consider these remarks:

> 308. "Knowledge" and "certainty" belong to different categories. They are not two "mental states" like, say "surmising" and "being sure." (Here I assume that it is meaningful for me to say "I know what (e.g.) the word 'doubt' means" and that this sentence indicates that the word "doubt" has a logical role.) What interests us now is not being sure but knowledge.

Knowledge, unlike certainty, is the public outcome of using conventionally accepted epistemic practices properly. And those are practices that we learn as we mature and are brought into the community of knowers. We must learn what needs to be justified, what can and what cannot be reasonably doubted, when a justification is complete, and so on. If we cannot master these skills, we cannot come to know; if we do master these skills, we are accepted as members of the community of knowers. Wittgenstein also notes:

> 141. When we first begin to believe anything, what we believe is not a single proposition, it is a whole system of propositions. (Light dawns gradually over the whole.)[4]

> 142. It is not single axioms that strike me as obvious, it is a system in which consequences and premises give one another mutual support.

[4] This is an inadvertent echo of verse 3.1 of *Introduction to the Middle Way* in which Candrakīrti describes the practitioner's developing awareness as like the glow of sunlight illuminating the world as a whole.

> 143. I am told, for example, that someone climbed this mountain many years ago. Do I always enquire into the reliability of the teller of this story, and whether the mountain did exist years ago? A child learns there are reliable and unreliable informants much later than it learns facts which are told it. It doesn't learn at all that that mountain has existed for a long time: that is, the question whether it is so doesn't arise at all. It swallows this consequence down, so to speak, together with what it learns.

That is, we don't learn a set of basic truths, even truths about our epistemic practices, and then erect an edifice of knowledge upon that foundation. Instead, we are socialized into a web of epistemic practices and common knowledge, all of which are mutually supporting, and which together constitute the standards of conventional truth. That set of epistemic warrants is governed by social conventions, conventions that are revisable and self-correcting, but practices that cannot be grounded in themselves, on pain of regress. Wittgenstein makes the anti-foundationalist thrust of this account explicit:

> 95. The propositions describing this world-picture might be part of a kind of mythology. And their role is like that of rules of a game; and the game can be learned purely practically, without learning any explicit rules.
>
> 96. It might be imagined that some propositions, of the form of empirical propositions, were hardened and functioned as channels for such empirical propositions as were not hardened but fluid; and that this relation altered with time, in that fluid propositions hardened, and hard ones became fluid.
>
> 97. The mythology may change back into a state of flux, the river-bed of thoughts may shift. But I distinguish between the movement of the waters on the river-bed and the shift of the bed itself; though there is not a sharp division of the one from the other.
>
> 162. In general I take as true what is found in text-books, of geography for example. Why? I say: All these facts have been confirmed

> a hundred times over. But how do I know that? What is my evidence for it? I have a world-picture. Is it true or false? Above all it is the substratum of all my inquiring and asserting. The propositions describing it are not all equally subject to testing.

And if we ask, what holds all of this together, what accounts for the success of this epistemic enterprise, Wittgenstein's account, like those of Sextus and of Candrakīrti, is the surprising, "nothing." Or perhaps, to put it another way: they hold themselves together through their mutual support. Our epistemic life is nothing but a set of groundless conventions, delivering a conventional world in which each piece validates the others. To be a knower is to participate in these groundless conventions.

> 204. Giving grounds, however, justifying the evidence, comes to an end; but the end is not certain propositions' striking us immediately as true, i.e. it is not a kind of seeing on our part; it is our acting, which lies at the bottom of the language-game.

> 205. If the true is what is grounded, then the ground is not true, nor yet false.

> 248. I have arrived at the rock bottom of my convictions. And one might almost say that these foundation-walls are carried by the whole house.

Wittgenstein observes here that part of the incoherence of foundationalism lies in the failure to see that to take something as *true*, as an object of *knowledge*, always requires justification, and so to say that there are claims that are both *foundational*—hence ungrounded and so unjustified—and *known* is inconsistent. This rejection of foundations, he also points out, does not undermine, but instead vindicates scientific reasoning, which is part of that structure of mutually supportive practices:

> 324. Thus we should not call anybody reasonable who believed something in despite of scientific evidence.

> 325. When we say that we know that such and such . . . , we mean that any reasonable person in our position would also know it, that it would be a piece of unreason to doubt it.

To the extent to which one thinks that the endorsement of warrants amounts only to an observation that those practices are in fact used by a community, one will think that this endorsement does not amount to a recognition of knowledge. On such a view it would be no more than an anthropological observation about a way that people happen to talk or organize their academic affairs. But to the extent that one thinks that practices themselves—at least if they are articulated properly and are successful— can have normative force and constitute warrants, one will think that this endorsement amounts to a theory of knowledge.[5] Hume's account of justification in the *Treatise* comes to mind as another example of this approach (Garfield 2019a).

Candrakīrti on *Pramāṇa*

We therefore turn first to Candrakīrti's conception of *pramāṇa*. As we will see, he adopts a view that anticipates the conventionalism, or communitarian pragmatism, of Hume and Wittgenstein, allowing him a positive epistemological project in the context of a Madhyamaka ontology of emptiness, as well as a route to understanding how we can make sense of justification as normative and norm-responsive, despite being a human practice that can be studied empirically. This is a central task of naturalized epistemology, and one in which Candrakīrti can help us.

Most Buddhist epistemologists appear to have accepted the definition of *pramāṇa* offered by Dignāga and Dharmakīrti in their epistemological works. Taktsang and his followers ascribe this view of *pramāṇa* to Candrakīrti himself, and Tillemans presupposes that

[5] Wittgenstein's externalism regarding justification hence contrasts with Cartesian internalism. *Mutatis mutandis*, Candrakīrti's conventionalism is a kind of justificatory externalism that contrasts with the internalist account of justification we find in the Pramāṇavāda tradition of Dignāga and Dharmakīrti.

Candrakīrti adopts it. To attribute this epistemological position to Candrakīrti, however, is unwarranted: in fact, Candrakīrti is distinctive in his *rejection* of this framework.[6] In *Clear Words*, Candrakīrti levels sustained critiques of Dignāga's and Dharmakīrti's definition of *pramāṇa*, specifically on the grounds that those definitions presuppose foundationalism, and on the grounds that the Pramāṇavādin account assumes in its very definition of another epistemic warrant that cognition can be completely non-deceptive. Candrakīrti insists instead that if we are to have any rational basis to accept the Madhyamaka framework, we must make sense of knowledge and justification in a non-foundationalist way, and that we must allow that deceptive cognitions can nonetheless take us to knowledge (Thakchöe 2012, 2013).[7] In *Commentary on Seventy Stanzas of Reasoning*, Candrakīrti writes:

> In this context, things fall into one of the two truths according to whether they are apprehended by a reifying cognition or a non-reifying cognition. According to the epistemic conventions of the exalted ones, these are the conventional truth and the ultimate truth, respectively. But it is not only exalted beings who employ the convention of defining the two truths. Among ordinary beings, there are those who are experts in the matters of worldly convention and who can do so as well. (verse 1, dBu ma, ya: 268a)[8]

[6] Indeed, it is plausible that Candrakīrti's explicit critique of what was to become for centuries an orthodoxy in Indian Buddhist thought—the Pramāṇavāda of Dignāga and Dharmakīrti—was a principal reason for his being marginalized in that tradition.

[7] See Arnold (2008: 144–158 and 175–183) for a meticulous treatment of Candrakīrti's critique in *Clear Words* of Dignāga's foundationalism. Arnold helpfully clarifies the close relation between Candrakīrti's reply to the Pramāṇavādins and that Nāgārjuna advances in *Reply to Objections* against his imagined Nyāya interlocutor. Just as the Nayaiyikas presupposed that knowledge must have a foundation in self-warranting epistemic instruments, Dignāga argued that perception and inference could serve as self-warranting foundations for knowledge.

Arnold notes that Candrakīrti sees that this requires that these be in contact with self-presenting intrinsic characteristics (*svalakṣana*). And that, he points out, amounts both to a commitment to intrinsic nature, violating the Madhyamaka doctrine that all phenomena are empty of intrinsic nature and a commitment to givenness that makes the source of warrant mysterious. See also Salvini (2022: 417).

[8] 'dir dngos po rnams phyin ci log dang phyin ci ma log pa'i shes pa'i dbang gis bden pa gnyis te | kun rdzob kyi bden pa dang don dam pa'i bden pa zhes bya bar 'phags pas tha snyad mdzad la| 'phags pa 'ba' zhig kho na bden pa gnyis rnam par 'jog par mdzad pa ma yin te | 'jig rten pa 'jig rten gyi tha snyad la mkhas pa rnams kyang bden pa gnyis kyis tha snyad byed do||

Candrakīrti is clearly committed to the veridicality of ordinary as well as expert epistemic practices. He is also explicit about the interdependence between epistemic instruments and the knowledge and objects they deliver, and the emptiness of each of them of any intrinsic nature:

> We explain that mundane objects can be apprehended by means of the four epistemic instruments, each of which exists in virtue of mutual interdependence. Wherever there is an epistemic instrument, there is also an epistemic object; wherever there is an epistemic object, there is an epistemic instrument. Neither the instrument nor the object exists intrinsically. Therefore, mundane objects are just things as they are perceived. (*Clear Words* 1.3; Skt. text ed. Vaidya 1960: B75.27–27; dBu ma, 'a: 25b; 2003: 55)[9]

In these passages, Candrakīrti is following Nāgārjuna's account of the two truths in chapter 24 of *Fundamental Verses on the Middle Way* (*Mūlamadhyamakakārikā*) Nāgārjuna famously writes:

> The Buddha's teaching of the Dharma
> Is based on two truths:
> A truth of worldly convention
> And an ultimate truth. (24.8)
>
> Those who do not understand
> The distinction between these two truths
> Do not understand
> The Buddha's profound teaching. (24.9)
>
> Without depending on the conventional truth,
> The meaning of the ultimate cannot be taught.

[9] tāni ca parasparāpekṣayā sidhyanti-satsu pramāṇeṣu prameyārthāḥ satsu prameyeṣvartheṣu pramāṇāni | no tu khalu svābhāvikī pramāṇaprameyayoḥ siddhiriti | tasmāllaukikamevāstu yathādṛṣṭamityalaṃ prasaṅgena | 3||

Tib: de'i phyir de ltar tshad ma bzhi las 'jig rten gyi don rtogs par rnam par 'jog pa yin no | | de dag kyang phan tshun ltos pas 'grub par 'gyur te| tshad ma dag yod na gzhal bya'i don dag tu 'gyur la| gzhal bya'i don dag yod na tshad ma dag tu 'gyur gyi| tshad ma dang gzhal bya gnyis ngo bo nyid kyis grub pa ni yod pa ma yin no || de'i phyir mthong ba ji lta ba bzhin du 'jig rten pa nyid yin la rag ste| spros pas chog go|

> Without understanding the meaning of the ultimate,
> Nirvana is not achieved. (24.10)

Here it is pretty clear that Nāgārjuna asserts that there are two *truths*. There is therefore a real burden of proof on anyone who would assert that he takes only the ultimate to be true. And it is equally clear that he takes a grasp of the conventional truth to be a necessary condition of understanding ultimate truth. It would appear to follow that, according to Nāgārjuna, at any rate, the conventional truth is not only a domain of truth—indeed, something upon which one can and must *depend*—but a soteriologically important domain.[10]

It follows that within the Madhyamaka tradition, some account is needed of how the conventional truth can provide a stepping stone to the ultimate, as well as an account of the respect in which that truth is in fact *true*. This is why, we will see, when Candrakīrti rejects the Pramāṇavādin account of *pramāṇa*, he does not reject the importance or the possibility of epistemic warrant and knowledge *tout court*; he only rejects a particular *account* of warrant and knowledge. His own Prāsaṅgika epistemology is a deliberate attempt to move away from any commitment to epistemological and ontological foundationalism. And, therefore, Candrakīrti defines *pramāṇa* simply as cognition that gives us access to the world in virtue of its agreement with ordinary epistemic convention, that is, in accord with what is commonly accepted in everyday epistemic practice (Thakchöe 2011, 2012).[11]

[10] Those who read Candrakīrti as a transcendentalist or nihilist typically agree that the conventional is soteriologically significant, as a kind of ladder to the ultimate that must be discarded once one reaches a transcendent understanding of reality. They might say that conventional reality and conventional practices can play this role despite being entirely false, and despite therefore not being a domain of possible knowledge. But this position faces two important difficulties. First, there is a need to explain why *these* practices and *that* apparent reality are soteriologically effective and not others. This is akin to the scientific realist argument that appeal to an explanatory construct presupposes that if it really explains anything, there is a presumption in favor of the truth of the theory in which it figures and of the reality of the entities it posits. Second, to grant the soteriological efficacy of the conventional is to grant that it does not deceive us with regard to the path to awakening, and to be nondeceptive is to be *true*, at least in one respect. It is therefore difficult to maintain both that the conventional is soteriologically efficacious and that there is no sense in which it is true.

[11] See also Newman (2024), Powers (2021), Salvini (2014, 2019), and Walsh (2015), each of whom argues that Candrakīrti presents us with a non-foundationalist, but not

Candrakīrti distinguishes three levels of epistemic conventions: (1) conventions not accepted in the world (*alokasaṃvṛti* = *'jig rten ma yin pa'i kun rdzob*) associated with the defective epistemic instruments, (2) ordinary mundane convention (*lokasaṃvṛti* = *jig rten gyi kun rdzob*) associated with the proper use of functioning epistemic instruments, and (3) exalted convention (**ārya-vyavahāra* = *'phags pa'i tha snyad*) associated with the epistemic practices of highly realized beings, or what we might regard as the epistemic conventions of expertise. This provides the framework necessary to distinguish error from truth, but also expertise from inexpert judgment, allowing not only the correction of trivial error by a second look, but also of persistent popular error by appeal to those who know better (Forman 2020; Newman 2024; Garfield and Thakchöe 2015; Thakchöe 2024). And he asserts explicitly that the views of ordinary people are not authoritative. Commenting on verse 21.10 of *Fundamental Verses on the Middle Way*, he writes, "It is not the case that whatever anyone sees as existent in fact exists" (Vaidya 1960: B418.12–419; 2003: 371).

Candrakīrti also distinguishes between two kinds of causes of epistemic errors: (1) adventitious causes of epistemic error and (2) innate or pervasive causes of epistemic error. The first of these comprise underminers such as defective senses, including blindness, deafness; environmental underminers, including mirages and fog; or other subjective impairments, including intoxication or illness. Causes of the second kind include evolved susceptibility to illusion, such as well-known optical or auditory illusions, and most importantly, the illusion of intrinsic existence—our tendency to perceive things that only exist interdependently and are empty of essence as existing intrinsically and independently.

This second category of error is vast, and errors of these kind undermine the authority of much or our unreflective experience. It is what allows us, for instance, to see momentary pleasures as sources of happiness instead of suffering, to see our own interests as independent of those of others, and so to see egoism as rational. To eliminate errors like

a relativist, or nihilist, account of epistemology, as well as chapters 2–5 of Cowherds (2011). And see Salvini (2022: 415) for a discussion of the two kinds of error. Vose agrees that Candrakīrti ascribes use of these four *pramāṇas* to ordinary agents, but denies that they actually function as warrants, given massive delusion (2024: 3).

this, we need to rely on philosophical experts, whose analysis shows us that our judgments in these cases—like judgments that the earth is flat, or that the sun rises in the east and sets in the west—are as deceptive as they are natural.[12] Nonetheless, as we will see, Candrakīrti will argue that even when we are epistemically impaired by underminers of the second kind, we might be free of the first kind of underminer, and that this may permit us to warrant claims about conventional reality, the knowledge of which—as Nāgārjuna points out—is the precondition of the elimination of the illusion of intrinsic existence.

Commenting on Nāgārjuna's *Fundamental Verses* 24.8 in *Clear Words*, Candrakīrti begins to draw these distinctions:

> Suppose someone were to ask, "why should the use of epistemic instruments be called *mundane convention* (*lokasaṃvṛti* = *jig rten gyi kun rdzob*); does this imply that there is some non-mundane (*alokasaṃvṛti* = *'jig rten ma yin pa'i kun rdzob*) convention from which it is distinguished?"
>
> We would reply, "mundane convention is that which (1) takes things just as they are (*yathāvasthita*), and (2) it *does not engage* in analysis (*cintā*) here." (*Clear Words*, 24.8; Skt ed. Vaidya 1960: B493.9–10; dBu ma, 'a: 163a; 2003: 440)[13]

The first criterion—to take things "just as they are (*yathāvasthita*)"—can mean either that mundane conventions take things as they *really are* or that these conventions take things for granted *as they appear to be*. The Sanskrit is ambiguous, and in this context, either reading works. On the first, it is to *accept* things conventionally as they *are* conventionally, and not to pursue any analysis into a deeper, ultimate mode of being. On the second, it is to accept that *in* the conventional,

[12] Thanks to José Cabezón (personal communication) for emphasizing the importance of the vastness of this source of error and the role of authoritative philosophers in our epistemic life.

[13] loke saṃvṛtirlokasaṃvṛtiḥ | kiṃ punaralokasaṃvṛtirapyasti yata evaṃ viśiṣyate lokasaṃvṛtiriti? yathāvasthitapadārthānuvāda eṣaḥ, nātraiṣā cintāvatarati |

Tib: 'jig rten gyi kun rdzob ni 'jig rten gyi kun rdzob bo zhes 'jig rten kun rdzob ces gang las de ltar khyad par du byed pa 'jig rten ma yin pa'i kun rdzob kyang yod dam zhe na| 'di ni dngos po ji ltar gnas pa rjes su brjod pa yin gyi| 'dir dpyad pa de mi 'jug go | |

there is no gap between appearance and reality—once again, that our conventions don't require that we inquire into the essences of things. In either case, the point is simply that mundane epistemic conventions generally get things right, and they do so without requiring analysis (hence taking us to the second criterion).

This second criterion raises an important question: What kind of analysis do we forego when we remain in the conventional domain? On one reading—that adopted by Tillemans, for instance—this criterion requires us to forego *every* kind of analysis: mundane epistemic practice on this reading is just the acceptance of whatever appears to be the case. This would, as we noted in the previous chapter, take us straight to the dismal slough, and would effectively undermine any epistemic distinctions. But in this context, that is a highly uncharitable and unwarranted reading. After all, to take things as they are—to get it right—often requires investigation; so, to read the second clause this way would issue in a serious tension between the two clauses.

This requires us to rethink what Candrakīrti means when he accepts *what is accepted by the world.* The everyday practices of ordinary people and those of the Mādhyamika are conducted in the same shared epistemic framework, encompassing activities such as seeing, hearing, and experiencing and interacting with the world and with one another, as well as theorizing, drawing inferences, and so forth. Since these are all common sets of practices, they are the ones we accept when we engage in mundane epistemic activity. Our ordinary epistemic activity also includes all kinds of investigation, including the kinds of investigations undertaken by police officers and those undertaken by scientists. It would not be coherent to *accept* mundane practices and to *reject* these kinds of analysis, and Candrakīrti never advises us to draw such a distinction.

A more plausible and more charitable reading—that suggested by Tsongkhapa—is that *analysis* in this context means *Madhyamaka* analysis, that is, analysis meant to reveal the ultimate nature of things, and hence that to remain at the conventional level is simply to forego analysis into the ultimate nature of reality. Tsongkhapa puts it this way:

> [S]ince it is said that the meaning of "nondeceptive" is *true,* and since that is also the case according to nominal convention, and since the

> sūtras also say that the meaning of "nondeceptive phenomena" is *truth*, and since the meaning of "unreal" in "all compounded phenomena are unreal, deceptive phenomena," is *deceptive*, the meaning of *true* should be understood as *nondeceptive*.
>
> Thus the "truth" in "conventional truth" means *true from the perspective of grasping things as truly existent*. It does not have the same meaning of "truth" in "ultimate truth." (Tsongkhapa 2006: 488)

Tsongkhapa's argument is subtle and compelling. When we assess whether an epistemic instrument is deceptive in the context of conventional truth, we ask about whether it is nondeceptive with regard to how things appear to those who grasp things as truly existent, that is, to those who do not engage in ultimate analysis. On this reading, these two clauses are not only consistent, but are pulling in the same direction, and a plausible one. Mundane epistemic practices are those that get things right; they do not concern themselves with the transcendent question of what the intrinsic nature of things are, only with their properties that figure in the world of interdependent phenomena.[14] The fact that on this reading there is no obvious tension between the two clauses in Candrakīrti's criterion speaks in its favor.

Together, then, it makes sense that these two criteria constitute the definition of the worldly *pramāṇa* as a *nondeceptive cognition*. In *Clear Words*, Candrakīrti explicitly distinguishes mundane epistemic warrants from practices that do not meet the criteria for epistemic warrant.

> Since they present the objects that appear to them erroneously, defective sensory faculties such as a visual faculty afflicted by ophthalmia, vision obscured by cataracts, or by jaundice are not even accepted by mundane convention (*alokasaṃvṛti*); hence, they are not regarded as veridical according to mundane convention (*lokasaṃvṛtsatya*). This is how we distinguish the veridical from

[14] Mathura (2024) points out that Tsongkhapa is following Jayānanda closely here. Jayānanda argues that in Candrakīrti's system, mundane pramāṇas are those that are coherent, methodologically appropriate to their object, beneficial, and non-deceptive (6:3; dBu ma, ra: 114b; 2021: vol. 2, 10–20).

> the non-veridical within mundane convention; the use of defective senses is not considered veridical even in the context of mundane convention. (*Clear Words* 24. 28; Skt. ed. Vaidya 1960: B75.20.21; dBu ma, 'a: 163ab; 2003: 440)[15]

As we noted above, the causes of epistemic error are those that arise from the malfunctioning of epistemic instruments, including the sensory faculties and our cognitive capacities. Defective sensory cognitions present deceptive objects, such as a visual field full of falling hairs when in fact there are none in the immediate environment (only bits of protein in the vitreous fluid that we mistake for hairs), or the appearance of a yellow conch, when in fact there is a white one in front of the eyes. This is not to say that these sensory cognitions are erroneous with respect to what appears to them—falling hairs and a yellow conch do appear—but only that they are erroneous with regard to what would appear to a normal, healthy human observera member of the epistemic community that constitutes the relevant epistemic conventions. This is why they are not epistemic warrants with respect to their objects, even though they may be warrants with respect to their appearances: our senses might deliver correct information about how the world *appears to us and to others*, but incorrect information about how it *is*, or how it would look if we were not impaired. Candrakīrti puts this point this way: "Such things as a double moon are not perceived in non-disordered cognitive states, even though they are perceived by disordered states" (*Clear Words* 1.3, Skt. ed. Vaidya 1960: B75.20.21; dBu ma, 'a: 25b; 2003: 55).[16] Candrakīrti emphasizes the veridicality and the interdependence of the epistemic warrants on one another and on their objects when he writes:

[15] athavā | timirakāmalādyupahatendriyaviparītadarśanāvasthānāste'lokāḥ, teṣāṃ yā saṃvṛtirasāvalokasaṃvṛtiḥ | ato viśiṣyate lokasaṃvṛtiriti |

Tib: rab rib dang ling tog sngon po dang| mig ser la sogs pas bdang po nyams pas mthong ba phyin ci log la gnas pa de dag ni 'jig rten ma yin te| de dag gi kun rdzob gang yin pa de ni| 'jig rten kun rdzob bden pa ma yin pas| jig rten kun rdzob bden pa dang| zhes de las khyed par du byas so||

[16] dvicandrādīnāṃ tu ataimirikajñānāpekṣayā apratyakṣatvam, taimirikādyapekṣayā tu pratyakṣatvameva ||

Tib: zla ba gnyis la sogs pa dag ni rab rib can ma yin pa'i shes pa la ltos nas mngon sum nyid ma yin la| rab rib can la sogs pa la ltos nas ni mngon sum nyid kho na'o| |

> We explain that mundane objects can be apprehended by means of the four epistemic instruments, all of which exist in mutual dependence. Where there is an epistemic instrument, there is also an epistemic object; where is an epistemic object, there is also an epistemic instrument. Neither of these two have any intrinsic nature. Therefore, the world consists exactly in things as they are observed. (*Clear Words* 1.3, Vaidya 1960: B75.26–28; dBu ma, 'a: 25b; 2003: 55)[17]

This statement not only makes it clear that Candrakīrti endorses an epistemology of some kind, and that he is a (at least a moderate) realist regarding the object of our experience, but also that the epistemology he endorses is not that of Dignāga or Dharmakīrti. He neither takes perception and inference to be the *only* epistemic instruments nor grants these or any other such instruments a *foundational* status. Instead, he is open to multiple sources of knowledge—including analogy and testimony—and he regards the instruments as validated by one another and by their success in delivering objects.[18]

We can now see what is wrong with Vose's epistemological arguments for reading Candrakīrti as a nihilist scouted in the previous chapter. Let us begin with his argument grounded in his interpretation

[17] tāni ca parasparāpekṣayā sidhyanti-satsu pramāṇeṣu prameyārthāḥ, satsu prameyeṣvartheṣu pramāṇāni | no tu khalu svābhāvikī pramāṇaprameyayoḥ siddhiriti | tasmāllaukikamevāstu yathādṛṣṭamityalaṃ prasaṅgena | prastutameva vyākhyāsyāmaḥ |
Tib: de'i phyir de ltar tshad ma bzhi las 'jig rten gyi don rtogs par rnam par 'jog pa yin no| |de dag kyang phan tshun ltos pas 'grub par 'gyur te | tshad ma dag yod na gzhal bya'i don dag tu 'gyur la| gzhal bya'i don dag yod na tshad ma dag tu 'gyur gyi| tshad ma dang gzhal bya gnyis ngo bo nyid kyis grub pa ni yod pa ma yin no| |de'i phyir mthong ba ji lta ba bzhin du 'jig rten pa nyid yin la rag ste| spros pas chog go| |

[18] Mathura (2024) notes correctly that Jayānanda in his commentary to 6.170cd argues that Candrakīrti is refuting what he regards as the foundationalism of the Pramāṇavāda tradition on the grounds that it presupposes a substantialist ontology that no Mādhyamika can accept. Jayānanda also writes that "scripture with completely pure objects is non-deceptive and authoritative, following mundane conventions according to which words with pure objects are authoritative" (2012: vol. 2, 17) and "This is the nature of mundane epistemic instruments: whatever is understood based on the details of what is taught in scripture is non-deceptive, just as objects of perception and inference are understood. . . . Scripture is authoritative because it is non-deceptive . . . and is not contradicted by perception or inference" (18). He thus affirms that authoritative texts count as *pramāṇas*, and that they are *pramāṇas* in exactly the same sense as perception and inference.

of *samvṛti*. We can grant that *a* principal meaning of this term is *deceptive*, which is the standard Sanskrit gloss on *false*, while bearing in mind that this is only *one* of its semantic ranges. But we can now see that even if we grant for the sake of argument that this is the principal meaning of the term as Candrakīrti uses it, it is fallacious to infer from the fact that everything in the conventional world is false, or deceptive, that nothing is true *in any sense*, and so that the conventional world is entirely nonexistent. To say that conventional phenomena are false *in the relevant sense* is to say merely that they exist in one way, and appear in another, in this case, that they are conventionally real, but appear to ordinary subjects as though they are ultimately real.[19]

With this in mind, if we return to the passage from *Clear Words* that Vose quotes in support of the claim that to be conventionally true is to be nonarisen, and hence nonexistent, we see that that passage does not support his reading. Let us recall the passage:

> The very emptiness characterized as nonarising by intrinsic nature is posited to be the middle path. For that which does not arise by intrinsic nature has no existence; and since there is no cessation of that which is nonarisen by intrinsic nature, it has no nonexistence. Thus, since it is devoid of the two extremes of being and nonbeing, emptiness characterized by the nonarising by the intrinsic nature of all is said to be the middle path. (dBu ma, a': 167b; 2003: 450–451, quoted at 2024: 14)

The crucial words here are *by intrinsic nature*, which qualify the verb *to arise*. Candrakīrti is glossing Nāgārjuna's verse to mean that dependently originated phenomena—the phenomena of the conventional world—do not arise with, or in virtue of, any intrinsic nature, or essence; that is precisely that of which everything is empty. For that reason, they exist only dependently, and so are unarisen *ultimately*.

[19] Here we have bracketed the question of what to make of the second semantic range of *samvṛti*, on which it means *by agreement*, or *nominal*. If we take that range to be primary, our case is even stronger. And given the continuity of that second range with the Pāli *sammuti*, there is good reason to take that range very seriously indeed on philological grounds, in addition to the good philosophical reasons for reading Candrakīrti as emphasizing that range of meanings.

This avoids the two extremes: essential or ultimate existence, and complete nonexistence. There is nothing nihilistic about this passage, and indeed it suggest that things are conventionally real, when *conventionally* (*samvṛti*) is read as *interdependently*, or *nominally*, another gloss that Candrakīrti provides in *Clear Words*.

This in turn undermines the claim that ordinary people cannot be epistemically warranted in their beliefs. This is because the basis of that conclusion is the premise that ordinary beings are *entirely* deluded, and we now see that even though they may be deluded with regard to the mode of existence of phenomena, this does not entail being deluded with respect to their conventional properties.

Finally, this suggests that Jayānanda's and Patsab's conclusion that buddhas have no experience at all on the basis of the claim that they do not *fabricate* is also unwarranted (Thakchöe and Wilshire, 2019). While it is true that nothing appears to buddhas as intrinsically existent, or as having an essence—that is, a buddha has no fabricated or deceptive appearances, nothing precludes a buddha seeing things just as they are—as dependently arisen and conventionally real, but ultimately empty. Having dispelled these plausible arguments for these nihilistic or transcendentalist arguments, we can turn to Candrakīrti's positive account.

Candrakīrti's Pragmatic Coherentism

The fact that the use of each of our conventional epistemic instruments is integral to our epistemic practices also means that to accept these practices is to accept certain normative features that they share. Among those are the recursivity of self-correction and the division of epistemic labor. The first comprises the practices we employ to assess our practices, allowing us to sharpen our tools and to improve our grindstones as we go along, using increasingly finely calibrated tools to advance science, and using our advanced science to refine and to recalibrate our tools in a virtuous epistemic spiral; the second involves our deference to experts, and our ability to determine who in our community to trust regarding which matters: physicist tell us about forces and atoms, art historians about genres and brushstrokes.

Philosophers may have views about these matters, but whatever they say must be treated with healthy suspicion. These two features are now widely accepted in contemporary coherentist and naturalized epistemology, and we see each at work in Candrakīrti's own thought. This is a non-foundationalist, conventionalist, and coherentist approach to knowledge. And it is not nihilistic: one could only draw that conclusion if one thought that foundationalism is the only cogent epistemology, and therefore that such a virtuous spiral is in fact a vicious circle or regress. Given the dialectical context—the principled rejection of foundationalism by the Mādhyamika—this would be to beg the question.[20]

On Candrakīrti's view, the conventional world is that which is delivered by non-defective conventional epistemic instruments. This conventional truth is distinguished from that which is conventionally false because the false is that which is delivered by defective epistemic instruments. This much makes it clear that Candrakīrti not only has the resources to draw a distinction between truth and falsity, between warranted and unwarranted claims within the domain of the conventional, but also draws these distinctions explicitly. And in doing so, he appeals to the crucial distinction between how something appears to a single epistemic agent and how it appears to a typical member of the epistemic community. This distinction allows him to explain warrant in terms of epistemic convention, and then to draw the distinction between truth and falsity on the basis of the Peirceian spiral that arises from the account of warrant (Thakchöe 2024).[21] Candrakīrti can

[20] See also Forman (2020) for a detailed Sellarsian defense of Candrakīrti's coherentism that makes plain his commitment to the mutual dependence of the various *pramāṇas* and defends this framework as non-relativistic.

[21] According to Peirce, the process of warrant involves three elements: perception, judgment, and reasoning. These elements form a spiral because each one leads to the next, creating a continuous and evolving process of inquiry and justification. Perception provides the initial data, which leads to judgment about the significance of the data, and then reasoning is used to draw further conclusions and to refine the initial perception. Perception is only a warrant when it leads to a judgment, and when that judgment is confirmed rationally. Judgment is warranted by perception and reason, and reason must be justified by judgments regarding validity and perceptual confirmation. This virtuous spiral constitutes the dynamic and self-correcting nature of inquiry and justification (chapter 3, 1955: 23–41; Atkin 2023).

hence help us to deepen a defense of coherentism, opening a middle path between foundationalism and relativism.

As Newman (2024) argues persuasively, when Candrakīrti understands what it is to be accepted by mundane conventions, he has in mind not a poll of what ordinary folks believe, but rather our conventions regarding confirmation, including the consultation and deference to experts, a kind of early anticipation of Putnam's account of the division of epistemic labor: Candrakīrti escapes "the dismal slough of relativism [through a model of *lokaprasiddhi* that] distinguishes expert knowledge about mundane reality from the untutored notions of the *hoi polloi*" (76). This appeal to a self-correcting process allows us collectively to pull ourselves from the slough by our own bootstraps.[22]

Mundane epistemic conventions may be the way ordinary beings distinguish truth from falsity in conventional reality, but they are inadequate to provide a complete understanding of that conventional reality, and this by their own lights. Again, the analogy between common sense and science is helpful here. Common sense might tell us that the sun rises in the east, traverses the sky, and sets in the west. But common sense also tells us that in matters of astronomy, science trumps the most naïve deliverances of common sense itself. So, when science teaches us that in fact the Earth revolves clockwise on its axis while the sun remains still at the center of the solar system, common sense tells us to correct our naïve understanding.

We therefore do *not* say that it is conventionally *true* that the sun traverses the sky from east to west, only that it *appears* to do so. And this is why we come to take our ordinary way of talking to refer to *appearance*, not to *reality*. Candrakīrti, by analogy, tells us that our mundane epistemic conventions include the convention of refining our views in response to sophisticated Madhyamaka analysis that can lead us to see that conventional truth is deceptive, and so to distinguish what is mere appearance from reality. As we would put it, deference to experts is built into mundane epistemology; as Candrakīrti would put it, deference to the perspective of more realized practitioners is built into the

[22] Salvini (2019) makes much the same point in his perceptive discussion of the etymology of *lokaprasiddhi*.

epistemology of ordinary people.[23] While modern science may be very different from classical Indian meditative practice, the homology remains: in each case, our epistemic practices involve deference to those we regard as experts, at least in their respective domains of expertise.

Candrakīrti thus rejects the global error theory ascribed to him by so many of his canonical and contemporary commentators. No global error theory can distinguish truth from falsity or provide an account of warrant. And so, when Candrakīrti affirms that there is one moon, not two, and there is no creator god, he does so because he also affirms that conventional epistemic warrants deliver a single moon, and not two moons, and that no warrant that we recognize conventionally delivers the existence of a creator god.

Conventional and Ultimate Pramāṇas

Thus far, we have shown that Candrakīrti distinguishes between truth and falsehood, and between warranted and between unwarranted assertions in the context of the conventional. But a Madhyamaka epistemology requires more than that: we need an account of the relation between the judgments of ordinary epistemic agents whose minds are obscured by primal confusion regarding the fundamental nature of reality and the judgments of noble beings or buddhas, experts whose minds are free from that distortion. Here Candrakīrti introduces the device of an *exalted conventional truth* as opposed to an *ordinary conventional truth*. This exalted truth is the final stepping stone to the realization of ultimate truth. It also provides the model for ordinary appeal to expertise in the domain of the conventional.

In order to explore this next level of Candrakīrti's epistemology, we turn to Candrakīrti's *Commentary on Nāgārjuna's Seventy Stanzas on*

[23] See Arnold (2008: 158–162) for a discussion of why Candrakīrti rejects the idea that our conventions need to have convention-independent foundations. And see Garfield (1990) and Garfield and Dreyfus (2011) for a discussion of how this insight connects Madhyamaka to Pyrrhonism. It is also worth noting that on this point Tsongkhapa appears to disagree with Candrakīrti. He takes sensory evidence and reasoning to be sufficient to allow us to eliminate errors of this kind. We side with Candrakīrti: our epistemic landscape is too complex for any of us to navigate it on our own.

Emptiness (*Śūnyatasatativṛtti*), which addresses the distinction between two approaches to conventional truth, calling them "the inflationary approach" (*sgro btags pa'i don*) of the ordinary beings and "the deflationary approach" (*sgro ma btags pa'i don rig pa*) of the exalted beings:

> When the meaning of *truth* is unclear to ordinary beings, they talk about it through an inflationary convention. This is what is called "conventional." When the meaning of *truth* is clear to exalted beings they talk about it through a deflationary convention. This is what is called "ultimate." When ordinary beings use the term *conventional* as a convention, we should not assume that this is based on their understanding of the falsehood of conventional objects. The truths accepted as valid by ordinary beings are understood to be conventional truths only from the perspective of exalted beings. The truths accepted by worldly beings that are based on falsehood are simply nonsense, as when one describes a non-existent entity. (*Commentary on Nāgārjuna's Seventy Stanzas on Emptiness*, verse 1, dBu ma, ya: 268a–268b)[24]

To adopt an *inflationary* understanding of epistemic conventions is to appreciate that a claim can be warranted conventionally, but to do so without understanding the deeper implications of the fact that the warrant is only conventional, or that the truth affirmed is only conventional truth. That is, it is to understand that warrant is conventional, but to fail to understand *what it is to be conventionally true*. This stance

[24] 'dir dngos po rnams phyin ci log dang phyin ci ma log pa'i shes pa'i dbang gis bden pa gnyis te | kun rdzob kyi bden pa dang don dam pa'i bden pa zhes bya bar 'phags pas tha snyad te mdzad la | 'phags pa 'ba' zhig kho na bden pa gnyis rnam par 'jog par mdzad pa ma yin te | 'jig rten pa 'jig rten gyi tha snyad la mkhas pa rnams kyang bden pa gnyis tha snyad byed do || 'di ltar bden pa'i don ni mi snang la sgro btags pa'i don rigs par tha snyad byed pa la 'di ni kun rdzob pa'o zhes tha snyad byed do || gang du bden pa'i don mi snang ba ma yin la sgro ma btags pa'i don rig pa'i tha snyad la | de la 'di ni don dam pa kho na'o zhes rnam par 'jog go || re zhig gang la 'di kun rdzob ces tha snyad byed pa de la mi bden pa'i don 'di 'jig rten pas khong du chud pa nyid kyis de'i yul la bsam pa gtang bar mi bya'o ||gang yang 'jig rten gyi tha snyad la bden par 'dod pa de yang 'phags pa rnams 'jig rten kun rdzob kyi bden par bzhed de | med pa'i don la tha snyad 'dogs pa ltar don med pa nyid du [268b] brjod do ||de yang brdzun pa nyid du rtogs par byed pa | 'phags pa nyid kyis 'chad par 'gyur ba'i 'jig rten pa rab tu grags pa'i rigs pa nyid kyis nye bar ston par mdzad de |

is inflationary because one who adopts it engages non-analytically with things, and so takes them to exist intrinsically, inflating their ontological status. Moreover, to understand warrant this way is also implicitly to take the warrants to be independent, inflating their epistemic status. This is what it means to formulate epistemic judgments based on how things appear when one apprehends them naïvely, without critical analysis.

To take this inflationary stance is also what it is to occupy Sellars' "manifest image" (1963: 6), "the framework in terms of which man came to be aware of himself as man-in-the-world" (2007: 374). This is the image of reality and of our place in it in terms of which we naïvely observe and explain the world around us. It contains persons and things, as well as the norms that persons institute as the standards of truth and falsity. Importantly, the manifest image does *not* include the theoretical resources in terms of which to understand the true nature of the entities we encounter in the world, or to provide deep theoretical explanations of their appearance to us.

To occupy this image is to explain what one sees in virtue of regularities, but not to engage in the deep analysis that would take us into the scientific image (Sellars 1963; Garfield ed. 2019b: part 1). The mundane epistemic conventions to which Candrakīrti refers are non-philosophical and pretheoretical, and many of those who employ them, however successfully, never reflect on what they are or why they are useful—unless, perhaps, they enroll in an epistemology class. But this does not mean that this stance is dispensable: without using these basic epistemic resources, we could never pursue science or epistemology, and so could never come even to a deeper understanding of those conventions themselves. Just as the manifest image is methodologically less rigorous than the scientific image, but nonetheless both pragmatically useful on its own and necessary as the normative context for science, the mundane conventional truth is pragmatically useful and provides the context for the deeper philosophical analysis that takes us toward ultimate truth.

Exalted epistemic convention takes us further. It, Candrakīrti tell us, involves "genuine insight into the conventional status of epistemic convention." Powered by deeper analysis and by more profound understanding of the nature of reality and of epistemology, this kind of analysis penetrates our innate, pretheoretical understanding of our conventions. To see things in this way is to comprehend things as they are: to acknowledge that their reality is merely conventional and to realize that they are illusory, empty of intrinsic nature and dependently originated. It is also to recognize that our conventional epistemic warrants are warrants only with respect to their appropriate objects—entities apprehended as dependently originated and empty of intrinsic existence.

It is important to see that this expert analysis does not entirely undermine our pretheoretical conventional knowledge of the world. While it corrects errors in that understanding, and while it reframes that knowledge as merely conventional, it preserves the distinction between truth and falsity in the conventional, and the possibility of epistemic warrant in that framework; it respects the conventional as the necessary basis for the ultimate.

Consider two crucial passages in which Candrakīrti defines *the world* with reference to *mundane convention* (*lokavyāvahāra*). In *Clear Words*, commenting on verse 24.8 of *Fundamental Verses*, he writes: "The world is known to be the psychophysical clusters, / The world definitely depends on them. / It follows that the world comprises a person (*pudgala*) designated in dependence on the clusters" (Skt ed. Vaidya 1960: 492.6–9; dBu ma, 'a: 163a; 2003: 439).

In this passage, Candrakīrti gives us two senses of the term *the world* (*loka*). In the first sense the world comprises the five psychophysical clusters—matter, sensation, perception, personality traits, and consciousness—because it is designated dependently upon them. In the second sense, the world comprises, among other things, persons (*pudgala*) that are designated dependently upon those clusters. Candrakīrti makes the same point in the *Commentary on Seventy Stanzas on Emptiness*: "So, what is it that which we describe here as 'mundane convention'? We describe the world, in this context, as persons designated in dependence upon the clusters, just as fire is designated dependently upon the fuel" (*Commentary on Nāgārjuna's Seventy Stanzas on Emptiness*, verse 1, dBu ma, ya: 268b).[25]

[25] yang na ci zhig la 'dir 'jig rten gyi tha snyad ces bya zhe na | de la re zhig bud shing la brten nas me bzhin du phung bo la brten nas brtags pa'i gang zag la 'jig rten zhes brjod do ||

The world comprises persons; it follows that mundane convention consists in that instituted by persons, including, in Candrakīrti's view, both ordinary and highly accomplished persons. For anything to exist or to be known conventionally, we need persons to institute the relevant conventions, even as persons themselves are instituted by those very conventions. Here we have a nice anticipation both of Hume's emphasis on the recursive dimensions of custom and of Sellars' account of the transition from the manifest to the scientific image, a transition that does not discard, but instead supplements that image.

Sellars points out that while the manifest image of the world raises questions that demand explanation in the scientific image, the scientific image can never replace the manifest image. This is because even though the scientific image is more authoritative with regard to the nature of things, and while it provides deeper explanations of nature and of thought than are possible in the manifest, the categories of normativity and the moral, linguistic, and epistemic conventions that make human society, discourse, and therefore that make science itself possible demand the existence of communities of *persons*—the beings that constitute the manifest image.

We therefore cannot dispense with either image; they are deeply interdependent, and truth in each is responsive to the practices and standards that define each. Just as the manifest image cannot be refined or corrected without science, the scientific image cannot get off the ground without the questions posed and the normative standards instituted in the manifest. A world, or a *loka*, cannot be understood completely without a binocular vision that merges these two images into a single reality.

Just so, Candrakīrti emphasizes a millennium and half before Sellars that while ultimate truth may provide a deeper account of reality than conventional truth, it cannot supplant it; the two truths are two sides of the same coin. The ordinary mundane perspective on the world raises metaphysical questions that can only be answered by the

Candrakīrti, *Commentary on Nāgārjuna's Seventy Stanzas on Emptiness*, dBu ma ya 268b: yang na ci zhig la 'dir 'jig rten gyi tha snyad ces bya zhe na | de la re zhig bud shing la brten nas me bzhin du phung bo la brten nas brtags pa'i gang zag la 'jig rten zhes brjod do || (See Thakchoe 2011: 39–55). On the last point, being a nonanalytic cognitive process, Candrakīrti says mundane convention "(i) it posits things as they are conventional, and (ii) it does not engage in the analysis" (*Clear Words* 24.8 *dBu ma* 'a 163a).

deep analysis that the exalted perspective makes possible. And just as the scientific image does not eliminate the manifest image, but instead illuminates it to a greater degree than the manifest image can illuminate itself, the deflationary exalted perspective does not *eliminate* the reality of the conventional world, but instead *illuminates* it in a brighter light (Sellars 2007: 386).[26]

Candrakīrti writes that the exalted perspective allows us insight into the two truths:

> Things fall into one of the two truths depending on whether they are apprehended through a reifying or a non-reifying cognition. They are defined according to the epistemic conventions of the exalted beings (*'phags pas tha snyad mdzad*) as the conventional truth and the ultimate truth, respectively. There are also ordinary beings who are experts in the matters of worldly convention and who can, as well, employ this convention for defining the two truths. (*Commentary on Nāgārjuna's Seventy Stanzas on Emptiness*, verse 1, dBu ma, ya: 268a)[27]

This statement provides convincing evidence that Candrakīrti rejects the account of *lokaprasiddha* that Taktsang, Tillemans, and others in their camp attribute to him, as he does *not* take whatever ordinary beings think to be the measure of conventional truth or take us into the dismal slough (Thakchöe 2024). Candrakīrti here explicitly rejects that view, endorsing the perspective of experts as that from which we determine what conventional truth is, and the perspective of non-defective conventional cognition as that which delivers its content.

Just as Sellars emphasizes that neither of these images is foundational to the other and that each image is successively enriched in dialectical relationship to the other—with deference to science built

[26] See Chadha (2019), Duckworth (2019), and Tillemans (2019) for more discussion of the relationship between the two images and the two truths.

[27] 'dir dngos po rnams phyin ci log dang phyin ci ma log pa'i shes pa'i dbang gis bden pa gnyis te| kun rdzob kyi bden pa dang don dam pa'i bden pa zhes bya bar 'phags pas tha snyad mdzad la| 'phags pa 'ba' zhig kho na bden pa gnyis rnam par 'jog par mdzad pa ma yin te| 'jig rten pa 'jig rten gyi tha snyad la mkhas pa rnams kyang bden pa gnyis tha snyad byed do|

into the very idea of the manifest image—Candrakīrti emphasizes that neither of the two truths is foundational to the other: the ultimate is what we find when we ask after the final nature of the conventional; but the conventional is the source of the practices that enable that inquiry. While realization of the ultimate is soteriologically necessary, conventional truth constitutes the normative framework that makes its realization possible: the two truths are intertwined.

Candrakīrti takes *that which is accepted in the everyday world* to comprise the things we visually observe, the sounds we audibly hear, the aromas and savors we smell and taste, as well as the ideas and thoughts we conceptualize, the stuff of the manifest image. But it also comprises the epistemic instruments and practices that allow us to know these things, and to correct our errors. These are the stuff of the scientific image. He takes these entities to constitute *that which is accepted in the everyday world* because they are epistemically warranted in virtue of the success they afford us, and because they are collectively endorsed in our epistemic practices. To engage in these practices is to participate in the conventions of gaining knowledge and of justifying our claims and so constitute the conventional truths. They are therefore, according to Candrakīrti, *pramāṇa*--epistemically warranted (*Commentary on Āryadeva's Four Hundred Stanzas* 5.24; dBu ma, ya: 105a, 2019: 153–154). And they warrant one another, just as do the two Sellarsian images.

Recursivity and Realism

To say that epistemic practices are recursively self-correcting is to say that we can recognize that we often use fallacious reasoning, misperceive, rely on mendacious sources, succumb to illusions, and so on, and that when we do recognize errors such as these, we correct them using the very epistemic instruments that we discover ourselves to have misused. In doing so, we engage in a process of self-correction. An inference may lead us to see that we must have misperceived: that couldn't have been a polar bear in the pasture; it must have been a Maremma. Perception may correct an inference: based on your normal travel patterns, we were sure that you were in Kyoto, but here you are in front of us in Benares.

Testimony may correct either perception or inference, as is often the case when we are studying a subject about which we know too little with an expert teacher. You might have thought that that animal was a squirrel, but in fact it was a chipmunk; your perception was not as authoritative as you thought it was, and it was corrected by the testimony of the biologist. We once thought that disjunctive syllogism is valid, but now have come to learn that it only preserves truth in a consistent domain; skilled logicians corrected our inferential practices. To become a competent knower is not to have reached the apogee of the epistemic spiral,[28] but to have learned to participate effectively in it, and this participation includes openness to correction.

This spiral, which defines our epistemic practices, depends upon a division of epistemic labor. Part of the reason to include *śabda*, or testimony, as one of the *pramāṇas* is the recognition that we can, do, and indeed *must* rely on those who we collectively regard as experts in order to know much of anything. Just think for a moment about all of the things about which you legitimately claim knowledge. How many of those are known independently of the testimony of relevant experts? Some of us even rely on our ophthalmologists to let us know in what circumstances we can trust the evidence of our visual faculties. And when we get to astronomical, geographical, medical, or historical facts, we recognize that everything that we know implicates expert testimony at some point. As we have seen, such testimony may correct our naïve reliance on even *prima facie* warrants such as perception and inference. This is why foundationalism in the theory of knowledge is a non-starter, and this is why Candrakīrti rejects it.

This approach to the conventional allows Candrakīrti to endorse an epistemology that provides an account of the *pramāṇas* without succumbing either to the foundationalism of the Nyāya tradition or to that of the Buddhist Pramāṇavāda tradition. It is an epistemology that recognizes that the normative status of the *pramāṇas* neither derives from infallibility nor is *sui generis*. Instead, it derives from the various fallible epistemic conventions that constitutes these as *pramāṇas* in the first place, which include those for mutual correction. Despite

[28] Most Buddhist epistemologists would claim that only a Buddha achieves that status.

its fallibility, this is an epistemology sufficient to establish a clear distinction between that which is warranted and that which is not in the context of mundane convention, and so a distinction between the true and the false—between that which is trustworthy and that which is not.

Candrakīrti *explicitly* warns us against what Tillemans calls the "typical reading" of the error theorist in order "to avoid misrepresenting *conventional truth* to mean the perspective of the ordinary beings, for that would," Candrakīrti says, "require committing to the assumption that ordinary beings have the knowledge that the objects are unreal (*mi bden pa'i don*)" (*Commentary on Nāgārjuna's Seventy Stanzas on Emptiness*, dBu ma, ya: 268a). This understanding of conventional truth is *not* "easy-easy truth." While ordinary folk lack the epistemic sophistication necessary to deflate conventional truth, they nonetheless know that expert analysis trumps their own. Expert Mādhyamikas, or exalted beings, directly understand the deflationary meaning of *conventional truth*, and so their understanding becomes the *measure* of truth (Newland 2011).

Candrakīrti states his distinctions between the two approaches carefully and concisely this way in the *Commentary on Seventy Stanzas on Emptiness*. He does so by contrasting two terms, each of which is often translated as *conventional* in English: *samvṛti*, which can mean either *by agreement* or *concealing*, and *vyavahāra*, which means *everyday*, or *transactional*. The first term, as we have noted, connotes the deceptiveness of conventional truth—its tendency to *conceal* the fact that it is *nominal*, or that it is established through our practices; the second connotes the fact it is just what emerges from our everyday commercial, interpersonal, and discursive practices.

> Thus, ordinary people do not take the terms *samvṛti* and *vyavahāra* to be synonymous. The first has its basis in the idea of convention in the context of the *saṃvṛti/paramārtha* (*conventional vs. ultimate*) distinction: *saṃvṛti* denotes one side of this binary: it denotes ordinary convention but not *reality*. It therefore makes perfect sense that it only exalted beings can assert that *saṃvṛti* is not reality. Only exalted beings understand that these two terms—*vyavahāra* and *saṃvṛti*—are coreferential and this is not inconsistent with the fact

that ordinary people do not see this. (*Commentary on Nāgārjuna's Seventy Stanzas on Emptiness*, dBu ma, ya: 268b)[29]

Here Candrakīrti states that only realized experts are capable of fully understanding the implications of *saṃvṛti*. They see that to be conventional is to be deceptive. Folks like us naïvely take the things that exist conventionally to be *more* real than that—to exist independently, and ultimately. We hence fail to see them as deceptive (even when we *know* that they are), and so do not fully apprehend them *as conventional*. The expert sees through their deceptiveness, is not deceived, and so sees them *as conventional*. But this is not to fail to seem them at all; instead, it is to see them *just as they are* (Garfield and Thakchöe 2011). Once again, this is powerful evidence that Candrakīrti does not take ordinary epistemic agents to be the final arbiters of conventional truth. And this is to take conventional truth to outstrip "easy-easy" truth, or mere consensus.

Out of the Slough

We have seen that exegetes from Taktsang to Tillemans, when Candrakīrti says that the Mādhyamika endorses mundane conventions, he means that a Mādhyamika is doing nothing more than reporting on the naïve realism of ordinary beings, a view that he himself must reject. On this purely anthropological reading of the Mādhyamika's understanding of conventional reality, the Mādhyamika can report on how ordinary people conduct their inquiries, on what they say is true, on what they say is false, and on what they claim to be warranted or unwarranted. But on this view, these reports are opaque: one cannot infer from the fact that ordinary people say these

[29] kun rdzob kyi sgra ni 'jig rten pa'i tha snyad kyi rnam grangs ma yin te| kun rdzob dang don dam pa'i dbye bas de ni rnam pa gnyis su gnas pa'i phyir dang tha snyad kyi phyogs gcig la kun rdzob kyi sgras brjod pa'i phyir ro| |rigs pa'i stobs kyis 'di'i don ni gang zhig 'jig rten gyi tha snyad la kun rdzob kyi sgras brjod la| de ni 'di ltar na 'jig rten gyi tha snyad 'di ni 'jig rten kun rdzob ste| de ni de kho na nyid ma yin no zhes 'phags pa kho na gsungs par rigs la| tha snyad dang kun rdzob kyi sgra dag kyang rnam grangs nyid de| de la skyon med do| |

things that any of them are true, or warranted, or even that there is warrant in the ordinary world.

The Mādhyamika epistemologist of the conventional would be in the position of a contemporary epistemologist explaining how an astrologer or a palmist justifies their predictions. Such an epistemologist might describe procedures for reading the stars or the lines on our hands, but they do not take those procedures to confer warrant on the conclusions drawn from these practices; they only take the participants themselves to ascribe warrant to those conclusions, and they take them to do so erroneously.

If Candrakīrti genuinely took the mere consensus of ordinary people to be the measure of conventional truth, then there would be no reason for him to offer his sustained rejection of the naïve realism reflected the philosophies of Indian orthodoxy. Candrakīrti rejects the logical and epistemological realism of Gautama's Nyāya, the realistic metaphysical pluralism of Kaṇāda's Vaiśeṣika, the dualism of Kapila's Sāṃkhya, the meditation practices of non-Buddhist systems, the Vedic hermeneutics of Jaimini's Pūrva Mīmāṃsā, and of Bādaryāṇa's Uttara Mīmāṃsā. The ontological, epistemological, cosmological, creationist, and empirical presuppositions represented in the orthodox Hindu systems are far more representative of the naïve realism and of the intuitions entrenched in the ordinary worldview than any of the views couched in Buddhist philosophical schools, most of which are, in fact, radically counterintuitive. So, if Candrakīrti really intended to dive into the slough, he would endorse those views. But he does not. To explain his own critique of commonly held views, we need to attribute to Candrakīrti the more sophisticated epistemological view that we have now seen that he embraces.

Let us sum up our account of Candrakīrti's epistemology of the conventional as revealed by a careful reading of his texts: (1) Defective sensory or cognitive faculties are the sources of mundane epistemic errors, and their objects are mere fictions, not conventional truths. (2) Mundane conventional truth is that which is delivered by faculties free from such adventitious epistemic defects; there is thus a difference between getting it right and getting it wrong with respect to the conventional, and conventional truth is a kind of truth. But mundane conventional truth is not the final truth; even healthy sense faculties and cognitive processes are afflicted by the pathology of primal confusion and so mistakenly reify conventional truth, inflating it by attributing to it an ultimate status. Those same conventional truths, however, are seen to be deceptive from the perspective of realized epistemic authorities—expert perceivers of reality. (3) It is possible to understand the conventional truth free from the pathology of the second-order causes of epistemic defects; therefore, it is possible to be fully authoritative with respect to conventional reality. That understanding is the final standard of conventional truth, and the stepping stone to the conceptual understanding of ultimate truth: to the realization that the ultimate truth is that there is no ultimate reality and that there is only conventional reality.[30]

This generates an epistemic spiral that leads to a kind of Peircean stability at the limit, even though conventionalism and a commitment to the recursivity of epistemic conventions guarantee that prior to that limit everything is unstable, impermanent, provisional—qualities that Buddhist philosophers ascribe to all phenomena. Epistemic conventionalism is a significant aspect of Candrakīrti's epistemology, and it is one of his most important contributions to Indian philosophy. It is unique in the medieval Indian philosophical landscape in its coherentist and pragmatic account of knowledge. It defies the dominant foundationalism in Indian epistemology, and it represents the most coherent application of Nāgārjuna's own sense of conventional truth that one could imagine.

Candrakīrti on the Nature of Epistemic Normativity

Candrakīrti's epistemological conventionalism—a view that Hume would rediscover in his *Treatise* a millennium later (Garfield 2021), and that Feyerabend (1924–1994) and Wittgenstein (1889–1951) would so forcefully articulate in the twentieth century in *Against Method* (1975) and *On Certainty* (1969) respectively,—is the view that our epistemic practices are not *just* social practices that are

[30] It does not follow, however, that everyone sees conventional truth in the same way. Highly realized practitioners and ordinary people see things very differently, as texts like the *Vimalakīrti-nirdeśa-sūtra* make clear. See Cowherds (2011: ch. 1).

embedded in a wider network of social and linguistic conventions; they are the social practices that constitute the normativity we expect of an epistemology. They gain this power from the fact that they are self-correcting, and that they involve not only basic commitments to perception and immediate inference, but also deference to experts.

This epistemic framework requires us to adopt a healthy skepticism about each conclusion to which we come, in virtue of an awareness of our own fallibility. But it also grounds a confidence that careful analysis and collective activity can improve our understanding over time, and that the conventional knowledge we obtain can help us to understand ultimate truth and so advance us on the path to liberation. Buddhist soteriology and a progressive philosophy of science are not as different as they might appear, and they might well illuminate each other.

All of this takes us to a deeper understanding of *truth* (*satya*) as it figures in Candrakīrti's philosophy. As we observed, Candrakīrti distinguishes between two classes of epistemic defects that are the targets of the corrective mechanisms built into our epistemic conventions. Adventitious epistemic defects allow us to distinguish veridical perceptual or conceptual episodes from non-veridical ones. Bad vision, deafness, or drunkenness impair us as epistemic agents, as do environmental conditions such as solar glare, ambient noise, or distractions. If we are affected by such adventitious conditions, our perceptual or conceptual states fail to be epistemically authoritative. We have conventions for discounting what they deliver in these states; when they are unimpaired, we assume their authority.

But there are also impairments to which we are subject simply because we are human beings. For instance, we do not see infrared wavelengths or ultraviolet. The range of frequencies that we can hear is limited. And we do not, like sharks or birds, sense magnetic fields. These are the kinds of impairments that are species-specific and distinguish us from other animals. Candrakīrti would have understood these in terms of the different realms of existence exhibited in the Bhavacakra—the wheel of life.[31] That icon reminds us that different

[31] The *Wheel of Life* is a common Indo-Tibetan icon that represents the relation between the causes of suffering in in cyclic existence, the six realms of rebirth (or psychological moods, if taken more metaphorically), the twelve links of dependent origination, and the fear of death. The largest part of the central area of the icon is devoted to the

kinds of beings inhabit different worlds, worlds that may overlap partially with ours, or not at all, and to which different epistemic standards apply.

So, for instance, a flower that is monochrome to our eyes may be variegated to a bee. If a normal human being sees such a flower as white, then for me to see it as white is an example of a veridical perception; to see it as yellow is to see it falsely. If I see it as variegated, I am also just wrong. But for a bee to see that same flower as monochrome would be erroneous; by the standards appropriate to bees, it should appear variegated. This is one respect in which the failure to detect an aspect of the world may not constitute an epistemic defect at the conventional level. And this shows us that our perceptual apparatus can be deceptive in one respect, but non-deceptive—*pramāṇa*—in another, even conventionally. It can be conventionally true that the flower is white, even though in the world of a bee it is conventionally true that it is variegated; our eyes and a bee's eyes might yield different perceptions, but each is a warrant in its respective domain.

But there is a second pervasive kind of epistemic failing that—while it does not undermine conventional warrant—traps us in primal confusion. That is the innate tendency to take the phenomena we perceive to exist intrinsically, and to have properties independent of our perception. This is to take what Husserl called the *natural attitude* toward the objects of our awareness. When we do not consciously interrogate our experience, the flower that appears red to us, or the vibrations that impinge on our ear that cause us to hear C# on the oboe are experienced as the direct detection of properties that are there in the object, and that would be there even if we were not detecting them. We know that is wrong, and that the properties we perceive are constructed by complex cognitive and neural processes, not simply detected.

depiction of the six realms: the hells, the world of the hungry spirits (*pretas*), the world of the animals, the human realm, the realm of the *asuriyas* (or honor-seeking semi-divine beings), and the divine realms. Part of the point of the iconography is that there is a deep sense in which the world one inhabits depends upon the kind of being one is. So, for instance, a dog inhabits a largely olfactory world, whereas our world is experienced primarily through vision, and a shark's through magnetic sensors. While we might naïvely take our senses and cognition to deliver the world to us as it is, this icon suggests, in fact we construct that world, and can only construct a world to which our kind of being is subject.

This kind of natural error is the tip of a larger iceberg, which can be described as the superimposition of intrinsic reality on that which is empty of that intrinsic reality, and which exists only interdependently. And this is the Madhyamaka characterization of the primal confusion that is the root of the pervasive suffering of samsara. Candrakīrti observes that we are constantly subject to this illusion, and that the essence of this illusion is to take what exists only conventionally to exist ultimately. According to Tsongkhapa, only full awakening can free us from this illusion. Therefore, only a buddha can be a complete *pramāṇa* with respect to the ultimate truth, understanding the nondual nature of the two truths, recognizing that there is only conventional reality.[32]

That means that all of our perceptions are deceptive at the conventional level; they are not authoritative with respect to the ultimate mode of existence of things. And that, as we have seen, is why Taktsang takes Candrakīrti to believe that our epistemic instruments are never authoritative with respect to our objects, and that there is no truth in the conventional world, and, hence, no knowledge. But we can also see that to draw Taktsang's conclusion is to miss the distinction between adventitious and pervasive epistemic defects and so the distinction between authority with respect to the conventional and authority with respect to the ultimate. When Candrakīrti says that the deliverances of unimpaired sense faculties trump those of impaired sense faculties and that those of the noble beings who do not impute intrinsic reality to the objects of their experience trump those of competent, but ordinary, epistemic agents, this is what he has in mind.

One can be authoritative with respect to the conventional without being authoritative with respect to the ultimate, just as a person might know that this Calla lily is white because they see it and know that their eyes are good and that they are in standard conditions, without knowing that other organisms correctly see it differently. That is, they might know this not only if they don't know that it would be multicolored to a bee, but also if they don't know how, or even that, their

[32] See Garfield (2020, 2022c, 2023, 2024) for discussions of the relation between conventionally warranted understandings of the ultimate, and the more complete authority of nonconceptual apprehension of emptiness.

brain constructs the representation that constitutes this experience. They might even know that the lily is white despite having never studied Madhyamaka and so not knowing that it is empty of intrinsic identity. Each of these dimensions of ignorance reduces their epistemic expertise, but none of them undermines the fact that they know that the lily is white.

We can make this point clearly by returning to one of Candrakīrti's favorite analogies for primal confusion: the perception of floaters in the visual field by someone with retinal disease. While the person afflicted with this illness sees hairs floating through their visual field, there are no such hairs in reality. The perception by the person with the illness is trumped by that of the person with healthy eyes. But this does not mean that there is no fact of the matter about what is perceived. When the patient goes to her ophthalmologist, the doctor will begin the initial interview by asking her how many hairs she sees in her visual field. Note that the doctor is not endorsing the reality of the hairs—she knows that they are only bits of protein—but she is accepting the patient's word that he sees hairs. If the patient says that she only sees one or two, the doctor may well tell her that there is no need for treatment yet, but that if the number increases, she should come back.

And indeed, the patient may well come back a few months later saying that there are now dozens of floaters in her visual field, at which point the doctor schedules surgery. The point here is that even though there are no actual hairs floating through the air around our patient, there is a real difference between her seeing two or three and seeing dozens, and she can be right or wrong about that; indeed, she is authoritative with respect to how many she sees, and the doctor respects her authority in that domain, despite knowing that the hairs she sees are illusory.

It is just so with respect to the phenomena we find in the conventional world. Although they might be illusory—appearing to exist intrinsically and to have their natures intrinsically despite being interdependent and merely conventional—there is a difference between being right and wrong about them. And that difference can be captured by the fact that we can legitimately claim authority regarding them and their properties. We do so through the use of epistemic instruments such as perception, inference, analogy, and testimony. And we do so despite the fact that our own view might be trumped either by those more expert than we are regarding the relevant conventional phenomena, or more to Candrakīrti's point, by those who directly perceive interdependence and emptiness where we see intrinsic reality and independence. It is the fact that we can use our epistemic instruments in this way—despite their fallibility—that allows us to escape the dismal slough. And because we are not left in the slough, because we do have the capacity to draw relevant distinctions in the conventional world, practice, progress on the path, and liberation can be seen to be possible; if we could never get it right about the conventional, it is not clear how one could even begin to understand the potential efficacy of Buddhist practice, or of anything else, for that matter.

Back to Truth

And this leads us to a reassessment of truth itself as Candrakīrti understands it, which allows us to see in a different light why the dismal reading of Candrakīrti is inapposite, a reading that might be characterized as transcendentalist or nihilistic, depending on one's perspective. Heidegger, thinking through the Greek *aletheia*, asks us to understand truth as disclosedness (*Erschlossenheit*) (2001: 44). Truth is, on this view, not primarily a property of sentences, but the reality of the world and that which is in it. It is simply the way things show up, both in ordinary experience and in scientific inquiry. Sentential truth is a special case: true sentences disclose the world to us, whereas false ones conceal it from us. This understanding also comports with the semantic range of *satya*, which can be a property of sentences or of things.

This is important for our understanding of Madhyamaka philosophy. Many scholars have urged that *satya* is ambiguous between *truth* and *reality*. This relies on a view that truth can only be a property of representations such as sentences, propositions, and thoughts, and that it is some kind of relation between those representations and something in the world external to them. We think that the ambiguity thesis is false, and that the view of truth on which it rests is mistaken.

When we see that to be true is to be *disclosed*, we see that truth can be a property of things as much as of sentences.

A table can be disclosed to us in perception, as can the fact that it is a table or that the sentence "this is a table" is acceptable. Moreover, when Heidegger says that a table can be *disclosed*, he is pointing not only to the fact that perception can make us aware of a table, but also to the fact that our understanding of even simple objects is deeply embedded in our way of being in the world: objects reveal themselves to us in different ways depending on our mode of engagement with them. Not only are single objects disclosed to us when we apprehend conventional truth; the rich web of meanings and relationships that constitute our lived experience of the world is also disclosed, offering us insight into dependent origination as conventional truth.[33]

But, as we noted in Chapter 1, there is another route to this understanding of *truth*, through the English etymology of that term. A true sentence is one on which we can rely in reasoning or in communication, and it is relatively recently that the use of *true* as a property of sentences becomes first primary, and then seen as the only correct usage. Seen this way, *satya* just means *trustworthiness.* Conventional truth is then that which we are in the habit of trusting. While it might be deceptive from the ultimate standpoint, it does not let us down in ordinary practice. Ultimate truth is ultimate because it is completely non-deceptive; it never lets us down, no matter how deeply we inquire into it. This is how we think that *satya* and its cognates should be understood, and this defuses completely the ambiguity thesis.

So, Candrakīrti does not take truth to consist in a "correspondence" between a statement and a set of facts as did many of his orthodox Indian interlocutors, and as do many contemporary Western philosophers, following the lead of the Stoics. Candrakīrti rejects the traditional Indian correspondence theories of truth on the ground that such truth theories are foundationalist at their core, taking for granted the cogency of an agreement between two independent entities: language and reality, as though language is not part of reality, and as though reality is not shaped by language.

[33] Arnold draws our attention to another affinity between Candrakīrti's and Heidegger's thought: the temporality of persons (forthcoming: 288–289).

Instead, like Hume, Candrakīrti takes truth to be trustworthiness, and so bound to human conventions; like Heidegger, he takes it to disclose our world, and to disclose the role we have in constituting that world. He thereby draws a distinction between truth and falsity, both within the domain of the conventional and within the domain of the ultimate. There is a difference between getting it right and getting it wrong; and our epistemic practices can and must track that difference. To take truth as conventional is therefore not to become mired in the slough of epistemic nihilism. It is to adopt a sane approach to the truth itself. To adopt this approach is to recognize that although a world can only be understood in relation to a form of subjectivity, once that form is fixed, the world appears to it in a determinate way. This is so whether or not its subjects recognize either that relativity or that determinacy.

Candrakīrti's epistemology takes seriously both the idea that justification is a human activity, not a transcendental property, and the idea that this does not undermine its normative force. And, as we will see in Chapter 5, what goes for epistemology goes for ethics. This conventionalism will allow Candrakīrti to take the normative force of ethics seriously while locating the agent, the patient, and conduct, as well as the ground of evaluation, squarely in the domain of the conventional. To take conventional truth seriously is to explain why Mahāyāna ethics is cogent.

3

Firm Ground

Candrakīrti's Metaphysics and the Two Truths

The Two Truths

Let us now turn to Candrakīrti's conception of the world and of its relation to the knowing subject as he understands it through the doctrine of the two truths. As we saw in the previous chapter, in his *Commentary on Nāgārjuna's Seventy Stanzas on Emptiness* Candrakīrti tells us that the world (*loka*) is that which shows up for a person, relativizing the world itself to the psychophysical clusters that determine subjectivity.[1] It follows from this and from the fact that there are many different kinds and loci of subjectivity that there are many worlds, which overlap with one another to varying degrees. We will need an account of how this plurality of worlds makes sense of ordinary life and of the path to liberation.

There are various metaphysical positions that have been ascribed to Candrakīrti in the contemporary literature (and—although they are not so clearly distinguished there—by implication in the classical literature). In particular, Candrakīrti has been called both a realist

[1] Salvini (2022) points out that Candrakīrti uses the term *loka* or *world* in a number of different ways: "First *loka* may mean the 'world' of ordinary experience. But it can also mean a 'person' in that world, conceptually imputed upon the 'five aggregates . . . ' Last, Candrakīrti takes *loka* to mean a 'perceiver,'" and this allows him to a distinction not explicitly found in Nāgārjuna: some people in the world do not even qualify is *loka*, since they are not genuine 'perceivers', and these 'false-perceivers' are of two types: those with impaired sense faculties and those with distorted views" (414). Salvini hence draws our attention to the fact that Candrakīrti does not understand the world as a pre-given reality that we apprehend from outside, or a reality not already saturated with human purposes, but rather an interdependent complex of subjects and objects, saturated with normativity, and always relativized to the interests of those subjects embedded in it. This also reminds us that not everyone in the world is authoritative regarding even their own experience. This all demonstrates the deep connection between the epistemology discussed in the previous chapter and the ontology we address in this chapter.

By the Light of the Moon. Jay L. Garfield and Sonam Thakchöe, Oxford University Press.
 DOI: 10.1093/oso/9780197830741.003.0004

and a global anti-realist. There is truth and falsity in each of these descriptions. Everything depends on how these labels are understood. If we take *realism* to be the thesis that entities we find in the world exist substantially and independent of minds and perceivers, Candrakīrti has to be an anti-realist: like any Mādhyamika, he takes all entities to be empty of that kind of existence. The only kind of existence anything—including emptiness itself—has, on his view, is conventional, interdependent existence, with identity dependent on the subjectivity that apprehends it.

If, on the other hand, we take realism to be the thesis that the entities we encounter in the everyday world are empirically real—that there are facts about them, and a difference between getting them right and getting them wrong, and that those facts are independent of our particular beliefs about them—then Candrakīrti is emphatically a realist. For while he denies ultimate reality to all phenomena, he insists that conventional reality is a kind of reality, and that we don't each get to make up our own version of it. The two truths are each *truths*, not a truth and a falsehood. And this means that to the question, "is he a realist or an anti-realist?," the only possible answers are both or neither. Each is equally good, so long as one keeps in mind the right sense of *realism*.

Candrakīrti has also been called a reductionist (Siderits 2007, 2015), an eliminativist (Ferraro 2017), and a supervenience theorist (Garfield 2015) with regard to conventional entities. To get a handle on his position on this continuum it will help to contrast his views with those of other Buddhist philosophical positions. Reductionism about persons in contemporary philosophy is expressed, as Mark Siderits explains it, as "the view that while it is not wholly incorrect to say that persons exist, the existence of a person just consists in the existence of a brain and body and the occurrence of a series of physical and psychological events" (2016: 78). In the Buddhist context, Siderits notes that reductionism must be understood within the framework of the two truths. In that context, he cites Vasubandhu's *Handbook of Metaphysics* (*Abhidharmakośabhāṣya*):

> That is a conceptual fiction the idea of which does not occur when it is divided into parts. Like a pot: there is no idea of a pot when

> it is broken into shards. And that is also to be known as a conceptual fiction the idea of which does not occur when properties are stripped away by the mind. Like water: there is no idea of water where properties such as shape and the like have been excluded by the mind. And with respect to these, the convenient designations being formed through the power of convention, saying that pot and water exist is true, one does not speak a falsehood, this is conventional truth. What is other than this is ultimate truth. Where there is the idea even upon division, as well as upon exclusion of other properties by the mind, that is ultimately real. Like *rūpa* (physical things): even when it is divided up into atoms, and even when the mind takes away properties such as taste and the like, there is still the intrinsic nature (*svabhāva*) of *rūpa*. Feeling, etc., should be seen in the same way. Because this exists in the highest sense, it is called ultimately real. As one grasps that by a transcendent cognition, or by a subsequent convention, it is ultimate truth. (Pruden vol. 3, 6.4; 1988: 910–911; trans. Siderits 2007: 112)

Siderits argues that Buddhist metaphysics must be read as reductionist on the grounds that no partite entities are ultimately real; they are not real because they are reducible into still smaller units of spatial parts or temporal moments. It follows, he argues, that since partite entities are only real by the standards of common sense, they are only *conventionally* real. Nonetheless, Siderits argues, their conventional reality—as opposed to complete unreality—according to Buddhist theorists, consists in the fact that they are reducible to ultimately real momentary, impartite dharmas, and to be ultimately real is to have intrinsic nature.

In the Abhidharma framework, only ultimate particulars to which conventionally real partite entities reduce are ultimate real. So, we might say, on this view there are forests conventionally, but only because there *really* are trees and forests *reduce* to trees. To take this position is to claim that there are ultimately real simples, and that conventional reality depends upon that more fundamental reality. It is also to take the position that conventional reality is not really dependent upon conventions, but instead on reductive relations that in turn ground linguistic conventions. So, on this view, conventional reality is a kind of second-class reality—false, fiction, and illusory;

ultimate reality is the first-class reality—ultimately real, nonfiction, non-illusory—that grounds it.

While Siderits is correct that many in the Abhidharma tradition can be read as reductionists, Candrakīrti rejects that position, and with it the thought that there are entities with radically different ontological status. Like all Mādhyamikas, he follows Nāgārjuna in asserting that nothing exists ultimately, and that conventional existence is the only kind of existence that makes any sense. But while he rejects ultimate reality, he does not conclude that nothing is real at all. This is because by denying that there is a difference between a first-class and a second-class reality, he is able to take conventional reality seriously as the *only* reality. The doctrine of emptiness is thus, in the hands of the Mādhyamika, both a key to a kind of anti-realism and a key to a plausible, but robust, realism about the conventional.

All of this is grounded in Nāgārjuna's framework of the two truths. We have seen that Candrakīrti asserts that each phenomenon has two natures: a conventional nature and an ultimate nature. The *locus classicus* is *Introduction to the Middle Way* 6.23–6.25 and the autocommentary on these verses:

> Through seeing all phenomena both as real and unreal
> One apprehends the two natures (*ngo bo gnyis*) of the objects that are perceived.
> The object of correct perception is the way things really are.
> The object of false perception is called *conventional truth.* (6.23)

> Thus, the Buddhas, and the noble beings, who inerrantly understand the nature of the two truths, have said that all internal and external phenomena, such as personality characteristics and sprouts, have two natures of their own: a conventional nature and an ultimate nature. Of these, the ultimate nature is the one that is the object specifically of the primordial wisdom of those who see things correctly. Even though it does not exist essentially, it is the same in all things. The other is the nature that is perceived by ordinary people whose wisdom is impaired by the cataracts of primal confusion. These fools see things as having intrinsic reality when in fact they

do not. Therefore, it has been shown that all phenomena have two natures....

> It is also said that there are two kinds of false perception:
> Perception by clear sense and by impaired senses.
> The cognitions of impaired senses are said to be wrong
> When compared with those of healthy senses. (6.24)

... In the same sense that these two kinds of perception are regarded as falling into two categories— wrong and non-erroneous—their objects are as well.

> Whatever the six unimpaired sense faculty apprehend—
> All such objects are regarded
> As true in the everyday world.
> The rest are taken to be false in the everyday world. (6.25)
> (dBu ma, 'a: 253b–54a; 1992: 98–100)[2]

Let us examine this important passage with care, as it provides the crucial bridge between Candrakīrti's epistemology and his metaphysics. At 6.23, Candrakīrti explicitly affirms that every object has two *natures*, not that there are just two ways of seeing the same thing. Conventional and ultimate natures are each affirmed as real natures of things, each of which is the object of a certain kind of understanding. Tsongkhapa glosses this very nicely:

> Each of the internal and external phenomena has two natures: ultimate and a conventional nature. The sprout, for instance, has a nature that is found by a rational cognitive process, which sees the real nature of the phenomenon as it is, and a nature that is found by a conventional cognitive process, which perceives deceptive or unreal objects. The former is the ultimate truth of the sprout; the latter is the conventional truth of the sprout.... But this does

[2] See Salvini (2022: 414–416) for further discussion of the different kinds of error possible regarding conventional truth, and of what it is to be incorrect regarding the conventional.

> *not* show that a *single* nature is in fact two truths in virtue of the two *perspectives* of the former and latter cognitive processes. (Tsongkhapa 2006: 483)

We do not quote Tsongkhapa because of a prior commitment to a Geluk position, but because his commentary is the clearest gloss of what Candrakīrti says in these verses and the autocommentary. The central point is that according to Candrakīrti, the two truths represent two natures of phenomena, *not* two perspectives on them. This is to say that they are each *real.* When Candrakīrti uses the term *false,* he follows Nāgārjuna (*Fundamental Verses* 13.1) and most of the Indian tradition in understanding it to mean *deceptive.* As we saw in Chapter 2, the conventional nature is deceptive according to Candrakīrti, because when ordinary beings apprehend conventional phenomena, they take them to exist ultimately; but those conventional phenomena, like a deceptive mirage—which appears to be water, but which in reality is only a refraction pattern—are real. Otherwise, they could not cause us to take them to exist intrinsically (see Cowherds 2011: ch. 2, 5, for an extended treatment of this issue).[3]

The thesis that the truth is independent of what we think is a hallmark of realism; once our epistemic conventions are in place, they determine an account of truth, and so determine our ontology. As we have seen, Candrakīrti insists that not everything that anyone says—or everything that anyone takes to be real—counts as conventional truth; we can distinguish what exists conventionally from what does not, even if some people think that it does. Candrakīrti is therefore not a nihilist, but a kind of realist about both of the two truths. This is so despite the fact that he is also a global anti-realist inasmuch as he thinks that neither of them is real ultimately.

[3] One might object at this point that the claim that each object has two natures contradicts the claim that conventional reality is the only reality. But it doesn't. The ultimate *truth* is emptiness, which is the absence of any intrinsic nature, and so the fact that nothing—not even emptiness—exists ultimately. So, while in the Prāsaṅgika Madhyamaka framework there are two *truths,* there is only one *reality,* and that is conventional reality. The ultimate truth is that there is no more than that (Garfield 1994, 2002; Garfield and Priest 2009, 2021).

The tension between this moderate but robust realism and a global anti-realism or panfictionalism is resolved by the insight that conventional reality is the only kind of reality that anything can have. This realism about both natures thus provides the key to the unification of multiple lifeworlds into a single conventional reality in which lives can be lived successfully despite the pervasiveness of illusion and ignorance. And we will see that this understanding of the conventional is what makes sense of the emptiness of all phenomena.[4]

Conventional truth is constituted by our ways of talking, interacting, perceiving, and organizing our lives—that is, its *vyavahāra*, or *transactional, everyday* aspect. Nonetheless, this truth presents itself to us as though it is more than that—as though it is independent of those conventions and that our conventions simply conform to a pre-existing reality. That is the sense in which even though we constitute the world in which we live, it presents itself to us in costume,[5] deceiving us into believing that it is not something that we collectively brought into existence, but something that we just found and now perceive just as it is. That confusion is the superimposition of intrinsic reality, a superimposition that is the root of samsara.

This means that even though conventional truth is a kind of *truth*, it is not truth in the same sense—or to the same degree as ultimate truth. A trick-or-treater may deceptively appear to be a ghost at our doors, but he is nondeceptively begging for candy. We do not conclude from the fact that there are no ghosts that there are no little kids in sheets. Similarly, a conventional tree may appear to exist intrinsically and to be presented to my consciousness just as it is, even though it is dependently arisen, and apparent to me only subject to the conditions of my subjectivity. It is deceptive in that respect, and so false; it betrays us if

[4] Salvini points out correctly that this account of the relation among multiple conventional worlds (*lokas*) and between the conventional and the ultimate rests in part on the fact that, by using a non-affirming negation (*prasajya*), we can deny a statement without affirming a contrary position. So, we can deny that the conventional world is ultimately a particular way without asserting that it is ultimately some *other way*. This makes sense of the Madhyamaka idea that there is *no way* that the world is ultimately, and so that there is *only* conventional truth, once again bringing us to the conclusion that conventional truth must be understood as a kind of *truth* (2022: 408).

[5] Hence the Tibetan translation of *saṃvṛti* as *kun rdzob* (*disguised*, or *costumed*).

we accept our naïve understanding of it. But in virtue of the fact that it functions as a tree in all of our ordinary interactions, satisfies the definition of a tree, is indeed growing in the field, and so on, it is conventionally a tree that depends on appropriate causes and conditions, on its parts, and so on, and so is non-deceptive in that respect; it does not appear to be a building, for instance. And so we do not conclude from the fact that there are no intrinsically existent trees that there are no trees at all. This is the ontological dimension of the epistemological fact that deceptiveness in one respect does not entail deceptiveness in all respects: to be real in one sense does not entail being real in all senses.

So, when those of us who need eyeglasses perceive the tree with our glasses on, we are not deceived to the degree that we might be if we left our glasses at home; but we are deceived when compared with the experience of an adept who directly perceives its dependently originated status and hence its emptiness. In comparison with the tree they perceive, our tree is *false*. Candrakīrti puts the point this way in his *Commentary on Āryadeva's Four Hundred Stanzas*:

> It makes no sense to claim that ordinary perception should cancel exalted beings' perception of reality. For one thing, it is a warrant only with respect to mundane reality. Its apprehended object has the property of existing falsely and deceptively. (13.1; dBu ma, ya, 202b; 2019: 349)[6]

So therefore, not only does conventional truth not undermine ultimate truth, but ultimate truth does not undermine the reality of conventional truth. In *Commentary on Nāgārjuna's Seventy Stanzas on Emptiness*, Candrakīrti states:

> Linguistic expression (*tha snyad*) is conventionally (*kun rdzob*) true when what it expresses conceptually represents reified reality (*sgrog*

[6] 'jig rten pa'i mthong bas de kho na nyid mthong ba gsal bar rigs pa yang ma yin te| de ni 'jig rten pa kho na las tshad ma nyid yin pa'i phyir dang| des dmigs pa'i don yang brdzun pa bslu b'i chos can nyid du sgrub pa'i phyir ro|

> *btags pa'i don*) despite the fact that this reality does not appear as it truly exists. (v. 1, dBu ma, ya: 268a)[7]

This contrasts with the perception of accomplished beings, the perception that Mādhyamikas take to be free from error: "it alone is ultimate truth (*don dam pa'i bden pa kho na*) when what it expresses constitutes the comprehension of the reified reality while at the same time comprehending reality as it is" (v. 1, dBu ma, ya: 268a).[8] This complex relation between ultimate and conventional reality and the very specific understanding of the ultimate nature of emptiness enable the realism that Candrakīrti advances, and thereby provide his rejoinder to the charge of nihilism. When commenting on verse 24.7 in Nāgārjuna's *Fundamental Verses on the Middle Way*, in which Nāgārjuna rejects the charge of nihilism on the grounds that his opponent does not understand the meaning of *emptiness*, Candrakīrti emphasizes that to say that all things are empty cannot be to say that they are non-existent. Quoting the *Questions of the King of Anavatapta* (*Anavatapanāgarājapariprcchā-sūtra*) verse: "Whatever has arisen from conditions is unarisen: / There is no arisen essence. / Whatever depends on conditions is said to be empty. / Whoever understands emptiness is careful." Candrakīrti comments:

> Therefore, the meaning of *arising dependent on causes* is exactly the same as the meaning of *emptiness*. But the meaning of *nonexistent* is not the meaning of *emptiness*. You criticize us because you assign the meaning of *non-existence* to the term *emptiness*. This shows that you don't know the meaning of the term *emptiness*. (*Clear Words* 24.7; Skt. Vaidya: 1960: B491.23–26; dBu ma, 'a: 162b; 2003: 438–439)[9]

[7] 'di ltar bden pa'i don ni mi snang la sgro btags pa'i don rigs par tha snyad byed pa la 'di ni kun rdzob pa'o zhes tha snyad byed do| |

[8] gang du bden pa'i don mi snang ba ma yin la sgro ma btags pa'i don rig pa'i tha snyad la| de la 'di ni don dam pa kho na'o zhes rnam par 'jog go| |

[9] iti bhagavato gāthāvacanāt | evaṃ pratītyasamutpādaśabdasya yo'rthaḥ, sa eva śūnyatā śabdasyārthaḥ, na punarabhāvaśabdasya yo'rthaḥ sa śūnyatāśabdasyārthaḥ | abhāvaśabdārthaṃ ca śūnyatārtha mityadhyāropya bhavānasmānupālabhate | tasmācchūnyatāśabdārthamapi na jānāti | Kevin Vose (personal communication) argues that Candrakīrti's commentary to *Fundamental Verses on the Middle Way* 24.18 undercuts this reading, as, Vose argues, Candrakīrti glosses *dependent origination* as *non-origination* and *non-ceasing*, and therefore as non-existence. Here is what Candrakīrti says:

Candrakīrti's meaning could not be plainer: *if* one were to understand *emptiness* as *non-existence*, the doctrine that all phenomena are empty would be nihilistic. But that is *not* what *emptiness* means; instead, it means *dependently arisen*. And if one understands it this way, it is

> Emptiness itself is explained to be dependent designation. A chariot is designated in dependence on its parts, such as its wheels. That which is designated on its parts is essentially unarisen; and whatever is essentially non-arisen is empty. That which is essentially unarisen has the nature of emptiness, and this is explained to be the middle way. Therefore, whatever is essentially unarisen is without existence. Since it is essentially unarisen, is is unceased, and therefore also is without nonexistence. Therefore, being free from the two extremes of existence and non-existence, this very emptiness characterized by the absence of essential production is the Middle Way—the path of the Middle. Therefore, in this way, these terms "emptiness," "dependent designation," and "Middle Way" are simply different names for dependent origination itself." (Skt. Vaidya 1960: B504.32–33, 1–5; dBu ma, 'a: 167b; 2003: 450–451)
>
> yā ceyaṃ svabhāvaśūnyatā sā prajñaptirupādāya, saiva śūnyatā upādāya prajñaptiriti vyavasthāpyate | cakrādīnyupādāya rathāṅgāni rathaḥ prajñapyate | tasya yā svāṅgānyupādāya prajñaptiḥ, sā svabhāvenānutpattiḥ, yā ca svabhāvenānutpattiḥ, sā śūnyatā | saiva svabhāvānutpattilakṣaṇā śūnyatā madhyamā pratipaditi vyavasthāpyate | yasya hi svabhāvenānutpattiḥ, tasya astitvābhāvaḥ, svabhāvena cānutpannasya vigamābhāvānnāstitvābhāva iti | ato bhāvābhāvāntadvayarahitatvāt sarvasvabhāvānutpatti lakṣaṇā śūnyatā madhyamāpratipat, madhyamo mārga ityucyate | tadevaṃ pratītyasamutpādas yaivaitā viśeṣa saṃjñāḥ - śūnyatā, upādāya prajñaptiḥ, madhyamā pratipad iti ||
>
> Tib: stong pa nyid gang yin pa de ni brten nas gdags pa ste| stong pa nyid de nyid ni brten nas gdags pa zhes bya bar rnam par gzhag go| | 'khor lo la sogs pa shing rta'i yan lag la brten nas shing rtar 'dogs la| de'i rang gi yan lag la brten nas btags pa gang yin pa de ni| rang bzhin gyis ma skyes pa yin la| gang rang bzhin gyis ma skyes pa de ni stong pa nyid yin zhing*| rang bzhin gyis ma skyes pa'i mtshan nyid can gyi stong pa nyid de nyid ni dbu m'i lam yin zhes bya bar rnam par gzhag ste| 'di ltar gang zhig rang bzhin gyis ma skyes pa de la ni| yod pa nyid med la| rang bzhin gyis ma skyes pa la 'jig pa med pas med pa nyid med pa de'i phyir| yod pa dang med pa'i mtha' gnyis dang bral ba de'i phyir| rang bzhin gyis ma skyes pa'i mtshan nyid can gyi stong pa nyid de nyid ni dbu m'i lam ste| dbu m'i shul zhes bya'o| |de'i phyir de ltar na stong pa nyid dang| brten nas gdags pa dang| dbu m'i lam zhes bya ba 'di dag ni rten cing 'brel par 'byung ba nyid kyi ming gi bye brag yin no||.

The crucial terms here are *essentially unarisen (svabhāvenānutpattiḥ)* and *without existence* (*astitvābhāvaḥ*). In this context, it is clear that Candrakīrti, echoing the homage verses of *Fundamental Verses*, is referring to *essential* existence, and *arising with an essence*. This is confirmed by his conclusion that dependently originated empty phenomena are *free from the extremes of existence and nonexistence*. So, when he says here that they are without existence, that must be taken in the context of his assertion that they are without nonexistence as well. This is therefore not the nihilistic claim that dependently originated phenomena are nonexistent, but the more moderate claim that they lack essence.

simply the doctrine that all phenomena arise in dependence on causes and conditions. That is not a nihilistic doctrine, but a realistic doctrine, according to which the empirical world is real, but comprising only essenceless phenomena. The essencelesssness of phenomena does not undermine, but rather constitutes, their reality, while at the same time constituting their unreality *ultimately*.[10] And Candrakīrti emphasises as well that conventional reality does not undermine efficacy. In his commentary on verse 1.3 of *Fundamental Verses on the Middle Way*, he writes:

> One should understand how things that have a false nature can nonetheless function both as the cause of pathology and of liberation on the basis of the explanation I provide in *Introduction to the Middle Way*. There I put the problem this way: Since things arise neither from themselves, nor from others, nor from both, nor causelessly, why did the Buddha say that ignorance is the cause of our dispositions? And I reply that this is so conventionally, not in ultimate reality.
>
> One might then ask how we set out the conventional framework. We maintain that conventional existence is simply dependence on conditions. But this does not entail acceptance of any of the four corners of the tetralemma. That would absurdly entail that things have intrinsic nature, which would make no sense at all. Since we maintain only mere dependence on conditions, since cause and effect are mutually dependent, they do not exist intrinsically. So, we do not maintain that anything exists intrinsically. This is why it is also said:
>
> > Sophists say that
> > Suffering is self-caused, caused by another,
> > Caused by both, and that it is uncaused.
> > But you have explained that it is dependently arisen,

[10] Salvini notes that Candrakīrti sees that if to exist ultimately is to be found at the end of an analysis aimed at determining a thing's intrinsic nature, then *nothing* exists ultimately, including the emptiness of ultimate reality (2022: 413).

And also:

> The agent depends upon action,
> And action depends upon the agent.
> If they are not conceived in terms of dependent origination
> There is no way that they could exist.
> (1.3; Skt. Vaidya: 1960: B54.20–25; B55.1–4; dBu ma, 'a: 14b–15a; 2003: 39–40)[11]

[11] yathā ca mṛṣāsvabhāvānāṃ padārthānāṃ saṃkleśavyavadānahetutvaṃ tathā madhyamakāvatārādvistareṇāvaseyam || atrāha- yadi svataḥ parataḥ ubhayato 'hetutaśca nāsti bhāvānāmutpādaḥ, tatra kathamavidyā pratyayāḥ saṃskārā ityuktaṃ bhagavatā? ucyate | saṃvṛtireva na tattvam || kiṃ saṃvṛtervyavasthānaṃ vaktavyam? idaṃpratyayatāmātreṇa saṃvṛteḥ siddhirabhyupagamyate | na tu pakṣacatuṣṭayābhyupagamena sasvabhāvavādaprasaṅgāt, tasya cāyuktatvāt | idaṃpratyayatāmātrābhyupagame hi sati hetuphalayoranyonyāpekṣatvānnāsti svābhāvikī siddhiriti nāsti sasvabhāvavādaḥ | ata evoktam-

svayaṃ kṛtaṃ parakṛtaṃ dvābhyāṃ kṛtamahetukam |
tārkikairiṣyate duḥkhaṃ tvayā tūktaṃ pratītyajam ||

ihāpi vakṣyati-pratītya kārakaḥ karma taṃ pratītya ca kārakam | karma
pravartate nānyatpaśyāmaḥ siddhikāraṇam || iti ||

Tib: dngos po brdzun pa'i rang bzhin can rnams ji ltar kun nas nyon mongs pa dang| rnam par byang ba'i rgyu nyid yin pa de ltar ni rgyas par dbu ma la 'jug pa las nges par bya'o| 'dir smras pa| gal te bdag dang gzhan dang gnyi ga dang rgyu med pa las dngos po rnams skye ba yod pa ma yin na| ji ltar bcom ldan 'das kis ma rig pa'i rkyen gyis 'du byed rnams zhe gsungs| bshad par bya ste| 'di ni kun rdzob pa yin gyi de kho na nyid ni ma yin no|| ci kun rdzob kyi rnam par gzhag pa brjod par bya ba yin nam zhe na|

rkyen nyid 'di pa tsam gyis kun rdzob grub par khas len gyi| phyogs bzhi khas blangs pa'i sgo nas ni ma yin te| dngos po rang bzhin dang bcas pa smra bar thal bar 'gyur ba'i phyir dang| de yang rigs pa ma yin pa'i phyir ro|| rkyen nyid 'di pa tsam zhig khas blangs na ni rgyu dang 'bras by gnyis phan tshun ltos pa'i phyir| ngo bo nyid kyis grub pa yod pa ma yin pas dngos po rang bzhin dang bcas par smra bar 'gyur ba ma yin no||

de nyid kyi phyir|
sdug bsngal ran gis byas pa dang||
bzhan gyis byas dang gnyi gas byas||
rgyu med trog ge bay is 'dod||
khyod kyis brtan nas 'byung bar gsungs||
zhes sungs so||
di nyid las kyang|
byed po las la brten byas shing||
las kyang byed po de nyid la||
brten nas 'byung ba ma gtogs pa||
grub pa'i rgyu ni ma mthong ngo||

The Unity of the Two Truths

In this context, it is useful to return to Sellars' account of the two images. Each of the images comes with its own epistemic practices, guaranteeing that we know about the phenomena we encounter in the manifest image despite the fact that they do not appear in the scientific image, and *vice versa*. Nonetheless, there is good reason to be metaphysically *realistic* about each of the two images. In "Philosophy and the Scientific Image of Man," he introduces the manifest and scientific images as follows:

> The philosopher is confronted not by one complex many-dimensional picture, the unity of which, such as it is, he must come to appreciate; but by two pictures of essentially the same order of complexity, each of which purports to be a complete picture of man-in-the-world, and which after separate scrutiny, *he must fuse into one vision*. Let me refer to these two perspectives, respectively, as the manifest and the scientific images of man-in-the-world.
>
> ...And let me explain my terms. First, by calling them images I do not mean to deny to either or both of them the status of 'reality.' I am, to use Husserl's term, 'bracketing' them, transforming them from ways of experiencing the world into objects of philosophical reflection and evaluation. (Sellars 1963: 4–5)

This qualified realism that Sellars recommends could serve as a nice recapitulation of Candrakīrti's version of realism about the two truths. As Sellars does with respect to the two images in a more contemporary European context, Candrakīrti takes the two truths to be distinct, to be equally real, to be constituted by the way we experience the world, and, following Nāgārjuna's *Fundamental Verses on the Middle Way* 24.18, in the end to require a kind of fusion. The fusion is important, for it is the identity of the conventional with the ultimate that forces us to take the conventional seriously, just as it is the identity of the world on which the manifest image is one perspective with the world on which the scientific image is another that forces us to take the manifest image seriously, even in the context of a robust scientific realism.

But this raises a question: How does Candrakīrti bring these worlds together to constitute a unified whole? That is, what makes it possible, on Candrakīrti's account, for human beings with diverse beliefs, desires, traditions, and priorities to achieve sufficient common ground to constitute the world and practices that enable human life? And what makes it possible for us to share a world with our non-human colleagues?

Candrakīrti's conception of a world (*loka*) is very much that of a *lebenswelt*, a lived world, the world of the manifest image. The world we inhabit—our conventional reality—is the world of objects, properties, and events that show up for us and that play a role in our lives. Our world is constituted by these phenomena, but we also constitute those phenomena and determine the structure of that world. Hence Candrakīrti's insistence that the five psychophysical clusters constitute the world.[12] For this reason, the *Wheel of Life* icon, as we discussed in the previous chapter, has ontological as well as epistemological import. When we read the icon phenomenologically, it even tells us that we inhabit different worlds in different moods (Garfield 2022b: 7–9). As Wittgenstein writes in the *Tractatus*, "The world of a happy man is different from that of an unhappy man" (1922: 6.43). This is a point that Heidegger makes forcefully as well:

> In interpreting, we do not, so to speak, throw a "signification" over some naked thing which is present-at-hand, we do not stick a value on it; but when something within-the-world is encountered as such, the thing in question already has an involvement which is disclosed in our understanding of the world, and this involvement is one which gets laid out by the interpretation. (1962: 190)

John Haugeland comments:

> moods/attunements disclose being-in-the-world as a whole–that is, as the whole unitary structure of who, being-in, and world. In particular, they are neither specifically "inner" (psychological) nor specifically "outer" (worldly) but instead arise in the course of

[12] See Deguchi, Garfield, Priest, and Sharf 2022: ch. 9; Thakchöe 2023: ch. 7.

> concrete interactive living amidst things and co-others... moods and attunements are the basic way in which intraworldly entities affect us... In findingness as affect, things matter to Dasein: the hammer is missing, business is booming, a friend lets you down, your health is improving—these are not just 'facts' that we register but things that we care about. (2013: 145–146)

A world is not something *given* to us, existing antecedent to our subjective encounter with it, but instead something that we construct as we interact with our environment and our culture. Its contours and contents depend partly on the structure of our own sensory apparatus cognitive systems, and partly on the causes and conditions that impinge on us. The primal confusion that Buddhist thought diagnoses as the root of samsara is in large part the illusion that the world as we experience it is given to us, and that we simply faithfully record reality as it is independently of our encounter with it.

We take Candrakīrti's diagnosis of this ubiquitous illusion and identification of its importance to philosophy to be of the first importance for any sensible account of human knowledge. Candrakīrti's understanding of the world might seem at first glance to be exotic, or at least naïvely idealistic. But it is not, and we can see this by seeing how close Candrakīrti's perspective is to that of such twentieth- and twenty-first-century philosophers as Goodman, who writes, "The uniformity of nature we marvel at or the unreliability we protest belongs to a world of our own making" (1978: 10), or Putnam, when he writes, "But the notion of a transcendental match between our representation and the world in itself is nonsense... In short, I am saying that the 'real world' depends upon our values (and, again, vice versa)" (1981: 134–135).

Candrakīrti is also an ally to Quine, who writes that "it makes no sense to say what the objects of a theory are, beyond saying how to interpret or reinterpret that theory in another" (1968: 202). Feyerabend points out that absent a theory, observation doesn't mean anything at all, that "bright dots as seen either through a telescope, or on a photographic plate" are not even data unless we have a theory about how they were produced (1981: 38). Emphasizing that neither theory nor observation can be taken as foundational, but that they each support each other, he writes:

> Considering that perceptions are influenced by belief in theories, this criterion would seem to be somewhat arbitrary. It is easily seen, however, that it cannot be replaced by a less arbitrary and more "objective" criterion. What would such an objective criterion be? It would be a criterion which is either based upon behaviour that is not connected with any theoretical element—and this is impossible (cf. my criticism of the theory of sense data above)—or it would be behaviour that is tied up with an irrefutable and firmly established theory, which is equally impossible. We have to conclude, therefore, that a formal and "objective" account of explanation cannot be given. (1981: 93–94)

This should convince us that Prāsaṅgika Madhyamaka is not simply an ancient Tibetan or Indian doctrine merely of interest to historians; it reflects a perspective that is strikingly similar to that which informs much of the most interesting recent work in epistemology and metaphysics in the West, even if not acknowledged. That means that a deeper understanding of Candrakīrti's development of this doctrine and of his commentators' adumbrations of his views could advance contemporary discussions. Let us conclude this parade of twentieth-century Western Mādhyamikas with Thomas Nagel:[13]

> It is difficult to understand what could be meant by the objective character of an experience, apart from the particular point of view from which its subject apprehends it . . . But if experience does not have, in addition to its subjective character, an objective nature that can be apprehended from many different points of view, then how can it be supposed that a Martian investigating my brain might be observing physical processes which were my mental processes (as he might observe physical processes which were bolts of lightning), only from a different point of view? (1974: 443–444)

[13] For a more detailed exploration of the connection between Sellars' account of the relation between the manifest and the scientific images of the world and Candrakīrti's account of the two truths, and of the implications of these accounts for realism about the conventional or the manifest, see Garfield ed. (2019b), esp. the essays by Arnold (chapter 8), Duckworth (chapter 4), Garfield (chapter 7), and Tillemans (chapter 5).

Back to Realism

This relativism to subjectivity—which we now see as the common property of the Indian Madhyamaka tradition and the contemporary phenomenological and neo-pragmatist traditions— raises a serious question: Does this kind of ontological relativism—whether Buddhist or Western—take us right back to the dismal slough, but in an ontological register? Do we each inhabit isolated solipsistic worlds in which there can be no standard other than ourselves for truth and falsity, right and wrong? Candrakīrti certainly does not think so, and we can now bring the resources we explored in the previous chapter to bear to see why. That account will enable us to appreciate Candrakīrti's understanding of the two truths as well.

Our human epistemic instruments—including perception, inference, testimony, analogy, and whatever other mechanisms we have to take the measure of reality—deliver the world to us with remarkable uniformity despite the variation around the edges. It is this brute biologically grounded uniformity—our belonging to the same realm in Buddhist terms—that makes it possible to constitute an epistemic community. And there is enough uniformity among our sensory and cognitive capacities that we can say what it is for a sense faculty or an analytical process to be functioning normally. 20/20 vision is normal, and it is normal only because it is the mean acuity of human vision. Anything worse constitutes an impairment. Our failure to see in the infrared does not constitute an impairment, although it would be an impairment for a bee. This relative uniformity in capacities, along with our ability to recognize deviations from optimality enable us to distinguish trustworthy perception, inference, testimony, and analogy from untrustworthy instances, and this immediately gives us an account of conventional epistemic warrant and so of the difference between conventional truth and conventional falsehood.

The fact that, as we saw in Chapter 2, testimony and analogy figure among our epistemic instruments—as Candrakīrti emphasizes in *Clear Words*—grounds the communitarian aspect of convention in this context. This is so in part because the testimony of others and inductive evidence of success grounds confidence in our own perceptual and inferential capacities and in those of others. But testimony is also important because it enables us to make sense of the role of expertise in correcting the views of non-experts. This deference to expertise is central to a metaphysics of the conventional. The world is what shows up for us through our epistemic instruments; that which shows up for correctly functioning epistemic instruments, and is not undermined by superior ones, is that in which we can trust; it is true. The rest is false. And this is exactly how Candrakīrti characterizes it *Clear Words* in his comments on *Fundamental Verses* 1.3. Candrakīrti begins by asking:

> One might ask: So dependently arisen things exist conventionally, but not ultimately. But isn't it necessary to explain how things are to be understood to exist conventionally? We accept mere arising conventionally. But this is not to accept arising in terms of the four extreme positions. That would be absurd: it would be to accept the position of those who take things to exist essentially, and that would make no sense at all. This is because when we accept that things are merely conditioned, we take causes and effects to be mutually dependent. Since we do not assert that they do exist essentially, we do not agree with the essentialists. This is what Nāgārjuna means when he writes:
>
> > Sophists say that suffering
> > Is self-caused, caused by something else,
> > Caused by both, or uncaused.
> > You have said that it is dependently originated.
> > (Nāgārjuna, *Praise of the Supramundane* [*Lokātītastava*], v. 21, bsTod tshogs, ka: 69a, cited in *Clear Words* 1.3, Skt. Vaidya: 1960: B54.20–25; dBu ma, 'a: 18b; 2003: 39)[14]

[14] saṃvṛtireva na tattvam || kiṃ saṃvṛtervyavasthānaṃ vaktavyam? idaṃpratyayatāmātreṇa saṃvṛteḥ siddhirabhyupagamyate | na tu pakṣacatuṣṭayābhyupagamena sasvabhāvavādaprasaṅgāt, tasya cāyuktatvāt | idaṃpratyayatāmātrābhyupagame hi sati hetuphalayoranyonyāpekṣatvānnāsti svābhāvikī siddhiriti nāsti sasvabhāvavādaḥ | ata evoktam-svayaṃ kṛtaṃ parakṛtaṃ dvābhyāṃ kṛtamahetukam |tārkikairiṣyate duḥkhaṃ tvayā tūktaṃ pratītyajam ||

Tib: 'di ni kun rdzob pa yin gyi de kho na nyid ni ma yin no || ci kun rdzob kyi rnam par gzhag pa brjod par bya ba yin nam zhe na | rkyen nyid 'di pa tsam gyis kun rdzob grub par khas len gyi | phyogs bzhi khas blangs pa'i sgo nas ni ma yin te | dngos po rang bzhin dang bcas pa smra bar thal bar 'gyur ba'i phyir dang | de yang rigs pa ma yin pa'i phyir ro

It is easy to misread Nāgārjuna's position in chapter 1 of *Fundamental Verses on the Middle Way* as the denial that anything arises dependently, since Nāgārjuna denies each of the four corners of the *catuṣkoṭi* in this verse. He denies that anything is self-arisen, denies that anything arises from anything different from itself, denies that anything arises from both self and other, and denies that anything arises without a cause. Acres of forest have been cleared to carve the woodblocks and then to make the paper devoted to debating the significance of this fourfold denial. And we do find both canonical and contemporary interpretations of Nāgārjuna's position according to which he means to deny the reality of any dependent origination or dependently originated phenomena.[15]

In this passage, Candrakīrti corrects this misreading by juxtaposing this verse with the verse he quotes from MMK 1.3 and with MMK 8.12 in which Nāgārjuna explicitly affirms the reality of dependent origination and its necessity to account for action, agency, and the effects of action.

> Agent depends upon action.
> Action depends on the agent as well.
> Apart from dependent arising
> One cannot see any cause for their existence. (8.12)

Tsongkhapa's summary of Candrakīrti's commentary on this verse is helpful:

> For you, who maintain that entities exist inherently, to say that an entity that existed previously does not exist later is to deprecate all entities, because if they existed essentially, it would be tenable for them ever to be nonexistent. As far as *we* are concerned, since

|| rkyen nyid 'di pa tsam zhig khas blangs na ni rgyu dang 'bras bu gnyis phan tshun ltos pa'i phyir | ngo bo nyid kyis grub pa yod pa ma yin pas dngos po rang bzhin dang bcas par smra bar 'gyur ba ma yin no || de nyid kyi phyir ||sdug bsngal rang gis byas pa dang ||gzhan gyis byas dang gnyi gas byas ||rgyu med rtog ge ba yis 'dod || khyod kyis brtan nas 'byung bar gsungs || zhes gsungs so ||

[15] See, e.g., Taktsang in Yakherds 2021; Wood 1995.

> they are dependently arisen, no entitles are seen as having essence. Therefore, how could this deprecate either ultimate or conventional existence since we maintain that nothing at all is ultimately existent, and that, conventionally, all phenomena arise dependently? (2006: 230)

The point is that in 1.1 Nāgārjuna is not denying the reality of causation or dependent origination; he is denying its *intrinsic* reality; 8.12 explicitly affirms its *conventional* reality. This, Candrakīrti points out, is not to deny the reality of the conventional work, but to affirm it. Prāsaṅgika Madhyamaka is not nihilism, but a realism about the empty conventional world. And the fact that this point is made in the context of the relation between agent and action reflects its significance as a ground for ethics.

Citing the same passage from Nāgārjuna in the autocommentary to *Introduction to the Middle Way* 6.114, Candrakīrti responds to an imaginary opponent. The opponent here argues that once the four positions of the *catuṣkoṭi* have all been rejected, there is no possibility of accounting for relations of causal dependence in the conventional world:

> You have argued against the arising of consciousness from self, other, both, and without cause from the perspectives of both the ultimate and conventional truths. Nonetheless, you claim that at the conventional level, consciousness arises from ignorance and actions, and that such things as sprouts arise from seeds. How do you reconcile these claims? (6.114; dBu ma, 'a: 290ab; 1992: 211)[16]

We reply as follows:

> Because entities do not arise causelessly,
> Nor through causes such as God (Īśvara),

[16] 'dir smras pa| gal te khyod kyis bdag dang gzhan dang gnyi ga dang rgyu med pa las skye ba phyogs gnyi gar yang bkag nas| ma rig pa dang 'du byed dang sa bon la sogs pa dag las rnam par shes pa dang myu gu la sogs pa kun rdzob tu skye ba de ci ltar nges par bya| de brjod par bya ste|

Nor from self, other, or both,
They arise entirely through dependence. (6.114)

As we have said before, *because* things do not come into being intrinsically or from a deity (Nārāyaṇa,) from time, from fundamental particles, from such causes as primal substance (*prakṛti*) or pure consciousness (*puruṣa*) nor from self, other; neither from both nor causelessly, it is fact that this arises depending upon that. That is what we mean when we do not deny the conventional existence of the world.

. . .

This explanation of dependent origination as nothing more than depending on conditions (*idampratyayatāmātra*) not only precludes one from coming up with the idea that there is uncaused production, but also demonstrates the incoherence of the other alternative conceptions of intrinsically existent arising. Each member of alternatives such as reification and nihilism, permanence and impermanence, existence and nonexistence is shown to be incoherent. (6.114; dBu ma, 'a: 290b; 1992: 212).[17] This is what I mean when I say:

Since all things entirely originate dependently,
No reification of causation can withstand analysis.
Therefore, the argument from dependent origination
Tears the net of all incorrect views into shreds. (6.115)

One can only understand how conventional entities can be found to have their actual identities (*bdag gi dngos po yod pa 'thob*) through

[17] de brjod par bya ste| gang phyir rgyu med pa dang dbang phyug gi |rgyu la sogs dang bdag gzhan gnyi ga las| |dngos rnams skye bar 'gyur ba ma yin pa| |de phyir brten nas rab tu skye bar 'gyur| |gang gi phyir ji skad bshad pa'i tshul gyis dngos po rnams kyi skye ba ngo bo nyid las byung ba yod pa ma yin la dbang phyug dang dus dang rdul dang rang bzhin dang skyes bu dang sred med kyi bu la sogs pa rnams las kyang ma yin zhing*| bdag dang gzhan dang gnyis ka las skye ba yang ma yin pa de'i phyir| 'di la brten nas 'di 'byung ba zhig ste| de tsam zhig la 'jig rten gyi tha snyad mi bcad pa'i don du brten to| || ...de ltar rkyen nyid 'di pa tsam gyi rten cing 'brel par 'byung ba bshad pa na| rgyu med pa las skye ba la sogs pa'i rtog pa 'di dag mi srid pa 'ga' zhig tu ma zad kyi| rtag pa dang chad pa dang rtag pa dang mi rtag pa dang dngos po dang dngos po med pa gnyis la sogs pa rtog pa gzhan dag kyang mi srid pa nyid do . . .

> the argument according to which, "depending on this, that arises," and not through any other, thus the argument from a mere conditionality of dependent origination, tears the entire net of faulty views into shreds. To understand that *mere conditionality* is the meaning of *dependent origination* is to be unable to accept that entities have any intrinsic nature whatsoever. (6.115; dBu ma, 'a: 290b–291a; 1992: 213)[18]

In these passages, Candrakīrti explains that to be empty is to be dependent on conditions, and so that dependent origination and emptiness are the same property. Those who charge Candrakīrti with nihilism confuse emptiness with nonexistence and confuse his denial of reificationism with nihilism. This interpretation, however, cannot be sustained if we read these texts with care. Candrakīrti, in *Introduction to the Middle Way* and its autocommentary, is committed to a moderate realism with regard to the conventional world: while he argues that it is dependently originated, illusory, and empty of any intrinsic nature, he does not conclude that it is nonexistent, but rather that to exist is to be dependently originated and empty of any intrinsic nature. He also emphasizes that a clear distinction between truth and falsity can be drawn within the conventional based not upon a poll of the ignorant, but upon the analyses of the learned: no matter how many people believe in a creator deity, the fact that conventional analysis shows that there is none means that it does not exist even conventionally.

Candrakīrti also argues that to apprehend the conventional world as existing in a more robust sense than that is to succumb to the illusion of reification. But to deny the reality of the world would be to make even the illusion that there is a real world incomprehensible. This is

[18] zhes bstan pa'i phyir bshad pa| gang phyir dngos po brten nas rab 'byung bas| |rtogs pa nyid dag brtag par mi nus pa| |de phyir rten 'byung rigs pa 'di yis ni| |lta ngan dra ba mtha' dag gcod par byed| |gang gi phyir 'di la brten nas 'di 'byung ngo zhes bya b'i rigs pas 'di tsam zhiggis dngos po kun rdzob pa rnams kyis bdag gi dngos po yod pa 'thob kyi gzhan du ma yin pa de'i phyir rten cing 'brel par 'byung ba rkyen nyid 'di pa tsam gyi rigs pa 'dis ji skad bshad pa'i lta ba ngan pa'i dra ba mtha' dag gcod pa yin no| |'di ltar rkyen nyid 'di pa tsam zhig rten cing 'brel par 'byung b'i don du rnam par 'jog pas ni dngos po 'ga' yang rang bzhin khas mi blangs te|

because since illusion is a discordance between mode of existence and mode of appearance, there must be some mode of existence to ground an illusion; otherwise, the illusory appearance would be a hallucination of the nonexistent. Consider this discussion in *Commentary on Āryadeva's Four Hundred Stanzas*:

> The wheel of a firebrand, a magical creation,
> A dream, an illusion, the moon in water,
> An echo one hears,
> A mirage, a cloud, and existence are similar (13.25).

> Since the swift spinning of the firebrand is the cause of mistaken perception of the nonexistent circle, it is indeed perceived in the form of a wheel. But in this case, the wheel does not have even the slightest nature of its own, just as women who arise magically due to the psychological conditions of meditative stabilization can—just like real women—cause unhappiness for the lustful . . . The nature of the self of the waking state is just like the nature of the self in the dream state: it is caused to appear by the somnolence that causes the mistaken attachment to the self.
>
> What is not seen in the waking state is not real. Just as the illusory women created by the magicians' tricks are empty of being real women, ignorant people are deluded regarding the nature of the mind. This is just like the moon in water: it is empty of being a real moon and comes to appear by the power of dependent origination; nonetheless it causes the naive to confuse it with the real moon. It is just like the fog that arises by the power of dependent origination at places, times and for particular reasons: it causes those at a distance to confuse it with smoke.
>
> Dependent origination is like echoes in mountain caves, mountain ravines, and in windy mountains: they produce the false impression of sounds that appear to people to be real. It is like a mirage, which is caused by the rays of the sun in particular times and places: it does not have the nature of water, but which causes those far away to confuse them with water. It is like the distant clouds, which can be confused with mountains. Things such as consciousness arise in cyclic existence in virtue of being conditioned by karma.

> Propelled by the ignorance and confusion of such craftsmen, they are like the firebrand and these other examples: they are false and deceptive. Although existence is empty of its own nature, it appears deceptively to fools. By knowing the nature of things, one becomes liberated through the complete exhaustion of attachment. Thus, we explain that the immutable state of cyclic existence is to lack intrinsic nature, like the circle of a firebrand. (13.25; dBu ma, ya: 207b–208a; 2019: 370–372)[19]

In this commentary, Candrakīrti never claims that the phenomena he discusses are nonexistent. Instead, he shows that they exist in one way and appear to exist in another. And in each case, the analogies

[19] gang gi phyir de ltar rang gi ngo bo ma nges pas rkyen ji lta ba de lta de ltar rnam par 'gyur ba'i phyir mkhas pa rnams la |
mgal me'i 'khor lo sprul pa dang ||
rmi lam sgyu ma chu zla dang ||
khug rna nang gi brag ca dang ||
smig rgyu sprin dang srid pa mtshungs ||ji ltar med dang bcas pa'i yog pa myur du bskor ba'i 'gros de mthong ba phyin ci log gi rgyu yin pa'i phyir 'khor lo'i rnam par dmigs par 'gyur mod kyi | de la 'khor lo rang gi ngo bo bag tsam yang yod pa ma yin pa 'gyur mod kyi | dang | ji ltar sprul pa'i ting nge 'dzin gyi rkyen las byung ba'i bud med dag yod par 'gyur ba'i bud med rnams ltar 'dod chags can rnams kun nas nyon mongs pa'i rgyur 'gyur 'gyur mod kyi | dang | zhing . . . | ji ltar sad pa'i bdag gi dngos po ltar gnyid dang mtshungs par ldan pa'i rnam par shes pa dang ldan pa'i bdag gi dngos po'i rkyen can rmi lam gyi bdag gi dngos po [208a] || bdag la chags pa phyin ci log gi rgyu yin la | zad pas de ltar mthong ba med pas de bden par gyur pa yang ma yin pa dang | ji ltar sgyu ma mkhan gyi 'khrul 'khor gyi rgyu can sgyu mar byas pa'i na chung rnams bden par gyur pa'i na chung gis stong bzhin du de'i rang bzhin rnam par mi shes pa rnams kyis sems rmongs pa lhur byed par 'gyur ba dang | ji ltar bden par gyur pa'i zla bas stong pa'i chu'i zla ba rten cing 'brel par 'byung ba'i stobs kyis de ltar byung ba na byis pa rnams la zla bar phyin ci log pa'i rgyur 'gyur ba dang | ji ltar yul dang dus dang rgyu mtshan rnam pa de lta bu dag la brten nas rten cing 'brel par 'byung ba'i stobs nyid las khug rna byung ba na rgyang ring po na gnas pa rnams la bden par 'gyur ba'i du bar phyin ci log pa'i rgyur 'gyur ba dang | ji ltar ri'i tshang tshing dang | ri khrod kyi sul dang | rlung gi zabs rnams kyi nang gi brag cas skye bo rnams la yod par gyur pa'i sgrar mngon par rlom pa skyed parji ltar yul dang dus kyi khyad par du nye bar lhags pa'i nyi ma'i 'od zer gyi rten can gyi smig rgyu chu'i rang gi ngo bos dben bzhin du thag ring ba rnams la chur phyin ci log skyed par byed pa dang | yang ji ltar sprin rnams thag ring po nas ri la sogs pa'i rnam par phyin ci log nye bar skyed par byed pa de bzhin du mkhas pa ji lta ba bzhin rten cing 'brel bar 'byung ba'i rang bzhin la bzo ba rnams la ma rig pa'i phyin ci log gis 'phangs pa las kyi rkyen can gyi 'khor ba rnam par shes pa la sogs pa'i skye ba phyi rol gyi snod dang bcas par skye bzhin pa mgal me'i 'khor lo la sogs pa ltar | brdzun pa slu ba'i chos can yin dang rang bzhin gyis stor par gyur du zin kyang byis pa'i skye bo 'drid par snang bar 'gyur te dngos po'i rang bzhin shes pas rnam pa thams cad du chags pa zad pas rnam par grol ba la brten par 'gyur bar 'khor ba mgal me'i 'khor lo la sogs pa ltar rang bzhin med do zhes bya ba 'di mi g-yo bar gnas so |

are meant to show that the confusion of their mode of existence and mode of appearance reflects a failure to see accurately the causes and conditions that give rise to their appearance, leading to an attribution of intrinsic nature to that which lacks it. In each case, we are led to confuse empty phenomena with intrinsically real phenomena, conventional reality with ultimate reality. But in no case are we ascribing reality to the completely unreal.[20]

Candrakīrti can be seen as navigating between the Scylla of reification of the conventional and the Charybdis of nihilism regarding the conventional. So far, we have been discussing his realism. In doing so, we have tried both to explain why—given how seriously he takes the conventional—he might be accused of reification, and why in the end that charge is misguided. But in demonstrating that the charge of reification is misguided, we have seen that it is important to Candrakīrti's understanding of the two truths that there is also a sense in which the conventional is entirely false, and it is essential to his position that no conventional phenomena exist intrinsically.

Rejecting Nihilism about the World

The position that the conventional is entirely false could easily be read as nihilistic. While many Mādhyamikas would see that nihilism as one of the extreme positions to be avoided, and so might fault Candrakīrti for a commitment to it, we have seen that others—such as Taktsang and his followers—might embrace that position as the true Prāsaṅgika position. Candrakīrti is alive to this possibility of misinterpretation and explicitly forestalls it. In the *Commentary on the Four Hundred Stanzas* (13.10), he anticipates a realistic opponent accusing him of nihilism: "If your analysis shows that things such as the eyes do not exist, then how do you establish that faculties of sense such as the eyes, etc. are the effects of actions (*karma*)?" Candrakīrti replies: "Have we denied that they are the effects?" Again the opponent objects: "By having denied the existence of the eyes, etc. have you not denied this?" (*Commentary on Āryadeva's Four Hundred Stanzas* 13.10; dBu ma,

[20] See also Garfield (1994: ch. 1; 1995) and Arnold (forthcoming: 256–260).

ya: 201b; 2019: 357).[21] Here the realist opponent accuses Candrakīrti of being a metaphysical nihilist in virtue of his analysis demonstrating the emptiness of the sense organs and sense faculties. Candrakīrti rejects the assumption that motivates the objection, pointing out that he has argued neither that sense organs and sense faculties are nonexistent nor that they are not valuable epistemic instruments; he has only argued that they are dependently arisen. Their dependent origination both entails their emptiness and explains their value. If they were not interdependent with their objects and with the consciousness to which they give rise, they would be epistemically inert:

> It is because our analysis is primarily concerned with *searching for the intrinsic natures of the objects*. In this context, we are refuting the existence of things that are established by their intrinsic natures. We do not refute the existence of things like the eyes, which arise as the effects of causal production and dependent co-arising. Thus, things such as the eyes do indeed exist, for we say that they are effects of actions. (*Commentary on Āryadeva's Four Hundred Stanzas* 13.10; dBu ma, ya: 201ab; 2019: 357)[22]

We have seen that Takstang, Tillemans, and MacDonald cite persuasive passages in Candrakīrti's corpus in defense of their interpretation of Candrakīrti as arguing not only that there are no epistemic warrants, but also that there is no sense in which the world we inhabit is real. We now see that they have taken these passages out of the context of Candrakīrti's larger project and that when we read them in the context of what Candrakīrti says in the neighborhood and elsewhere, it does not support their reading. We have shown that in those passages Candrakīrti is only denying the possibility of ascertainment

[21] gal te de ltar mig la sogs pa rnams mi srid na| de'i phyir ji ltar mig la sogs pa'i dbang po 'di rnams las kyi rnam par smin pa'i ngo bor rnam par gzhag ce na| ci kho bo cag gis 'di rnams kyi rnam par smin pa'i ngo bo nyid bkag gam| gal te mig la sogs pa rnams 'gog par sgrub pas de ji ltar ma bkag ce na| . . .

[22] kho bo cag gi rnam par dpyod pa don rang bzhin tshol ba lhur byed pa nyid kyi phyir ro| |kho bo cag ni 'dir dngos po rnams rang gi ngo bos grub pa 'gog gi mig la sogs pa byas shing rten cing 'brel par 'byung b'i las kyi rnam par smin pa nyid ni mi 'gog pa'o| |de'i phyir de yod pas gang zhig rnam par smin pa nyid du bsnyad pas mig la sogs pa yod pa nyid do| |

and epistemic warrant within the foundationalist epistemology of the Pramāṇavāda or of the Nyāya; he is only denying the *ultimate* existence of objects of knowledge while endorsing a nonfoundationalist epistemology that, in virtue of making sense of conventional warrant, also underwrites a non-reductive metaphysics that makes sense of ontology within the context of the two truths.

That is, when Candrakīrti declares that the Mādhyamika agrees with the world, he not only affirms that he accepts the epistemic practices acknowledged in our conventional practices, but he also accepts the ontology they confirm. That is an ontology comprising observable events, patterns of behavior, values, animals, persons, and the conventions they induce. But that is not all there is to the world. As part of the ascent to ultimate truth, we must consider the world not only as it presents itself to and is constituted by ordinary beings, but also as the world of the noble beings—those with deeper insight into reality. So, not only does Candrakīrti have the resources—and not only does he deploy them—to differentiate truth from falsity within the conventional, but he thereby also establishes a robust realism about the conventional world. To say that conventional is deceptive and false is only to contrast it with the ultimate truth, which is nondeceptive and which transcends convention.

Just as Sellars urges that there is a demand to unify the two images despite their very different and mutually irreducible ontologies, Candrakīrti shows that there is a sense in which ultimate truth and conventional truth are identical: the ultimate truth about things is that they are empty of intrinsic identity and only exist conventionally; there are not two domains of reality—that of conventional phenomena and that of emptiness—but a single domain of empty phenomena that appear to us to be non-empty. This is true despite the fact that there is another sense in which ultimate truth cannot be identical to conventional truth: conventional truth is, by definition, deceptive; ultimate truth is nondeceptive.

And this is another reason that Candrakīrti is *realistic* about conventional truth, despite recognizing that it is constructed, deceptive, and *ultimately* unreal, and also another reason why the dichotomy of realism versus antirealism is of so little use in understanding his ontology. Since there is no extensional distinction between the conventional and the ultimate, to deny the reality of the conventional would not be to affirm the reality of emptiness at its expense, but to deny the reality of the ultimate as well. That would be to fall into a complete nihilism that no rational person could accept. Candrakīrti argues that mundane epistemic convention can reliably draw a distinction between what exists from what does not exist; hence, it can determine what in fact exists conventionally and is ultimately empty.

Our realistic account of Candrakīrti's position is eloquently defended in Tibet by Tsongkhapa. As we have seen, Tillemans characterizes his reading as "atypical." We think that we have shown that it is *not* atypical: it is simply correct. In the *Great Exposition of the Path to Enlightenment*, Tsongkhapa presents three necessary conditions a thing must satisfy in order to exist conventionally:

> How does one determine whether something exists conventionally? We hold that something exists conventionally (1) if it is known to a conventional consciousness; (2) if no other conventional valid cognition contradicts its being as it is thus known; and (3) if reason that accurately analyzes reality, that is, which asks whether something intrinsically exists, does not undermine it. We hold that what fails to meet those criteria does not exist. (Tsongkhapa 2015: 178)

The first two criteria distinguish those entities that exist conventionally from those that do not exist even conventionally (horses and persons satisfy them; unicorns and souls do not), thereby setting the Prāsaṅgika's standard for conventional truth/reality. In other words, applying the first two standards, a Prāsaṅgika can distinguish conventionally real entities (such as a laptop computer) from those entities that do not exist conventionally (such as a unicorn). The third standard sets the Prāsaṅgika's criterion for ultimate truth/reality.

Tsongkhapa's first standard captures Candrakīrti's conception of *being known to exist in the everyday world* (*lokaprasiddha*).

> In a sense, conventional consciousness operates in a non-inquisitive manner. It operates only within the context of how a given phenomenon appears to it, without analyzing, Is this how the object actually

> exists, or does it just appear this way to my mind? [628] It is called non-analytical consciousness, but it is not the case that it is utterly non-inquisitive. It operates within the context of how things appear, how they are known, to a worldly or conventional consciousness. It does not operate via analysis of how things actually exist. Therefore, it is called mundane knowledge. (Tsongkhapa 2015: 178)

The second criterion establishes conventional reality.

> Other conventional valid cognitions do not contradict that which exists conventionally. For example, a consciousness that does not analyze how things actually exist may think that a rope is a snake or that a mirage is water. However, conventional valid cognition does contradict the objects apprehended by such consciousnesses, so those objects do not exist even conventionally. (Tsongkhapa 2015: 179)

This criterion encodes the fact that conventional reality is not simply what appears to us at first glance; to be real is to be corroborated by further analysis and not to be undermined by it. And the second criterion ensures that the kind of analysis relevant to establishing our conventional ontology is conventional analysis, not ultimate analysis, or analysis that reveals emptiness.

This is particularly relevant in the context of the distinction between the person and the self. Candrakīrti affirms the conventional existence of persons, while denying the existence of selves. The person is the interdependent continuum of psychophysical processes that constitutes our everyday identity; the self is the core identity in which we naïvely take ourselves to consist, and which rational analysis shows us does not exist in any sense (Garfield 2022b, chs. 1–3). But the point is perfectly general, that substantially existent entities fail to exist not only ultimately, but also conventionally. Candrakīrti distinguishes conventional existence in the *Examination of the Five Clusters* (*Pañcaskandhaprakaraṇa*).

> Substantial existence (*rdza su yod pa*) entails true existence (*bden par yod pa*), perpetuating craving. There is no substantial existence; things exist like a reflection. Samsara arises from craving. It does

> not follow from the fact there is no substance that there is nothing at all, because that would absurdly undermine the framework based on dependent origination. Therefore, insubstantial objects exist only conventionally and as, inherently empty; exalted beings do not crave them. Reifying them as objectively real is an error because they exist in one way and appear in another way, like apprehending a coiled rope as a snake. (dBu ma, ya: 248b; Pedurma, 2000: vol. 60, 1557)[23]

Candrakīrti makes this point explicitly in the same work, providing further evidence against an eliminativist or quietist reading.

> The explanation of the existence of a hut also illustrates the mode of existence of a garland, a forest, or a chariot. This explanation can also be used to explain the relation between the person and the dharmas: Just as a hut is dependently designated based upon such things as sticks and so on, the person is dependently designated based on taking the five psychophysical clusters—material form, feeling, perception, personality traits and consciousness—as one's own; alternatively it is designated dependently upon taking the six elements—earth, water, fire, wind, space and consciousness to be oneself; or it is designated dependently upon taking the six sensory domains—those of the eyes, the ears, the nose, the tongue, the skin, and the introspective faculty to be one's own. Such a person—like a hut and other things that do not exist intrinsically—does not exist without depending a conceptual framework in which its conditions explain it. If the person were independent, we should be able to apprehend it independently of its causes, but we do not apprehend it as such. Thus, the person does not exist intrinsically. (*Examination*

[23] rdzas su yod par gyur pa bden par yod pa nyid kyis zhen par yang 'gyur na| rdzas su med de gzugs brnyan lta bu'o| |zhen pa las ni 'khor ba na 'gyur ro| |dngos po med pas ye med pa nyid ces bya bar yang mi 'gyur te| rten cing 'brel bar 'byung ba la nye bar brten pa'i rnam par gzhag pa nyams par thal bar 'gyur b'i phyir ro| |des na 'di ltar rjes su med pa'i dngos po'i don rnam par gnas pa ni kun rdzob tsam du gnas pa ngo bo nyid kyis stong pa 'phags pa rnams kyis mngon par zhen par bya b'i gnas su ma gyur pa gang la bde b'i don du sgro btags pas ni phyin ci log nyid de| gzhan dag tu gnas la gzhan dag tu bzung ba nyid kyis thag pa bsdogs pa la sbrul du bzung ba lta bu'o| |

> *of the Five Clusters* dBu ma, ya: 248b–249a; Pedurma 2000: vol. 60, 1557–1558)[24]

Candrakīrti doubles down on this positive metaphysical account immediately:

> However, seeing the person as it really exists, correctly understanding it as existing in dependence on appropriation, does not lead to the two extremes of reification and nihilism, because, there is, in this case, no substance acting as the objective referent. We do not observe any substance as an objective referent of the word *I*, hence we are not committed to reification. Nor is this nihilism, because we do accept the person as merely designated in virtue of appropriating the aggregates. So, we avoid both these extremes. Instead we maintain—as the Madhyamaka system demonstrates—the person exists in virtue of appropriation and dependent origination. The exalted beings correctly understand the person as it really is, and thus abandon all self-grasping and thereby attain liberation from the samsara. This is the account of selflessness of persons. (the *Examination of the Five Clusters* dBu ma, ya, 249b; Pedurma 2000: vol. 60, 1559)[25]

[24] ji skad bshad pa'i khyim la sogs pa ltar bdag dang chos kyang bshad par bya'o| |ji ltar byas nas she na| de la rtswa la sogs pa la nye bar brten nas khyim rnam par gzhag pa de bzhin du gzugs dang | tshor ba dang | 'du shes dang| 'du byed rnams dang| rnam par shes pa zhes bya ba nye bar len pa'i phung po lnga la rjes su brten nas bdag ces nye bar 'dogs p'm| 249A| |khams drug pos dang| chu dang| me dang| rlung dang| nam mkha' dang| rnam par shes pa zhes bya b'am| reg pa'i skye mched drug po mig dang| rna ba dang| sna dang| lce dang| lus dang| yid ces bya ba la nye bar brten nas 'dogs so| |de lta bu'i bdag ni bdag tu rnam par 'jog pa'i rgyu la ma ltos par grub pa med pa nyid de khyim la sogs pa rang gi ngo bor med pa lta bu'o| |gal te yod na ni rang gi rgyu la ma ltos par nye bar dmigs par 'gyur ba zhig na de ltar dmigs pa yang med do| |des na rang gi ngo bor ni med pa nyid do| |

[25] gang gis nye bar len pa las rnam par gnas pa phyin ci ma log pa la ji lta ba bzhin du mthong ba de ni rtag pa dang chad pa'i mtha' gnyis su ltung bar mi 'gyur te| de'i rten du gyur pa'i dngos po nye bar mi dmigs pa'i phyir ro| |de yang rdzas rjes su ma dmigs pas ni rtag par lta bar mi ltung la| nye bar len pa las rnam par gzhag pa tsam gyis bdag khas blangs pas ni chad par lta bar mi ltung ngo*| |de lta bu'i mtha' gnyi ga spangs nas dbu ma pa'i sgrub pas brten nas 'byung bar nye bar len pa las rnam par gans pa'i bdag 'phags pas ji lta ba bzhin du rtogs pas bdag tu 'dzin pa rnam pa thams cad du spangs te 'khor ba las rnam par grol lo| |de ltar re zhig 'di ni gang zag la bdag med pa'o| | See also Arnold (2019, 2023) and Garfield (2015, 2022b) for more discussion of Candrakīrti's denial of any reality of the self while affirming the conventional reality of the person. Arnold and Garfield each argue that Candrakīrti understands the self as a substantially real, continuing entity that underlies our experience and agency, and that he takes there to be

Candrakīrti is no nihilist with regard to conventional reality. His ontology is interdependent with his non-foundationalist epistemology. While he rejects the ultimate existence of everything, he affirms the conventional existence of that which our best epistemic practices tell us exists. Candrakīrti urges that what is real is independent of the views of any *individual* knower and that the revisability built into epistemology guarantees certain level of objectivity to our ontology. This is no dismal slough, but a real world in which we exist as persons, and so do the phenomena around us.

Nonetheless, we must remember that our existence in that world is not what we might have thought it to be prior to Madhyamaka analysis. The world, while real, is—as many Madhyamaka philosophers note—like a mirage: it exists in one way and appears in another. Madhyamaka analysis transforms our appreciation of that world. But just as to see a mirage correctly is not to *fail to see it*, but to see it *as it is*—as a deceptive refraction pattern—as opposed to seeing it as it appears, to see the world correctly is not to fail to see it at all, but to see it as a dependently arisen continuum of impermanent, interdependent events in which we are embedded, *not* as a set of intrinsically existent objects of which we are subjects (Cowherds 2011: ch. 2). It is to see it as conventionally real, but ultimately empty, and to see these two characterizations as two sides of the same coin. This vision, Candrakīrti thinks, is soteriologically and ethically important—as we will see in Chapter 5.

Is Candrakīrti a Metaphysician?

There is one final exegetical point worth making in this context. Some, such as Ferraro (2017) and Siderits (2007), have argued

nothing that answers to this description, ultimately or conventionally. The person, on the other hand, is the indispensable conventional entity imputed on the basis of the psychophysical clusters that serves as the conventional referent of names and pronouns, and that functions as a subject and an agent. Also see Arnold (2008: 162–174) and Garfield (2022b: 21–23) for discussions of Candrakīrti's deployment of the chariot analogy in *Introduction to the Middle Way* as a defense of the conventional reality of the person in the context of the non-existence of the self.

that Mādhyamikas eschew metaphysics entirely in favor of a non-metaphysical, minimalist account of the ontological conventions of ordinary people. By now we can see that there is something right and something wrong about this. Here's what's right: if one understands by *metaphysics* the enterprise of articulating the fundamental nature of reality, or even the fundamental nature of any particular entity or class of entities, then there is an important sense in which Madhyamaka is anti-metaphysical. This is because the thesis that all phenomena are empty of any intrinsic nature, and the idea that nothing withstands ultimate analysis—that is, that we can never, when analyzing anything, find its essence—entails that the very quest for the ultimate nature of things is hopeless; one will always come up empty, so to speak.

This is the point of Candrakīrti's parable of the shopkeeper in his commentary in *Clear Words* on verse 13.8 of Nāgārjuna's *Fundamental Wisdom of the Middle Way*. That verse reads: "The victorious ones have said / That emptiness is the elimination of all views. / Anyone for whom emptiness is a view / Is incorrigible." At first blush, one might think that this is the ultimate in nihilism, asserting not only that everything is empty, but even that emptiness is non-existent. Candrakīrti's response is a nice example of Prāsaṅgika philosophical ju jitsu, turning the opponent's charge of nihilism against him, and revealing that it is only the Mādhyamika who takes seriously the existence of the conventional. Candrakīrti imagines a customer coming into a shop with empty shelves:

> We do not say that emptiness is another nature that one should ascertain once one has eliminated all false views. This is similar to a case where someone says, "I have nothing to sell you." And the customer replies, "give me some of what you call *nothing*." How would he manage to take hold of anything? (*Clear Words* 13.8; dBu ma, 'a: 83b; 2003: 226–227)[26]

[26] 'dir stong pa nyid ni lta bar 'gyur ba thams cad kyi mngon par zhen pa tham cad nges par 'byung ba ste log pa gang yin pa de yin la| lta bar gyur pa rnams log pa tsam ni dngos po yang ma yin no| gang dag stong pa nyid de la yang dnogs por mngon par zhen pa de dag la ni kho bo cag mi smras ste| 'di ltar gang zhig la khyod la zong ci yang mi ster ro zhe smas pa dang| kye bdag med pa zhes bya ba'i zong de nyid byin cig ces smra na| de zong med par 'dzin du gzhug par thabs gang gis nus|

Emptiness, Candrakīrti insists, is not an essence to be realized, something *more real* than the essences that Madhyamaka analysis refutes. It is the *absence of any essence.* To treat it as the *right essence*, as opposed to the wrong ones, would be to elevate the ultimate truth of essencelessness to an ontological status superior to that of the conventional world, and this would be to deprecate the mode of existence of the conventional world as a second-class reality. Just as "nothing" does not denote the goods the shopkeeper actually has to sell, but the absence of any goods, "emptiness" denotes the absence of any essence, not the *real* essence of things. As Westerhoff (2016) points out, this parable therefore constitutes a powerful critique of a nihilistic reading of Madhyamaka according to which the reality of emptiness eclipses that of the conventional.

So, while this *is* a refusal of metaphysics in one sense of that term, it is also a clear metaphysical thesis in another sense: Candrakīrti is arguing that everything—whether on the subjective or the objective side of things—is essenceless. And, paradoxically, as we have seen Candrakīrti aver elsewhere, this is a statement about the ultimate nature of things: it is the statement that the ultimate nature of things is to lack any ultimate nature. This is what Garfield and Priest (2003) as well as Arnold (2008: 183–188) have called "Nāgārjuna's Paradox," and it is a paradox that Candrakīrti embraces, hence doing metaphysics in the very register that he must deny that he is adopting. But whether we attempt to affirm consistently the claim to essencelesssness (as does Siderits) or concede that that claim is also a paradoxical one to an essenceless essence (as do Garfield and Priest), it is a claim that affirms the empirical reality of the dependently arisen conventional world.

So far, we have been concerned with Candrakīrti's defense of the reality of the conventional world against those who would argue that only its material foundations are real. But there is another Buddhist challenge to the reality of the conventional world—that from Buddhist idealists who would argue that the conventional world is entirely imaginary—nothing but a cognitive projection. In the next chapter, we will consider Candrakīrti's critique of Yogācāra, another prong in his defense of the reality of the conventional world, and so of the importance of taking that world seriously.

4

No Ground

Candrakīrti's Critique of Yogācāra

Introduction

One of the more puzzling—and some might say *troubling*—aspects of Candrakīrti's thought, and an aspect that turned out to be profoundly influential on Tibetan doxography once Candrakīrti's thought became normative in Tibetan understandings of Madhyamaka, is his antipathy to Yogācāra philosophy. It is puzzling because Candrakīrti's critique of Yogācāra seems so unfair in places, often relying on broad, flat-footed exegesis that elides all of the heterogeneity in that tradition, ignores its phenomenological focus as well as its sūtra foundation, and often appears to be the critique of a straw man. Careful attention to texts such as the *Sūtra Explaining the Intention ISaṁdhinirmocana-sūtra*), Asaṅga's *Bases of Yogācāra* (*Yogācārabhumi*), and Vasubandhu's *Thirty Verses* (*Triṁśikakārikā*) and *Treatise on the Three Natures* (*Trisvabhāvanirdeśa*) show both that this tradition was not entirely idealistic and that it is not antagonistic to Madhyamaka. The consistency of these positions was defended by, among others, Śāntarakṣita in his *Ornament of the Middle Way* (*Madhyamakālaṃkārakārikā*), and which was dominant in Tibet prior to the establishment of the doxographic hierarchy that subordinated Yogācāra to Madhyamaka by the fourteenth century.

We will address these issues in what follows, but we also note that in the context of that critique, Candrakīrti develops a very powerful critique of *idealism*, and there was an influential strain of idealism among Yogācārins. Sthiramati (510–570) and Dharmapāla (530–561) were influential idealists who taught at Vikramśīla and Nālandā, respectively, and whose work would have been familiar to

By the Light of the Moon. Jay L. Garfield and Sonam Thakchöe, Oxford University Press.
 DOI: 10.1093/oso/9780197830741.003.0005

Candrakīrti.[1] And while Candrakīrti's criticism of Yogācāra may not be apposite for the entire tradition, it is a fair response to Sthiramati, Dharmapāla, and their followers. In any case, this response is interesting in its own right, and it provides further confirmation of his moderate realism and further insight into the details of his understanding of the ontology and epistemology of the conventional.

There are five principal aspects to this critique. First, Candrakīrti charges Yogācāra idealists with deprecating the ontological status of external objects by treating them as entirely imaginary, and so charges them with falling into the extreme of nihilism with regard to the external world. In doing so, he takes Yogācāra thought implicitly to deprecate the conventional truth in general, thus undermining the identity of the two truths. Second, and closely related, he charges Yogācāra with the reification of the mind and even takes the tradition to be committed to the claim that the mind exists ultimately, hence falling into the extreme of reification with regard to the inner world.

Putting these two critiques together, we will see that at bottom, Candrakīrti's complaint against Yogācāra idealism is that it assigns completely different epistemological and ontological status to these domains. This is the third aspect of his critique. His criticism of this move foreshadows both Kant's *Refutation of Idealism* in the second edition of the *Critique of Pure Reason* and Sellars' critique of the myth of the givenness of the interior world in "Empiricism and the Philosophy of Mind." Like Kant, Candrakīrti takes the essence of an idealistic position to be the assignment of a greater degree of reality to the mind than to external objects, and to take the mind to be known directly, while external objects are only known indirectly, by inference from immediate experience. Like Sellars, he sees the latter to be a commitment to the *givenness* of the inner, and hence to be a form of foundationalism. And like Sellars, Candrakīrti also sees this to be an

[1] Sthiramati develops and defends an explicitly idealistic interpretation of Yogācāra in his *Commentary on the Thirty Verses* (*Triṃśikābhāṣya*) and in his *Commentary on the Discrimination of the Middle from the Extremes* (*Madhyāntavibhāga-ṭīkā*). Dharmapāla defends this position in his commentary on Vasubandhu's *Twenty Verses* and in his commentary on Dignāga's *Investigation of the Percept.* Vinītadeva's (c. 645–715) subcommentary on Dharmapāla's commentary on *Investigation of the Percept* is a good source for this reading (Duckworth et al. 2016). For a study of the *Twenty Verses,* including the Sanskrit and Tibetan texts, see Silk (2018).

incoherent theory of self-knowledge in virtue of divorcing intentional content from interpretation and function as a brute property of mental states.

This critique of givenness culminates in the fourth aspect of the critique: Candrakīrti's refutation of the reflexivity of awareness, a doctrine introduced by the Pramāṇavāda school of Yogācāra through the work of Dignāga and Dharmakīrti. This discussion, as will see, foreshadows another contemporary debate—that between reflexivists such as Husserl, Thompson, Zahavi, Kriegel, Gallagher, and other "new Husserlians" and higher-order theorists of self-knowledge who take their cue from Sellars. Candrakīrti argues that self-knowledge only makes sense when conceived as higher-order awareness, thus once again characterizing self-knowledge as structurally identical to and contingent upon knowledge of the external world. This position constitutes a final rejection of all aspects of subject-object duality in favor of a view of subjectivity as a causally determined process in a dependently arisen cognitive continuum. Finally, Candrakīrti charges the Yogācāra system with a commitment to the ultimate reality and foundational status of the dependent nature (*paratantra-svabhāva*), one of the three natures in Yogācāra thought. We will discuss these five critiques in turn.

Nihilism with Regard to the External World

As we have noted, not all Yogācāra philosophers or texts are idealist. But Yogācāra theory is united by two ideas that will be important to bear in mind as we examine Candrakīrti's refutation of idealism, as they figure both in his exegesis of Yogācāra and in his response to it. These are the doctrines of the three natures developed in the *Sūtra Explaining the Thought* and the doctrine that the foundation consciousness (*ālayavijñāna*) is the repository of the effects of previous actions and experiences and of the potential for future ones. The doctrine of the three natures is introduced as a phenomenological account of the nature of objects of experience, but then is elaborated by some Yogācāra philosophers, such as Jñānagarbha in his commentary to the *Sūtra Explaining the Thought* and Sthiramati in his *Commentary on*

Vasubandhu's Thirty Stanzas, as a metaphysical doctrine, and these two interpretations are not always clearly distinguished.

According to the seventh chapter of the *Sūtra Explaining the Thought* and other texts such as Vasubandhu's *Treatise on the Three Natures*, every object of experience has an imagined nature (*parikalpita-svabhāva*), a dependent nature (*paratantra-svabhāva*), and a consummate nature (*pariniṣpanna-svabhāva*). The imagined nature is the nature of the object as we imagined it to be in naïve experience: the object is experienced as dually related to the subject, and its properties appear to inhere in it independently of our subjectivity.

This nature is entirely a projection: we do not simply register the properties of an independent world; we are in the world, not dually related to it as subjects to a distinct object in reality; we apprehend objects only as they appear to beings like us, with sensory and cognitive systems like ours; we construct our experience. For example, when we see an apple, we naïvely experience it as being red independently of whether we see it, and we take ourselves to be experiencing a redness that is external to our subjectivity; we see the experienced apple as *in* the world, and ourselves as subjects as standing outside the world observing it. But this, Yogācārins argue, is just cognitive illusion. The redness of the apple is then an aspect of its *imagined nature*.

The dependent nature is the character of our experience as arising dependently on countless conditions. Our experience of the apple as red arises not only from interaction with the apple, but also from the properties of our visual system that has evolved over aeons, from the ambient light, from our attention, and so on. The apple we see is not an independent object that we simply register, but rather the confluence of a web of interdependent conditions, some internal to our bodies and cognitive processes, and some external to us.

The consummate nature is the fact that the dependent nature is empty of the imagined nature. That is, the causal process that results in our experience of the apple contains no red, smooth object outside of us, but rather a long history of causal processes, some physical, some psychological. To recognize this is to see that we are nondually embedded in the world we experience, and that the sense of a distinction between the inner and outer worlds, as well as the sense of the independence of the objects of experience from properties or own subjectivity, are also cognitive illusions.[2]

One of the similes for ordinary perceptual experience used in Yogācāra texts, such as *The Sūtra Unravelling the Thought* and Vasubandhu's *Twenty Stanzas*, but also in commentaries by Sthiramati and Vinītadeva on Vasubandhu's treatises, is that of a dream. When this simile is employed in the sutra and in Vasubandhu's texts, it is intended to illustrate the illusory nature of experience in a very specific sense: the objects that appear to be external to us—like the apple on the kitchen counter—are like the objects in a dream; they appear to exist and to have the characteristics we apprehend entirely independently of us, although they in fact arise as experienced objects, and their experienced properties appear in our conscious awareness, in virtue of our own cognitive processes. That is, they are constructions by our cognitive apparatus in response to causal interaction with our environments, and depend on the structure of that apparatus, its evolutionary history, and our own experience and situation.

Our natural disposition to take this constructed experience to be the perfectly accurate reception of a world that is just given to us thus fools us into thinking that the mode of appearance and mode of existence of the objects we experience are the same when in fact they are very different: indeed, there is no way that the world we experience *is* independent of our experience of it. The dream simile when thus deployed is to remind us that we are familiar with the fact that our own cognitive processes are both deeply involved in our experience and invisible to us in those experiences when we reflect on dreams. In that case we are not fooled (at least once we wake up). Reflection on this implication of our own subjective processes in the construction of experience can then lead us to see that the same is true of ordinary perceptual experience. Note that there is *nothing* idealistic about this: it is just sober phenomenological reflection on commonplaces of cognitive science, commonplaces that were obvious to classical Indian philosophers.

Sthiramati and Vinītadeva, however, take this simile in a more explicitly idealistic direction. They argue that the simile demonstrates

[2] See Garfield (2015); Gold (2015); Waldron (2023); Thakchöe (2015; 2023: 65–72) for more detailed discussion of three-nature theory.

that just as objects in a dream are entirely unreal and are purely constructions of consciousness caused only by our own internal cognitive processes and arising in the absence of any direct interaction with anything external to us, the objects we perceive in waking life—all apparently real physical objects—are in fact pure constructions of consciousness. On this reading of the analogy, it is meant to show that there is no external world at all: these cognitive processes constitute the evolution of the foundation consciousness in which every potential for experience matures with two aspects: a subjective and an objective aspect. But these two aspects are only aspects of *experience*: we take them to be the experiences of external objects by a subject, superimposing subject-object duality on that which is purely cognitive; these experiences in turn mature and give rise to new experiences; but all of these are nothing but ongoing cognitive activity, with sensory consciousness only occurring as the effect of unconscious processes in the foundation consciousness (Duckworth et al. 2016; Waldron 2003, 2023).

So, on the first understanding, the nonduality of subject and object is comprehended phenomenologically as the fact that experience is always constructed by a subject embedded in its world, and that can only deliver a world as experienced by that subject—that there is no world *just as it is*. On the second understanding, the dream analogy is making a metaphysical point, namely that there is no external world at all and that all that exists is the constant evolution of our consciousness. And it is this metaphysical understanding of the Yogācāra system against which Candrakīrti's critique is leveled, and against which it makes sense. It is *not* directed at the phenomenological side of Yogācāra. It is therefore meant to be a refutation of *idealism*, not of the entire Yogācāra school. Candrakīrti's purpose then in criticizing Yogācāra should be understood as continuous with the epistemological and metaphysical project we have explored in the previous chapter—it is part of a campaign to affirm the reality of the world in which we live, not a defense of a naïve realism.

This distinction is important in the present context because it helps us to make sense of the three principles regarding the dependent nature that Candrakīrti outlines in his autocommentary on verse 6.47 of *Introduction to the Middle Way*. He says that, according to the Yogācāra tradition, (1) it arises without any object, (2) it is not the referent of any conceptual fabrication, and (3) it is an ultimately real foundation of the imagined nature.

When Candrakīrti says that in the Yogācāra system "[the dependent nature] arises without any object, from propensities" (dBu ma, 'a: 264a; 1992: 131), he means that an idealist must take the causal processes that generate our experience to have exclusively psychological causes and must understand the experience to which they give rise to be unrelated to anything exterior to our minds. The "propensities" here refer to potentials carried in the foundation consciousness, the basic, subliminal level of cognition in which our most fundamental psychological processes unfold (Waldron 2003, 2023).

When Candrakīrti says that followers of the Yogācāra school take the dependent nature not to be the "referent of any conceptual fabrication" (Ibid.) he means that the idealist must take our language and thought to refer only to the imaginary objects we perceive as real, not to the dependent nature itself, which is entirely inaccessible to us, a point that Sthiramati makes in his commentary on Vasubandhu's *Thirty Verses* (Thakchöe 2023: 69–72; Tzohar 2017). These are two of the most obvious commitments of an idealistic position: the non-existence of the external world, and the fact that our intentional objects are entirely internal to consciousness.

Finally, and most importantly, when Candrakīrti says that according to Yogācāra the dependent nature is "the real existent that is the cause of imputed existents" (*Ibid.*), he means that the idealist must distinguish sharply between the ontological status of the dependent nature and that of the imagined nature. The former, because it has all of the relevant causal power and because it exists independently of and prior to our conceptual and perceptual processes, must be understood to exist intrinsically, or ultimately; the latter, because it is entirely illusory, must be taken to be completely non-existent (Thakchöe 2021; 2023: 72–77). The critique of this commitment will be the fulcrum for Candrakīrti's critique of idealism, which has both ontological and epistemological dimensions.

The anticipation of Kant's *Refutation of Idealism* is striking, and attention to Kant can help us to unpack Candrakīrti's critique. In that section of the second edition of the *Critique of Pure Reason*, Kant argues that the error common to what he calls Berkeley's "dogmatic idealism" and Descartes' "problematic idealism" is precisely that they assign distinct status to the inner and the outer worlds (in the first case distinct ontological status, and in the second case distinct epistemological status). In each case, the inner is given precedence over the outer, and the outer is reduced either to the status of being merely imaginary or to being unknowable.

Kant defends his own transcendental idealism on the grounds that it assigns the inner and the outer exactly the same ontological and epistemological status: each is empirically real while being transcendentally ideal; each is known only subject to the conditions of our sensibility. Similarly, Candrakīrti defends his Madhyamaka view on the grounds that it shows that and why mind and the external world have the same status: each is conventionally real, dependently originated, but ultimately empty and unreal; each is known in the same way, through our ordinary epistemic instruments.

Candrakīrti therefore presents as his target a position according to which there is no external world, a thoroughgoing idealism, such as that advanced by Vinītadeva in his *Commentary on Dignāga's Investigation of the Percept* (Duckworth et al. 2016: 78–104). He characterizes it this way in *Introduction to the Middle Way*:

> Since he has no object, he perceives no subject, understanding the triple world to be consciousness only,
> a bodhisattva who has attained the perfection of wisdom understands reality in terms of consciousness only (6.45).

> . . . One who understands reality . . . understands it to be consciousness only. This means that since no material form exists, mental episodes and mental factors are seen to be the only dependently arisen phenomena. Thus, he understands reality to be only consciousness. . . . Bodhisattvas therefore see that the apparent objects of consciousness do not exist . . . and understanding reality to be only consciousness. (dBu ma, 'a: 263a–b; 2005: 131–132)[3]

[3] gang gis de kho na nyid phyin ci ma log pa dang lhag par sgro ma btags par rtogs pa dang mthong ba dang khong du chud pa de ni de nyid rtogs pa ste| rnam par shes pa tsam du de kho na nyid rtogs par 'gyur zhes tshig rnam par sbyar ro| |gzugs med pas sems dang sems las byung ba rnams kyang rten cing 'brel par 'byung b'i dngos po tsam du

> Just like an ocean roiled by the wind, in which waves rise one after another,
> Mere consciousness arises through its own potential as the foundation consciousness with the seeds of all phenomena. (6.46)

Just as when the wind stirs the depths of the ocean, waves that appear to have been there all along take form and are stirred into motion. In the same way, consciousness has been present from beginningless time. We must deny that entities come into existence through the maturations of propensities in consciousness. But the maturation of these potentials in the foundation consciousness causes specific events in the relevant other consciousnesses to occur as their effects. But this is just the other-dependent nature and is taken by fools to be constituted by subject and object. But there is not the slightest thing here that is not mere consciousness. (6.46; dBu ma, 'a: 263ab; 2005: 133)[4]

> Therefore, the dependent nature arises, which is the cause of imputed entities.
> It arises without any external objects, it exists, and it is essentially beyond all fabrication and objects. (6.47)

One must accept this dependent nature. This is because it is the nondeceptive basis of the entire conceptual scheme. Just as you can't

rtogs pa'i phyir| rnam par shes pa tsam du de kho na nyid rtogs pa zhes bya'o| | . . . gang gi phyir byang chub sems dpa' 'dis 'chad par 'gyur b'i rigs pas sems la gzung ba yod pa ma yin pa nyid kyis 'dzin pa nyid kyang ma mthong zhing| khams gsum po 'di ni rnam par shes pa tsam mo zhes yun ring por goms par byed la| de goms par byas pa las kyang brjod du med pa'i dngos po tsam zhig rang rig pas mthong ste| de'i phyir rim pa 'dis rnam par shes pa tsam du de kho na nyid rtogs par 'gyur ro|

[4] ji ltar rgya mtsho chu rlabs kyi rten du gyur pa'i chu'i yan lag rlung gis kun nas bskyod pa las| rlung tsam gyis rkyen nye bar lhags pas gnyid log pa lta bu'i rba rlabs rnams 'gran pa'i sgo nas bdag gi lus rnyed pa ltar kun nas yongs su rgyug par rtogs pa de bzhin du 'dir yang rnam par shes pa gcig nas gcig tu brgyud pa thog ma med pa'i dus nas zhugs pa| gzung ba dang 'dzin par mngon par zhen pa'i bag chags yongs su smin pa las bdag nyid kyis dngos po yod pa thob par 'gag bzhin pas| kun gzhi'i rnam par shes pa la gang bag chags kyi khyad par rang gi rnam pa dang rjes su 'brel b'i rnam par shes pa gzhan skye b'i rgyur gyur pa gzhag pa rim gyis rang yongs su smin pa'i rkyen lhags pas yongs su smin pa thob pa de las gang yongs su ma dag pa gzhan gyi dbang tsam zhig nye bar bskyed pa de nyid la byis pa rnams gzung ba dang 'dzin pa'i rnam par rtog pa kun tu rtog par byed kyi| rnam par shes pa las tha dad par gyur pa'i gzung ba ni cung zad kyang yod pa ma yin no| |

> have the illusion that a rope is a snake without a real rope underlying the illusory appearance, . . . given that there are no external objects, the appearance of things like blue objects must have an actual cause. . . . We can also easily understand emptiness in these terms: . . . the dependent nature is not itself the referent of any conceptual fabrications. . . . In short, there are three principles regarding the dependent nature: (1) it arises without any object from propensities; (2) it is not the referent of any conceptual fabrication; (3) it is the real existent that is the cause of imputed existents. (6.47; dBu ma, 'a: 263b–264a; 2005: 134–135)[5]

Candrakīrti's Refutation of Idealism

With all of this in view, let us now examine Candrakīrti's response to the metaphysical version of the dream analogy: "Where is there an example of cognition with no external object? You might say, 'in a dream.' But since on our view, there is no cognition in a dream, Your example doesn't show anything" (6.48). In the autocommentary, Candrakīrti has the idealist presenting the example of a dream of a herd of elephants by one sleeping in a small room. In the dream, the idealist says, there is visual cognition of elephants, but no actual elephants. Visual cognition, they conclude, is consistent with the nonexistence of its putative external objects (dBu ma, 'a: 264ab; 1992: 132–133).

[5] gzhan gyi dbang gi ngo bo 'di ni gdon mi za bar khas blang bar bya ste| gang gi phyir de ni rtog pa'i dra ba ma lus pa'i gzhir 'dod pa'i phyir ro| |sbrul du 'khrul pa thag pa'i rgyu mtshan can ni de la ma ltos par mi rigs la| bum par 'khrul pa sa la sogs pa'i rgyu mtshan can ni sa la sogs pa la ma ltos par nam mkh'i khams su 'byung bar 264A| |mi 'gyur ba de bzhin du| 'dir yang phyi rol gyi don med na sngon po la sogs pa'i rtog pa ci'i rgyu mtshan can zhig tu 'gyur| de'i phyir gdon mi za bar rtog pa'i rgyu gzhan gyi dbang gi ngo bo khas blang bar bya ste| kun nas nyon mongs pa dang rnam par byang b'i rgyu yin pa'i phyir ro| |de ltar na gang gi phyir gang la gang med pa de ni des stong par yang dag par rjes su mthong la| gang zhig 'dir lhag mar lus par gyur pa de 'di na bden par yod pa yin no zhes yang dag pa ji lta ba bzhin du rab tu shes pa 'di ni stong pa nyid la phyin ci ma log par 'jug pa'o zhes bya ba la sogs pas stong pa nyid kyang legs par gzung bar 'gyur ro| |de ni spros pa thams cad kyi yul ma yin pa'i rang bzhin can yang yin te| mngon par brjod pa ni btags pa'i rnam pa 'dzin pa'i phyir te| ji srid mngon par brjod pa yod pa de srid du dngos po brjod pa ma yin no| |de'i phyir mdor bsdu na| 'dir gzhan gyi dbang gi ngo bo la gsum rnam par gzhag par 'gyur te| shes bya med par rang gi bag chags kho na las 'byung ba dang yod pa nyid dang spros pa'o| |gcig gi yul ma yin pa nyid do| |gdags par yod pa'i dngos po'i rgyu nyid ni yod pa nyid las grub pa'i phyir de ni gsum po las tha mi dad do zhe'o| |

Candrakīrti responds that this argument begs the question: in an attempt to show that we can make sense of objectless sensory cognition, the idealist presumes that in the dream the visual cognition is real, but the objects are unreal. But, Candrakīrti responds, this cannot be taken for granted: just as the dreamer dreams that there are elephants in the room, they dream *that they are seeing* the elephants: this is not a case of *real* seeing and *unreal* elephants; instead, it is a case of *dreamed* seeing as well as a case of *dreamed* elephants. The cognition and the cognized therefore in fact have the same status, that of dreamed events.

Thus, Candrakīrti argues, the dream analogy cannot demonstrate the possibility of cognition and its objects having different ontological status. This does not, as we will see, mean that he thinks that this analogy is useless, only that it cannot be used to defend metaphysical idealism. Moreover, inasmuch as nobody could deny that thought is real in some sense, this amounts to a defense against one line of attack on the reality of the external world, once again providing evidence that Candrakīrti is no nihilist.

After a brief skirmish on the question of whether the memory of dreams can help to establish the difference in ontological status, Candrakīrti offers a realistic use of the dream analogy:

> Just as you say that there are no external objects in a dream,
> The mental states of which you dream do not occur, either:
> The eyes, the visual object, and the visual cognition to which they give rise
> Are each false. (6.51)
>
> None of the remaining sensory triads, such as the auditory occur, either.
> This waking life is just like a dream:
> All things are false, including cognition,
> Since neither its objects nor the relevant organs exist. (6.52)
>
> All three of these exist in our normal waking state
> In the same way that they do when we are dreaming.
> And just as they disappear when we awake from a dream,
> They do so when we awake from the sleep of primal confusion. (6.53)

Some of the remarks in these three verses might invite a nihilistic reading, but by now we can see why that would be unwarranted. The sense of *false* (*mithyā/rdzun*), as we have seen, is always *deceptive*. Candrakīrti is leaning on the *deceptive* character of our experience of the world, not asserting that it does not exist. In the first of these verses, Candrakīrti affirms that the dream analogy does tell us something about the nature of our experience (thus *allying* himself with the phenomenological reading of Yogācāra to which we adverted above): it tells us that we should take seriously the fact that it is possible for all phenomena—whether physical or cognitive—to be deceptive, that is, to exist in one way, but to appear to us in another.

In the second and third of these verses, Candrakīrti emphasizes that this analogy forces us to reject the idea that the mind and its objects differ in status. They are all equally illusory, appearing to us to exist intrinsically, but in fact existing only dependently, empty of any intrinsic reality. That is, the sleep to which Candrakīrti takes ordinary sleep to be analogous is that in which we all slumber—the susceptibility to massive illusion about the nature of the world in virtue of our naïve tendency to take our senses and cognition to deliver the world to us veridically, just as it is, independent of our cognitive faculties. But illusionism is not nihilism: the fact that the world is *illusory* does not mean that it is *nonexistent*, nor there cannot be truth with regard to that illusion. Candrakīrti makes this point explicitly in his commentary to 6.71cd, where he concludes this discussion:

> Those who claim that consciousness is substantially existent, but who deprecate the ontological status of external objects will fall into the trap of belief in the self. In order to forestall this, caring practitioners should administer a stern and powerful regimen of scripture and reason. (dBu ma, 'a: 271b; 1992: 155)[6]

[6] de'i phyir rnam par shes pa rzas su smra ba'i brjod byed kyi gdon gyis gzung ba phyi rol gyi yul la skur pa 'debs pa 'di ni ci nas|bdag nyid gyang sar lhung bar byed par mi 'gyur par dam pa snying rje spyod pa rnams kyis lung dang rigs pa'i gsang sngags bzang po btab pas tshab cher mnan te gzung par bya'o|

The point is powerful: nihilism and reification may appear to be diametrical opposites, but in fact they are two sides of the same coin. To be nihilistic about the person—to ignore the contribution of subjectivity to the constitution of experience—is to reify the external world by taking the properties we experience to exist intrinsically in entities whose identity is intrinsic to them. But to be nihilistic about the external world—to adopt the idealistic position—is to reify the mind or consciousness as the only thing that truly exists and to ignore the interdependence of experience on its objects. The middle path that Candrakīrti recommends assigns the same epistemological and ontological status to the mind and its objects: each is ultimately empty and conventionally existent; dependently originated, and, although illusory, knowable. This is what moderate realism looks like in the context of the global anti-realism of Prāsaṅgika Madhyamaka.

The Reflexivity of Awareness

Up to this point, we have been focusing on the status of external objects, and Candrakīrti's response to the idealistic deprecation of their status in virtue of regarding them as entirely imaginary. We now turn to the status of cognition or awareness itself. On this side of the idealistic coin, we find Candrakīrti criticizing not deprecation but reification: the idealists within the Yogācāra tradition—and in this context we include not only Sthiramati and Vinītadeva, but also Dignāga and Dharmakīrti—argue that the mind has a special epistemological status in virtue of being directly aware of itself. That is, as Dignāga puts it, every episode of consciousness is at the same time an instance of self-consciousness, or reflexive awareness (*svasaṃvedanā, svasamvṛti/rang rig*): to be aware of an object is, *ipso facto*, to be aware of one's own subjectivity. This allows us to have immediate, incontrovertible knowledge of our own minds.

To put this in terms of the account of conscious experience as arising from the maturation of potential in the foundation consciousness, when any potential for conscious experience ripens, it does so with two aspects: the experience of the object and the experience of one's own subjectivity. To be aware is to be aware that one is aware.

This position is akin to that of Husserl and neo-Husserlians such as Kriegel (2009), Thompson (2007, 2017), and Zahavi (2005). Dignāga argues for this on two principal grounds: that this is the only way to avoid a regress when explaining the distinction between conscious and non-conscious states, and that this is the only way to explain memory. Candrakīrti helps us to understand the current debate between reflexivists and higher-order theorists.

The Regress Argument for Reflexive Awareness

The most common metaphor in Yogācāra literature for this reflexivity is an old one, probably predating its use in Buddhist literature, and also often used in Vedānta: self-illumination. While we need a lamp to illuminate objects in a room, we do not need a second lamp to illuminate the first: it is self-illuminating. Similarly, many Yogācārins argue, while we need subjectivity, or consciousness, to illuminate objects of knowledge, we do not need a second conscious state to illuminate the first: consciousness is self-illuminating. The metaphor is important and seductive: on this view, the structure of consciousness is like that of a lamp: it makes objects evident by shining a light of awareness on them. Once one buys into this metaphor, we can ask, "does this light need another light to make it evident?" Finally, if the analogy is taken seriously, we are forced to the conclusion that just as a lamp is self-illuminating, conscious awareness is self-illuminating, and so that awareness must be reflexive.

Proponents of this argument from analogy continue by asserting that it makes no sense to argue that a cognition becomes conscious in virtue of being the object of another higher-order cognition. This, they argue, would lead to a vicious infinite regress in which no mental state could ever be conscious unless it involved the simultaneous awareness of infinitely many states. The only way to avoid such a regress, they argue, is to accept reflexive awareness.[7]

[7] Indeed, Kriegel (2009), Thompson (2007), and Zahavi (2005) each advance nearly the same argument.

Candrakīrti responds obliquely to this argument in the following verse in *Introduction to the Middle Way* and its autocommentary:

> There is no reflexive awareness:
> How could one ever grasp the dependent nature?
> Action, agent, and, and object can never be identical.
> So, it makes no sense for any cognition to apprehend itself. (6.76)

> This so-called "reflexive awareness" entails the identity of action, object, and agent. This is because in coming to know, the knower, the known and the means of knowing are identical, and this entails the absurd consequence of identity of agent, action, and object. And such an identity is never observed. For example, a woodcutter, the wood he cuts, and the action of cutting can never be identical. So, because there can be no reflexive awareness, no cognition apprehends itself. (6.76; dBu ma, 'a: 273b–274a; 1992: 161)[8]

To understand Candrakīrti's argument here and its role in his philosophical program, it is useful to consider a few more examples used in Madhyamaka critiques of reflexivity: the blade of a knife may cut other objects but cannot cut itself; darkness can obscure other objects, but it cannot obscure itself. We should not over-read these analogies: any direct argument from these examples to the conclusion that reflexive action is always impossible would be straightforwardly fallacious. But that is not the point: the impossibility of reflexivity in the case of the knife and darkness is not intended to show that reflexive action is *impossible*, but only that we have to be careful about using an analogy to show that it is *always* possible, as there are good analogies on both sides of the ledger.

Candrakīrti's argument goes further. His explicit claim is that in the case of reflexive awareness, the idealist is identifying agent, object, and

[8] rig par byaba de nyid kyang byed pa po yin zhing| de'i bya ba yang tha mi dad pa nyid yin pas byed pa po dang las dang bya ba gcig tu thal bar gyur na| 'di dag gcig pa nyid du ni ma mthong ngo|| 'di ltar gcod pa po dang shing dang gcod pa'i bya ba gcig pa ni ma yin no|| 'di las kyang rang rig pa wong pa ma yin pas de nyid kyis de 'dzin pa ma yin no||

action. In pointing out this structure, he is charging that the metaphor of self-illumination fails to establish even the *possibility* of reflexive awareness, and when properly understood establishes its *impossibility*. While this extension is not as clear as it might be in Candrakīrti's text, attention to Śāntideva's presentation of this argument allows us to see what Candrakīrti has in mind.

Śāntideva makes this point explicit in chapter 9 of *How to Lead an Awakened Life*. In that context, he points out that a lamp does not illuminate an object *for itself*, but rather *for another who is seeing it*. That is, if we follow the agent, action, object model, the Yogācāra deployment of the analogy begs the question by illicitly identifying the subject of experience with the experience itself: the lamp may be the agent, but the act of illumination is the action, and the object is the visual awareness of one who sees the lamp. This suggests that introspective awareness has a different structure: the light causes the *person* to see the light as well as the objects it makes visible. Hence, Śāntideva argues, we should understand a conscious state as illuminating its object *to a subject* who is *different* from that state itself. So, the example, if spelled out explicitly, fails to be one of something that is *self-evidencing*, but rather is an instance of higher-order awareness.[9]

Why is this important? The consequence of a doctrine of reflexive awareness—whether it is mobilized by a Vedāntin, a Yogācārin, a Cartesian, or a Husserlian—is, as Kant pointed out, that there is a strong asymmetry between self-knowledge and the knowledge of the external world. The former is asserted to be immediate and therefore not subject to the distortion of mediating representations; it is supposed to give us certainty about our own mental states, even if not about their putative causes or objects; the latter is represented as mediated, uncertain. Moreover, this position is foundationalist: it

[9] Consider 9.18cd: a lamp does not illuminate itself, since darkness does not conceal itself.

This might seem just about as dark as Candrakīrti's text. But once we see how the argument works here, we find that Śāntideva has illuminated the point. Suppose that the lamp were truly self-illuminating. Then darkness would be self-obscuring, in which we would never perceive darkness. The fact that we do means that darkness does not conceal itself, but conceals other things from us; similarly, the lamp does not reveal itself to itself, but reveals other things to us.

regards knowledge of the external world—to the extent that there is any—as dependent on immediate self-knowledge.[10]

Candrakīrti is concerned with both of these issues. He rejects the asymmetry between self-knowledge and knowledge of the external world because it breaks the connection between the instruments of knowledge and knowledge itself. Epistemic instruments are established and derive their normative force through convention, and knowledge therefore requires participation in the public conventions that give them force. The idea of reflexive awareness, however, is the idea that we have a special non-conventional epistemic access to the inner. Candrakīrti therefore rejects the idea that self-knowledge grounds knowledge of the external world because this would entail that convention is irrelevant to justification and establishing self-knowledge as intrinsically self-validating.

Ironically, then, this immediate epistemology of the inner, which on this foundationalist model is supposed to make sense of knowledge, instead makes it mysterious. Candrakīrti then sees that the only way to make sense of the possibility of any knowledge at all is by articulating the conventions that we use to gain knowledge, and that requires that all justification is collective, public justification, and so all knowledge is mediated. Idealism denies that; Madhyamaka demands it.[11]

[10] This point is made explicitly in A. C. Mukerji's (1938) defense of self-illuminating consciousness as the only answer to what he sees as the sceptical abyss opened by Kant's denial of the possibility of immediate knowledge, and in particular of the possibility of knowledge of the transcendental ego.

[11] As Thurman (1980) also points out, Candrakīrti's argument has important affinities to Wittgenstein's Private Language Argument and his extension of that argument to the problem of other minds. Indeed, one of the virtues of Candrakīrti's account is that it shows us just why the problem of other minds does not arise in Madhyamaka philosophy: the very possibility of any knowledge, including knowledge of *one's own mind*, presupposes that we are members of epistemic communities; if we do not take other minds for granted, there is no knowledge at all. There is also an important affinity between Candrakīrti's attack on idealism and Sellars' attack on the Myth of the Given (Garfield 2019b, 2022b). In each case, a temptation to assert a privileged, immediate access to our own mind is resisted by reflection on the degree to which any knowledge of our own inner life must depend upon our participation in public epistemic practices, and so depends for its possibility on mastery of public conceptual categories in terms of which the mind can be understood.

The Memory Argument for Reflexive Awareness

The regress argument is not the only argument for reflexive awareness. In *Introduction to the Middle Way*, Candrakīrti also considers and refutes Dignāga's memory argument for reflexivity developed in his *Handbook of Epistemology* (*Pramāṇasamuccaya*). The argument is straightforward and well known, and—although it has also been resurrected by the "new Husserlians" (Kriegel 2011, Thompson 2017, and Zahavi 2005)—it is not very compelling. Nonetheless, Candrakīrti's response to it is noteworthy. The memory argument for reflexivity goes like this: to remember an event, one must have experienced it. When I remember seeing a blue sky yesterday, I also remember myself seeing the blue sky yesterday. But this is a single memory, not two. So, my current must be an experience of a single past event. So, that event must have been both seeing a blue sky and my awareness of my seeing a blue sky. So, to see a blue sky is also to be aware that I am seeing a blue sky, and all awareness is reflexive.

Our purpose is not to discuss all that is wrong with this argument. More interesting is Candrakīrti's refutation (also made more explicit by Śāntideva in *How to Lead an Awakened Life*, 9.23).[12] Candrakīrti argues that the entire model of memory presupposed by this argument is misguided. Memory is not the reproduction in consciousness of a past experience; instead, it is the causal consequence of a past experience. And that consequence may have little in common in content or structure with the original experience; what is important for memory is the causal continuum linking the original experience to the present recall. So, Candrakīrti concludes, although memory allows us to infer the past cognition of object, this does not entail that the original cognition was reflexive.

Candrakīrti's point is twofold: first, the fact that I recall the blue sky in a way that I would express as "I saw the blue sky" is simply a fact about how memory presents itself, not a fact about the structure of the initial perceptual experience that is the object of the memory; second, as just noted, memory is reconstructive, not preservative. Hence

[12] See Garfield (2006; 2015: 136–152; 2022b: 67–81) for more on both of these arguments, and 2006 for an extended treatment of the memory argument and of Śāntideva's refutation.

nothing whatsoever follows from the structure of memory about the structure of the event remembered. Āryadeva puts the argument this way in *Four Hundred Verses*: "Things that have been seen do not reappear. Nor does the same awareness arise again. Memory is of something that has ceased, Its object is always that which has dissolved" (11.25).

Candrakīrti's *Commentary* expands Āryadeva's argument: since both subjective states and their objects are transient, it is not possible for a present object to be the immediate object of a subsequently arising awareness; each cognitive state, he argues, has as its *immediate* object only its representational content. Therefore, no object that we saw in the past reappears in our future cognition; the object of memory is a reconstruction of a past experience, not that experience itself (*Commentary on Ārydadeva's Four Hundred Stanzas* 11.125, dBu ma, ya: 182b; 2019: 315–316). But then Candrakīrti asks rhetorically: "Does this imply that there is no episodic memory that recalls the past subjective experience?" To which he replies:

> Who would claim that there isn't? We do not deny the existence of a dependently originated memory. We accept the facticity of memory as Āryadeva has defined it: "Memory of that which has ceased; its object is always that which has dissolved." Therefore, the perceptual object of memory is always a bygone object....
>
> To say that something has *ceased* (*log pa*) is no different from saying that it lacks intrinsic reality or that it is dependently originated, because *cessation* does not mean *nonexistence.* Past things are not entirely nonexistent, since they are objects of memory and since their effects are observable. But nor are these ceased entities intrinsically real, for that would absurdly entail that they are eternal, and that they themselves would still be present. An occurrent memory represents the type of object that gives rise to it, and memory represents that very object. Therefore, since memory is of a ceased entity, its objects must be those that are ceased. It is like recalling when awake the objects experienced in a dream. (*Commentary on Āryadeva's Four Hundred Stanzas*, 11.25, dBu ma, ya: 182b–183a; 2019: 316–317)[13]

[13] yang ci 'das pa'i yul can gyi dran pa med dam | med do zhes de skad du su smra | kho bo cag ni rten cing 'brel par 'byung ba sel ba ma yin no || de ji ltar [83a] || yod pa de

Candrakīrti is simply making the point that memory is the effect of prior experience, and that it has as its indirect object the direct object of that prior experience. But it only takes that object indirectly in virtue of taking as its *direct* object a *representation* caused by that prior object through a continuum of causes originating in the original perceptual experience of the remembered object.

In the *Commentary on Introduction to the Middle Way*, Candrakīrti explains the relationship between an object that has ceased and a memory that arises from it. He does this with a dream analogy deployed in the *Sūtra on Samsaric Migration* (*Bhavasaṃkrāntisūtra*). In that sūtra, the king of Magadha approaches the Buddha and asks: "How does *karma* that was obtained a long time ago endure and get mentally appropriated during the time of death? Why is *karma* not temporally constrained given that all conditioned phenomena are empty?" (*mDo sde*, Tsa 284b, cited *Introduction to the Middle Way* 6.40; dBu ma, 'a: 260b; 1992: 121). The Buddha answers with the following analogy: a man dreams of having sexual intercourse with a beautiful woman. When he awakes the man remembers the woman from his dream and becomes infatuated with her. The man's recall of the woman from his dream—and the psychological processes including his arousal—continue after the cessation of the dream and are caused by the dream; although the woman does not exist, these are all actual experiences. Even though there is a considerable lapse of time between the dream and the recall, it is able to causally trigger memories to arise in the mind of the man who dreamed it.

Candrakīrti explains that the dream gives rise to a chain of subsequent mental events eventuating in the memory. Since the memory

ltar ni | des na | dran pa zhes bya log pa yi ||don la log pa kho na 'byung || zhes slob dpon nyid rnam par 'jog par mdzad do || de'i phyir dran pa'i dmigs pa ni 'das pa'i dngos po yin no || gal te de rang gi ngo | bos yod na ni de'i tshe dran pa de yod pa'i don la dmigs pa'i phyir rang gi ngo bos grub pa zhig na | gang gi tshe 'das pa'i dngos po de rang bzhin med pa de'i tshe de la dmigs pa'i dran pa yang rang bzhin med pa yin te | de'i phyir log pa yin no zhes bya bar grub po || log pa zhes bya ba ni rang bzhin med pa dang | rten cing 'brel par 'byung ba zhes bya ba dang | don gzhan ma yin pa ste | dngos po med pa'i don ni log pa'i don ma yin no || das pa'i dngos po rnam pa thams cad du med pa ni ma yin te | dran par bya ba yin pa'i phyir dang | de'i 'bras bu mthong ba'i phyir ro || rang gi ngo bos yod pa yang ma yin no || rtag pa nyid du thal ba'i phyir dang | dngos su 'dzin par thal bar 'gyur ba'i phyir ro || rnam pa de lta bu'i dngos po las skye ba na dran pa yang rnam pa de lta bu yin pas | des na;dran pa zhes bya log pa yi || don la log pa kho na 'byung || zhes bya ba grub ste | sad pa'i gnas skabs su rmi lam gyi gnas skabs su myong ba'i yul dran pa bzhin no ||

arises from a continuum of intermediate events, there is no temporal interruption or causal chasm between the past event we experienced and the future recollection of that event; nor is the past event somehow preserved and re-presented.

On the Madhyamaka view, the past experiences of the objects that seem to go out of existence are causally productive in triggering new memories, just in the same way as the disintegration of the dream woman, who has long ceased still causally produces a passion in the mind of the man, and the incident that initiates the memory—the past event—need not be all that similar to the memory itself; in this case, the past object was not even real, even though it is remembered as though it were. In *Introduction to the Middle Way* Candrakīrti concisely puts the argument this way:

> Since there is no intrinsic cessation,
> Even though there is no foundation consciousness, actions can
> produce effects.
> And so it makes sense that even if an action has ceased long ago,
> It will still produce effects. (6.39)
>
> Fools remain attached to the objects of their dreams
> Even after waking up.
> Just so, essenceless actions that have ceased
> Can nonetheless produce effects. (6.40)

Śāntideva makes a similar point. He uses the analogy of the hibernating bear bitten by a rat to point out that one may not even have been aware that one was in a particular state until one remembers it later (*How to Lead an Awakened Life* 9.23). While he is hibernating, a bear is bitten by a rat. He is unconscious of the bite, and the wound becomes infected. When the bear awakens in the spring, he experiences the pain of the infected wound. At this point he becomes aware that he was bitten.

Śāntideva's insight is simple: one can become aware of a past event in virtue of the causal continuum it initiates despite not having been aware of that event at the time it occurred. And that is how memory works: it is the downstream effect of an interaction with one's environment that gives one experience about it—not a replay of an experience in virtue of the preservation of a reflexive awareness of it. So *nothing* about the structure of a perceptual experience—including whether or not it was reflexive—can be inferred from the content of the memory of it. And this is exactly what Candrakīrti had in mind.

The Status of the Dependent Nature

Immediately after addressing reflexive awareness, Candrakīrti criticizes the Yogācāra tradition for reifying the dependent nature. He writes:

> If, despite its being unarisen and unknowable,
> You still suppose that your dependent nature exists,
> Why do you think that there is a problem with the existence
> Of other things that make no sense, such as the son of a barren woman? (6.77)

> I have already explained that the dependent nature can't arise from itself or from anything other. I have also shown that it would have to possess an unknowable nature. Therefore, if you maintain that something that is unarisen and whose nature is unknowable exists, why not accept other things that are just like the dependent nature, for instance the son of a barren woman? (dBu ma, 'a: 274a; 2005: 167)[14]
>
> Now you might reply:
>
> > If the dependent nature doesn't have a shred of existence
> > What could possibly give rise to conventional reality? (6.78ab)
>
> That is, you would have to think that conventional reality wouldn't have a shred of a cause. And if that were the case, what would the

[14] gzhan gyi dbang bdag dang gzhan las mi skye ba ni gong du cir bstan pa yin la| de lta ni ma shes pa'i bdag nyid can nyid du yang bstan pa yin no| |de'i phyir de ltar gal te skye ba med cing ma shes pa'i bdag nyid can gzhan gyi dbang gi ngo bo yod do zhes bya bar khas len na| gang las gzhan gyi dbang dang mtshungs pa'i chos can yin du zin kyang 'di yod pa nyid du 'dod par mi 'gyur ba| khyod la mo gsham gyi bus gnod pa ci zhig byas te| mo gsham gyi bu zhes bya ba spros pa thams cad las 'ads shing 'phags pa'i ye shes kyi spyod yul du gyur pa brjod du med pa'i rang bzhin can ci zhig yod do zhes 'di yang yod pa nyid du 'dod par gyis shig|

causal basis be of mundane conventions; they can't be self-caused! We respond:

> When you see the dependent that way, by clinging to a substantial ground
> You upend the entire framework of mundane convention. (6.78 cd)

Your lack of wisdom leads you to seize on to a substantial ground. You have poured your water into an unfired pot of dependent nature! (dBu ma, 'a: 274ab; 2005: 167–168)[15]

Candrakīrti is responding to an important strand of Yogācāra thought regarding the three natures, often referred to as the "pivot model" of the relation between the imagined and consummate natures to the dependent, a model clearly articulated in the sixth chapter of the *Sūtra Explaining the Thought*. It is easy to appreciate this model when we pay attention to the grammar of the names of the three natures. The first and third (*parikalpita* and *pariniṣpanna*) are each past participles: *imagined* and *consummated*. But the dependent (*paratantra*)—although that nature is situated between the other two in the order of understanding—is a nominal: *that which is dependent on another*. This suggests—and the *Sūtra Explaining the Thought* confirms—that the other-dependent nature in some sense grounds the other two natures: it is simply the reality of things, the world of dependently originated phenomena; the imagined nature is the way *we take that* reality to exist; the consummate nature is the way we *should take* it to exist, as empty of the imagined.

[15] gang yang dngos po btags par yod pa'i rgyur gyur cing zhes smras pa de yang gzhan gyi dbang yod pa nyid yin na| rigs pa zhig na|
gang tshe gzhan dbang cung zad yod min na| |
kun rdzob pa yi rgyur ni gang zhig 'gyur| |
kun rdzob pa rnams la rgyu cung zad kyang med do snyam du bsams pa'o| |de'i phyir 'di la 'jig rten gyi tha snyad kyi rgyu gang yin pa de rang nyid kyi yod pa ma yin pas kye ma kyi hud| gzhan gyi ltar na rdzas la chags pa yis| | 'jig rten grags pa'i rnam gzhag kun kyang brlag |shes rab med pas rdzas shas tsam la chags pa'i sgo nas gzhan gyi dbang gi bum pa so ma btang bar chu dang 'dra ba blugs nas rang ge blo gros kyi tshul ngan pa'i phyir 'jig rten pa'i rnam par gzhag pa 'jig rten kho na las grub pa 'dug shig |song shig byos shig tshos shig ces bya ba de lta bu la sogs pa dang| de bzhin du gzugs dang tshor ba la sogs pa gang yin pa de dag thams cad 'jig par rtogs te| de'i phyir 'di la rgud pa nyid 'ba' zhig srid par 'gyur gyi| mngon par mtho ba ni ma yin no| |

To see things this way is to give the dependent nature a privileged ontological status with respect to the other two: it is the nominal basis, and they are adjectival, describing ways that we apprehend that independently existent basis. We can get a feel for that when we consider the most natural way to think about how different organisms perceive the same environment: I might see a lily as white, while a bee, with its infrared and ultraviolet vision, may see that same lily as variegated in color. When we describe that situation, we think of an underlying physical reality—the lily as it is—apprehended in different ways by me and the bee. Each of us superimposes a distinct visual appearance on the lily (an imagined nature), when in fact, its causal structure is empty of that appearance (its consummate nature).

Candrakīrti takes this approach to amount to assigning the dependent nature intrinsic reality, and to adopting a version of foundationalism; he takes this to be both ontologically and epistemologically incoherent. In the terse two verse passage in which he addresses this problem, he first charges that the dependent nature is posited by Yogācāra philosophers as unarisen and unknowable. Note that in doing so, he explicitly introduces both the ontological and the epistemological dimensions of his dispute with Yogācāra on this point. This is because they are entangled. Candrakīrti asserts that the dependent nature can't be self-caused, on pain of explanatory circularity. But it can't be caused by something else, because that would presuppose that it is dependent, and that dependence would have to be explained, issuing in a regress. So, while the dependent nature is meant to be the causal nexus itself, or the stream of causally interdependent events, posited because every phenomenon must be explicable, it itself is inexplicable in the Yogācāra system.

When Candrakīrti says that the Yogācāra philosopher must take the dependent nature to be unknowable, he adverts to the fact that all of the objects of our knowledge are, almost by definition, in the *imagined nature*.[16] That is because we can only know things as they are present to us through the mediation of our sensory and cognitive

[16] We note that Vasubandhu makes exactly this point in verses 11 and 12 of *Treatise on the Three Natures*, when he asserts that we only know the dependent nature as we experience it—that is through the imagined nature.

faculties, and those faculties deliver things to us not *as they are*, in their bare causal nexus, but always *as they appear to us*. This is akin to the Kantian insight that we can never know noumena; our only objects of knowledge are phenomena, and those appear only in virtue of being synthesized subject to the conditions of our sensibility and understanding. So, when the Yogācārin talks about the dependent nature, they are talking about something that we cannot possibly know: the lily I imagine as the foundation of the bee's and my experience literally has no properties that either of us could ever experience or imagine.

So, Candrakīrti concludes, although it sounds like the dependent nature provides an explanation both of benighted and awakened experience through the imagined nature and the consummate nature, respectively, in fact—like the son of a barren woman—it turns out on analysis to be an incoherent construct in virtue of being causally inexplicable and uncharacterizable. While it looks like a necessary foundation, it can't explain anything at all, and itself is inexplicable, standing outside of the entire web of dependent origination, failing both to be conventionally real and to be ultimate real. It fails to be conventionally real because it is independent and unknowable; it fails to be ultimately real, because it is nothing but a sequence of dependently arisen events, and so entirely empty. This is why it can't hold water; it is a half-baked idea.

We leave aside here just how fair Candrakīrti is being to three nature theory, and we grant that there are formulations of this theory that make very good phenomenological sense (see especially Waldron 2023). But this much is sound: to the extent that one takes the dependent nature to be a final explanatory ground, one is in trouble. If it is taken to provide an epistemological ground, we effectively have the problem that Sellars developed for sense-datum theory: at best we confuse causation with justification, and we fail to see that something that cannot have propositional structure cannot serve as the premise in a justification. An uncognized dependent cannot be the epistemic basis for statements about imagined phenomena. And if it is taken to be an ontological ground, the very considerations that drive us to posit it lead to a regress or a circle; the search for a substantial basis as the final explanation for everything is always doomed.

The Point of these Refutations

Why are Candrakīrti's extended responses to the regress argument and the dream argument, his denial of the reflexivity of awareness, and his attack on three nature-theory important? In this entire discussion, we see Candrakīrti emphasizing the interdependence of the psychological and the physical domains and also the fact that these domains are identical in their causal structure and epistemic status. Candrakīrti's reason for rejecting idealism—as we have noted that Kant's would be a millennium later—is that it illicitly assigns status to mind distinct from that it assigns to material objects. In doing so, the Yogācāra presumes the immediate givenness of the mind and our ability to have non-deceptive access to our own cognitive life.

To do so is also to presuppose that this immediate, non-deceptive access can provide the foundation for our knowledge of the external world. This not only occludes the mediated, convention-dependent nature of our self-knowledge, but also undermines the warrant that we have for knowledge of the external world, reducing it to a second-rate knowledge. And to do this is both to deprecate the role of collective convention in the enterprise of knowledge generally—taking it to be only relevant in one domain—and to deprecate conventional epistemic warrant, taking it to be inferior to a mythic immediate knowledge.

Candrakīrti's arguments against idealism hence undermine one more version of foundationalism: the idea that our immediate knowledge of our own cognitive processes is the ground of our other knowledge, a view expressed not only in India, but also by Descartes and Husserl among many others in the European tradition. And this account rests squarely on the Madhyamaka account of dependent origination and on the conventional reality and ultimate emptiness of both mind and its objects.

There is also an ontological dimension to this refutation of idealism. Candrakīrti charges the idealistic wing of the Yogācāra school with assigning entirely distinct ontological status to the external world and to the mind, or to the dependent nature and to the other two. Idealists such as Sthiramati and Dharmapāla, he argues, are incorrect to treat external objects as entirely non-existent and treat consciousness as truly existent. Candrakīrti argues instead that external objects, while empty of intrinsic existence, exist conventionally, and that while the mind exists it does not exist intrinsically. Each is conventionally real, and ultimately empty; each is known only through the mediation of epistemic instruments. Candrakīrti summarizes this point in his *Commentary on Sixty Stanzas of Reasoning* (*Yuktiṣaṣṭīkāvṛtti*):

> To reject dependent origination is to undermine the reality of everything. All beings in samsara would be as nonexistent as the horns of a donkey. (45)
>
> To claim that things that we know to exist do not exist is irrational. One should therefore abandon both commitment to the objective existence and to the nonexistence of things that are dependently originated and should assert that they lack objective status, like reflections in a mirror. (45; dBu ma, 25ab; Loizzo et al. 2024: 200)[17]

So, let us review the five principal critiques Candrakīrti levels at Yogācāra:

(1) Yogācāra deprecates the status of external objects, undermining the status of conventional truth.
To this Candrakīrti replies that external objects are known, are intersubjectively available, and hence conventionally real.
(2) Yogācāra reifies the mind as ultimately real.
To this Candrakīrti replies that our mental states and processes are dependently originated, impermanent, and known only subject to our mental sense faculty; they are hence only conventionally real.
(3) Yogācāra assigns different ontological and epistemological status to the inner and outer worlds.

[17] rten cing 'brel bar 'byung ba dang 'gal na rnam par gzhag pa thams cad zhig par 'gyur ro| |bong bu'i rwa la sogs pa bzhin du 'gro ba yang mi dmigs par 'gyur ro| |.... de dmigs su yod bzhin du med par khas blang ba ni mi rigs so| |de bas na gang brten te 'byung b'i ngo bo nyid kyis yod pa dang med pa spangs pa ste| rkyen 'di tsam gyis grub pas gzugs brnyan bzhin du de ngo bo nyid kyis grub pa med par khas blang bar bya ste|

To this Candrakīrti replies that the mental and material worlds are each dependently originated, and that they are known only as they appear to us; they are each conventionally real and ultimately empty.

(4) Yogācāra treats cognition as reflexively aware.
To this Candrakīrti replies that self-knowledge is always fallible, higher-order awareness.

(5) Yogācāra treats the dependent nature as on ontological and epistemological foundation.
To this Candrakīrti replies that even though all phenomena are interdependent, to treat dependent origination itself as either a metaphysical or an epistemological foundation is incoherent; it is attempt to step out of the dependently originated world to explain it from the outside.

Now, we might question Candrakīrti's reconstruction of Yogācāra. The tradition is vast, and there is a great diversity of positions within it. While some Yogācāra scholars and texts are clearly idealist (e.g., Sthiramati, Dharmapāla, and Vinītadeva), others clearly are not (Asaṅga), and the positions of some are equivocal (Vasubandhu, Dignāga). There is as much reason to read Yogācāra as a phenomenological, rather than an idealistic, tradition.[18]

Our point here is that regardless of whether it is an attack on the entire Yogācāra position, as many Tibetan exegetes take it to be, Candrakīrti's refutation of idealism is correct: he insists that the ontological and the epistemological status of mind and of the external world are on a par—neither grounds the other; neither is more secure than the other. They are each possible only in the context of the other, and in the context of the conventions that enable epistemology and metaphysics. This is one more instance both of his realism and of his anti-foundationalism. And it is that realism that allows him to make sense of the ethical program of the Mahāyāna, to which we now turn.

[18] And once again, we must recognize that there are multiple approaches to unifying the Madhyamaka and Yogācāra traditions; Śāntarakṣita offers one model in *Ornament to the Middle Way*, and, as McNamara (2019) shows, Ranākaraśānti argues forcefully that Madhyamaka and three-nature theory are very much of a piece.

5
Higher Ground
Candrakīrti and the Bodhisattva Path

Ethics and Soteriology in Madhyamaka

Candrakīrti's focus on ethics is hardly *sui generis.* In the Buddhist tradition, ethics and soteriology are tightly intertwined. The fourth ennobling truth—that of the path—is the basis of all Buddhist soteriology, as it is the route to the release from suffering. Six components of that path—right action, right speech, right recollection, right intention, right effort, and right livelihood—are explicitly ethical. Others—such as right meditation and right view—are necessary cognitive conditions for developing and maintaining ethical motivation and so are also ethical: they constitute part of the practice by means of which we become more expert ethical agents. That is, they provide, respectively, the cognitive ground and the means of internalizing the more explicitly ethical aspects of the path. This is why the ven. Geshe Yeshes Thabkhas once remarked, "every syllable of Buddhadharma is about ethics" (personal communication).

The metaphor of path in the context of soteriology and of ethical cultivation runs through Buddhist doctrine (Garfield 2022d: ch. 7). In the Mahāyāna tradition the eightfold path is joined by the bodhisattva path as a further metaphor, this time as the metaphor for the path to full awakening based on the aspiration to liberate all beings (*bodhicitta*). It is in this context that Candrakīrti's ethical thought is articulated. The bodhisattva path is articulated in the *Sūtra on the Ten Grounds* (*Daśabhūmika-sūtra*). That account of the stages through which a bodhisattva passes en route to awakening and of the particular ethical qualities perfected on each of those stages comes to structure all subsequent path literature in the Mahāyāna tradition. This literature prominently includes Asaṅga's *Bodhisattva Grounds* (*Bodhisattvabhūmi*)

By the Light of the Moon. Jay L. Garfield and Sonam Thakchöe, Oxford University Press.
 DOI: 10.1093/oso/9780197830741.003.0006

and Candrakīrti's *Introduction to the Middle Way*, each of which follows the *Ten Grounds* structure and content very closely. Following Atiśa's transmission of Buddhist philosophy to Tibet, this structure becomes systematized in the extensive graduated path literature that dominates Tibetan understandings of Buddhist practice, especially as undertaken within the Prāsaṅgika Madhyamaka tradition.

For this reason, it is important to recognize that Candrakīrti's ethics and soteriology cannot be cleanly separated from each other. Prajñākaramati also points out in his commentary to *How to Lead an Awakened Life* that Śāntideva follows Candrakīrti very closely. *How to Lead an Awakened Life* is even more explicitly ethical in content than *Introduction to the Middle Way* (dBu ma, la: 41b1–288a7). We can therefore sometimes turn to Śāntideva for elucidation of ethical ideas that are expressed more obliquely by Candrakīrti. Finally, it is important to note that *Introduction to the Middle Way* is not the only text in which Candrakīrti takes up topics in ethics. His *Commentary on Āryadeva's Four Hundred Verses* (*Catuḥśatakaṭīkā*) and *Commentary on Sixty Verses of Reasoning* (*Yuktiṣaṣṭīkāvṛtti*) are also replete with ethical reflection. Only by reading these three texts together and in the context of the bodhisattva path can we get a complete picture of Candrakīrti's ethical thought.

It is also important to bear in mind the centrality of ethics to the Buddhist project as a whole, and so the fact that Candrakīrti's own project is bound up with the very structure of Buddhist ethics. That structure presupposes the broad background of illusion in our experience of the world and of our own place in it as well as a certain realism about the world that appears to us in this illusory form. As we have seen, each of these presuppositions is central to Candrakīrti's vision.

We must also bear in mind that Buddhist ethics is phenomenological: it aims not at enumerating duties or at the calculation of beneficial outcomes, but rather at transforming our experience of the world and of our place in it (Garfield 2022d; Harris 2024; Heim 2020). Ethical cultivation in the Buddhist tradition transforms us from egocentric agents who see ourselves as experiencing and acting on a world of objects into non-egocentric embedded agents who experience ourselves as elements of a network of interdependent beings and circumstances, none of which exists intrinsically or ultimately. Instead of taking ourselves to be outside of that network looking in, or at best occupying a privileged central spot in which our own desire satisfaction is a rational pursuit, we come to experience the entire world as a field in which our own well-being is of no different value from that of others and in which others afford not competition but cooperative benefit.

This approach reflects the conviction that our natural comportment to the world is entirely determined by illusion: the illusion of independence, that is, of existing external to the network of interdependence; the illusion that there is something morally special about *me*; and the illusion that others exist only as objects in relation to my own subjectivity. These are all versions of the overarching illusion of subject-object duality in its various manifestations, an illusion that we have been exploring in the previous two chapters. At the heart of both the Yogācāra and the Madhyamaka critique of the natural attitude toward the world is the idea that subject-object duality is an innate phenomenological framework that structures our experience, and, despite being natural, it is pernicious. To see the world this way is, as Wittgenstein felicitously puts it in the *Tractatus*, to experience the relation between our subjectivity and the world as like that between the eye and the visual field—as the transcendental, but empirically absent, precondition of all that we experience.

To adopt this standpoint is to take oneself as a kind of singularity, a point of subjectivity at once hyper-real as the condition of all experience of, and action on the world, and non-existent in that world. To see the world this way is hence, as we have seen in the previous chapter, to assign an ontological status to the self radically distinct from that assigned to all of its objects, and in the end, incoherent. Despite its incoherence, this stance has immediate ethical implications: it implicates a reason to be especially concerned with my own welfare, and to treat others as mere objects, less real and so less important than me. This is why, in *Introduction to the Middle Way*, Candrakīrti is so concerned to refute the version of idealism that encodes this view.

As we have noted repeatedly, illusion is always understood as a discordance between mode of appearance and mode of existence. So, when Candrakīrti argues that subject-object duality is illusory, we should take him to be claiming neither that subjects are non-existent nor that objects are non-existent, nor even that there is no relation between subjects and objects that distinguishes them from each other. Instead, we should take him to claim that subjects, objects, and the relation between them exist in one way but appear in another. The radical ontological disjuncture between subject and object that appears in our naïve experience of the world is the target of Candrakīrti's critical analysis—what Tsongkhapa calls "the object of negation"—in this case.

Instead of experiencing ourselves as standing outside the objective world, living it and acting on it, we are encouraged to experience ourselves as dependently originated phenomena *in* the world, subject to all of the same causes and conditions as anything else. That is to enter a kind of ethical flow state in which our engagement and manifestation of the virtues Candrakīrti identifies are spontaneous, not calculated, and in which our own position in the ethical landscape is not regarded as privileged. Subjectivity, on this view, is a real relation, a conventionally real, empirical relation, but not a transcendental relation. We are as much objects to ourselves as subjects, experienced by other subjects whose welfare and suffering matter just as much as ours, and whose welfare and suffering are deeply imbricated with our own.

To understand the illusion of subject-object duality this way is also to adopt the kind of moderate realism in the context of global illusionism that we have seen to be the defining characteristic of Candrakīrti's metaphysics and epistemology. This is because illusion requires the *existence* of that illusory object, despite our massive error regarding its *nature*. In this case, ethical conduct presupposes that we exist as moral subjects and as moral agents, that there are other sentient beings who matter, and that we are interdependent with them. That is, it requires the reality of the conventional world—the illusion is to misunderstand the nature of our moral subjectivity and agency, to grant ourselves a privileged position in the metaphysical and ethical order of things. The centrality of ethics to Buddhist thought is in the end what demands that Candrakīrti is realistic about that world.

Conventionalism and Relativism

As in the domains of metaphysics and epistemology, Candrakīrti's conventionalism has been taken by many classical and contemporary commentators to lead inexorably to a kind of nihilism according to which whatever anyone thinks is as true or as false as whatever anyone else thinks, and so there simply is no distinction between truth and falsity and hence in the end no reality. The analogue of this charge in the ethical domain is that Candrakīrti's conventionalism leads to a radical moral relativism that degenerates into nihilism. This, one might argue, follows from the fact that if there are no convention-independent moral facts, then whatever anyone believes to be good is good; whatever anyone believes to be bad is bad. And this eviscerates the distinction between good and evil of all content, reducing it to a mere distinction between that of which what some people happen to approve and that of which they happen to disapprove.

Bronwyn Finnigan raises this problem for Madhyamaka conventionalism specifically in the moral domain. She writes:

> [W]hile one might readily assume stability in folk *ontological* beliefs (where disagreement is left to the philosophers and scientists . . .), the same kind of stability in the *moral* assessments among "the folk" cannot be straightforwardly assumed. This is because it cannot be assumed that there *is* a general agreement in moral intuitions with which a Prāsaṅgika *could* straightforwardly agree. (2015: 771)

Finnigan argues that while it may be possible for the Prāsaṅgika Mādhyamika to avoid the dismal slough in the domains of epistemology and metaphysics, there is a special problem in the ethical domain generated by the phenomenon of widespread ethical disagreement in the world. She argues that this disagreement precludes the identification of any single convention that could constitute a standard of conventional morality, and that there is no reason to believe that any convergence on such a standard is forthcoming.

Finnigan gives several reasons for thinking this. First, she argues, one cannot appeal to any factual claims—even those on which all parties might agree—to ground moral consensus, as one would run afoul of a naturalistic fallacy, the failure of evaluative claims to follow from any purely factual claims (773–774). Second, she argues, there are no sufficiently widely shared intuitions to which one could appeal in order to avoid the dismal slough in this domain (775). Finally, she argues, non-cognitivism is blocked on the grounds that while non-cognitive claims might be *effective*, they could never be *justified* (775–778).

These are significant arguments, and they raise two important questions. First, is Candrakīrti nonetheless—whether justifiably or unjustifiably—a moral realist in the conventional domain? That is, does the qualified realism in the context of global anti-realism that we have encountered in the epistemological and ontological domains extend to the ethical domain? Second, if he is a kind of realist in this domain, is that realism justified?

The critique Finnigan mobilizes against conventionalism has a long history in the West, dating at least to Protagoras. Protagoras is best known for his statement that "man is the measure of all things, of the things that are, that they are, and of the things that are not, that they are not," expressing the view that each individual is the ultimate standard for their own moral, epistemic, and empirical judgments. While Protagoras apparently acknowledged that the law might establish a common order, he did not believe that there could be any objective standard for correctness in the law. The law, or our moral consensus, on this view, has no independent justification; it is just what we happen to prefer, and cannot be rationally defended against any alternative. This entails a radical relativism indeed, a slough more dismal than that even Tillemans envisions.

In the *Protagoras*, Plato argues against Protagoras that intersubjective knowledge is possible, and that knowledge can be a route to moral agreement. Candrakīrti takes a similar approach. He argues that epistemology leads ethics and soteriology, that moral vice derives from primal confusion about the nature of reality, and that moral development follows from the understanding of the emptiness and so the interdependence of sentient beings. Another way to put this is that on Candrakīrti's view—as the Buddha says in the second ennobling truth, and so as presupposed in all Buddhist ethical theory—moral vice is grounded in confusion, and virtue is enabled by the alleviation of that confusion. The bodhisattva path presupposes the possibility of moral progress, and Candrakīrti takes moral progress to rest on our realization of the nature of reality. And this demands a distinction between truth and error and between reality and unreality.

In this chapter, we demonstrate that Candrakīrti's ethics and soteriology are entirely coherent with his anti-foundationalist metaphysics and epistemology and so that his philosophical system constitutes a unity. We will show that in the ethical domain he rejects dismal relativism in favor of a robust commitment to moral standards that, despite being entirely conventional, in fact govern our lives.[1] We intend thereby to reply to Finnigan's critique and to show that there is no principled difference between the moral domain and the metaphysical and epistemological domains in the context of Candrakīrti's Prāsaṅgika Madhyamaka system. We begin by considering Candrakīrti's gloss on the term most often used to denote morality, *śīla*. This term has a slightly broader semantic range than the English *morality* or *ethics*, as it denotes all proper conduct, including what many Western theoreticians might regard as comprised by etiquette.

The Term *śīla*

Candrakīrti provides two etymologies for *śīla*. First, he claims, the term *śīla* derives from the root *śīta* meaning "soothing" or "cooling." This connects morality to the family of fire metaphors used to articulate Buddhist doctrine, including *skandha*, which has its root meaning

[1] Arnold makes a related point regarding the centrality of ethics to Candrakīrti's recovery of the reality of the conventional in the context of emptiness. He writes, "Candrakīrti's [*Introduction to the Middle Way*] is structured as it is because he thinks the cultivation of ethical and other virtues is necessary for ensuring Madhyamaka's doctrine of emptiness is not mistaken for nihilism" (forthcoming: 251). So, while we emphasize the importance of a moderately realistic understanding of emptiness and dependent origination as a foundation for Candrakīrti's ethics, and the continuity of his metaphysical and ethical positions, Arnold properly draws our attention as well to the importance of an ethical orientation for the understanding that emptiness does not amount to nonexistence. A bit later he writes, "the first five chapters of [*Introduction to the Middle Way*], though concerned with non-epistemic factors that are apt to be considered irrelevant to a philosophical assessment of the lengthy argumentation of Chapter 6 are after all relevant for understanding the sense of Candrakīrti's philosophical position" (Ibid., 252). This is because ethical cultivation transforms our instinctive comportment as agents and subjects to the world, making us more receptive to understanding the emptiness of subjects and objects, and less likely to disparage the ontological status of the world we come to inhabit. We would only add that this point applies not only to *Introduction to the Middle Way*, which is the subject of Arnold's study, but to Candrakīriti's corpus as a whole.

in the pile of wood heaped on a body on a funeral pyre, and *nirvāṇa*, the extinction of fire. This etymology, Candrakīrti hence reminds us, calls our attention to several characteristics of conduct: immoral behavior often has its origins in the heat of passion and so in our inability to coolly assess a situation and the most reasonable way to act in that situation. Ethically salutary behavior not only reflects a cooler attitude but also cools or soothes both the agent and those affected by the behavior, reducing the emotional temperature of a situation, calming things down.

Just as important, though, is the connection to soteriology suggested by this etymology and its connection to the larger network of fire metaphors. Samsara is characterized in places such as *the Fire Sutra (Ādittaparayāya-sutta)* as a situation in which we suffer like someone on fire, and in which the psychophysical clusters (*skandhas*) are the fuel for the flames. Nirvana, or the extinction of those flames, is thus a cooling. Ethical behavior is hence understood not only as good for both ourselves and for others in a mundane sense, but also as conducive to liberation. Jayānanda writes in his *Commentary to Introduction to the Middle Way* that the bodhisattva is "not under the sway of the psychopathologies" because "he is not under the sway of the psychopathologies that are responsible for causing misdeeds; the bodhisattva does not commit misdeed because "in the absence of cause, so will the effect be absent" (2.2; dBu ma, ra 86b; 2021: 426; pd, 61: 209–210). This connects directly to the second etymology Candrakīrti provides: *śīla* connotes well-being and happiness, and proper conduct is the cause of a happy life, whether understood cosmologically as a favorable rebirth or psychologically, as stability in a humane state of mind.

In chapter 2, verses 4–7 of *Autocommentary to Introduction to the Middle Way*, Candrakīrti divides *śīla* into three categories: ethical self-control (*saṃvara-śīla*), the cultivation of virtuous qualities (*kuśaladharma-saṃgrāhaka-śīla*), and the advancement of the welfare of sentient beings (*sattvārtha-kriyā-śīla*). Ethical self-control comprises the seven renunciations. The first three of these seven are the renunciation of three kinds of physical misconduct: killing, stealing, and sexual misconduct. This is accomplished through the pursuit of virtues such as patience, friendliness, charity, and control of one's emotions. The other four kinds of misconduct are comprised by the four misdeeds of speech: lying, slandering, harsh speech, and gossip. One abandons these vices by engaging only in truthful speech, positive speech, pleasant speech, and appropriate and timely speech.

But to see moral progress only in terms of salutary responses to particular ethical shortcomings is to miss the big picture. The cultivation of the bodhisattva path is not a matter of vice-by-vice self-help practices pursued until each vice is eradicated. Instead, it is the wholesale cultivation of a reorientation toward the world in which these vices lose their attraction and are replaced by the corresponding virtues, which are seen to be the only rational response to a correct vision of reality. And this transformation is accomplished in turn through renunciations of the three fundamental egocentric psychopathologies: attraction, aversion, and primal confusion, which together constitute the roots of suffering (Garfield 2022b). This is the route to resolving the problems Finnigan raises, for it replaces a challenge to *justify* moral judgments with an account of how to *see* moral agents and patients and of the consequences of that vision, hence grounding ethics in our experience of the conventional world.

Candrakīrti's positive ethical program involves the transformation of an agent's orientation to the world, replacing an egocentric, emotionally driven, and pathological egocentricity with one characterized by calm, non-egocentric care for others. All of this is based on the eradication both of the primal confusion that leads to the reification of self and of the objects with which we engage and of the egoism to which it leads and the replacement of that orientation with one grounded in an appreciation of interdependence and of the absence of self. That appreciation is achieved through reflection on the nature of reality and our place in the world. This orientation—while it affirms the illusory character of sentient beings as they are experienced in ordinary subjectivity—does not deny their reality or significance, but explicitly takes them as objects of concern and their welfare as something to pursue actively.

A realistic view of the conventional world hence undergirds a realistic conception of ethics, and a view of the world that refuses reification grounds an ethics that can take sentient beings and the cultivation of moral subjectivity seriously without reifying either the objects of our concern or the subject to be transformed. Once again, this does not presuppose convergence in ethical *judgments*, but rather that a deeper understanding of the interdependent nature of the conventional world inevitably leads to convergence in *how we experience our relationships* to others in that world.

This binds ethics much more closely to epistemology and to metaphysics than it would on the model presupposed by the Finnigan critique. It thereby sidesteps all three of her worries. The naturalistic fallacy is not in play simply because moral experience on this view does not involve deriving purely normative claims from purely descriptive claims: it involves seeing already normatively thick properties in the natural world.

Instead of understanding a common, conventional moral reality in terms of convergent *judgments*, a Madhyamaka understanding of ethics leads us to understand that common world as one of shared concerns and of interconnection. We expect disagreement regarding non-moral matters of fact, just as one might expect one's own and others' views about non-moral matters to change over time; but we also accept that that disagreement is only possible in the context of a shared background of broad agreements guaranteed by our similarities to one another, and we expect that resolutions of disagreement will be achieved by appeal to shared norms of discourse. This tells us that there is no *special* problem about the reality of the conventional raised by the fact of disagreement or change of view. For this reason, we should not expect there to be a special problem raised by the lack of unanimity in the ethical realm, and indeed we shall see that there is not. We now turn to Candrakīrti's analysis of that vision and of the path to its cultivation.

The Bodhisattva Path: Ethics and Nonduality

Since Candrakīrti's account of ethical cultivation is structured by the bodhisattva path as set out in the *Sūtra on the Ten Grounds*, a brief survey of that presentation, as it is articulated in *Introduction to the Middle Way* is useful. This will show us that the only way to understand Candrakīrti's exposition of ethical cultivation is to see him as taking the reality of the conventional world, together with its ultimate emptiness, seriously as the very condition of moral cultivation and of the pursuit of awakening. It is also important to see that while it is the second bodhisattva ground on which *śīla* is emphasized, the qualities cultivated on each ground are explicitly ethical, another reason to be cautious about translating *śīla* as *morality*, as opposed to *proper conduct.*

On the first of the ten grounds, the bodhisattva achieves an understanding of the world as empty and dependently arisen and cultivates generosity. These two—the realization achieved on this ground and the quality cultivated—are tightly linked. In the opening verse of *Introduction to the Middle Way*, Candrakīrti writes:

> Both the śrāvakas and pratyekabuddhas arise in dependence on the great sage, and buddhas are all born from bodhisattvas.
>
> The causes of the birth of these children of the victors are in turn are an attitude of care, non-dual insight, and the aspiration to awaken. (1.1)

Candrakīrti describes this non-dual insight as an understanding that in reality all things are of a single nature, and he comments that a bodhisattva's moral progress requires an awareness of this identity of nature. That is, we might say, ideal moral agency presupposes an experience of all phenomena—subjects and objects—as dependently originated, empty of intrinsic reality, conventionally real, and ultimately empty—hence the ethical importance of Candrakīrti's refutation of idealism explored in the previous chapter.

Tsongkhapa remarks that this recognition is not an ultimate awareness of the absence of all duality. Instead, he says, that it is an awareness free from extremes such as those of existence and non-existence (2015: 19). In drawing this distinction, he is emphasizing that the kind of non-dual awareness presupposed in ethical development is not a direct apprehension of emptiness of the kind attained in advanced meditative equipoise in which there is no object and no subject present to consciousness. Instead, to be free from extremes in this context means to refrain from the reification of the subject and of the denial of reality to the object. And this in turn means that ethical cultivation does not presuppose insight into ultimate reality, but rather is preparatory to that insight. Ethical cultivation presupposes insightful engagement with the conventional, an engagement that takes their emptiness into account, even if that emptiness is not directly experienced, but only understood reflectively and analytically, as it must be at early stages of the path.

Candrakīrti characterizes the vision of the first ground bodhisattva as one in which all things are seen to lack any intrinsic existence, and in particular a vision that comprehends the person as lacking any self. This enables and is reinforced by the cultivation of generosity. By overcoming the sense of self and the reification of things, one sheds the reflexive experience of the world in terms of a subject-object duality that privileges the subject as occupying a unique, central position and that takes our existence to be foundational to our world and our own happiness to be independent of the welfare of others.

By shedding this illusion, we come to see that we are not subjects *of* the world, but companions of others *in* the world, and that our own happiness is intertwined with and dependent upon the happiness of others. We thereby become able to give selflessly and spontaneously and to take joy in others' well-being. None of this would make sense unless one is committed not only to the fact that those to whom one gives lack any self, but also to their *reality*.

Candrakīrti makes this explicit in verse 4: "Sentient beings are like reflections of the moon on rippling water. Seeing that they are fleeting and essenceless, bodhisattvas, with their wisdom governed by an attitude of care, strive to liberate these beings" (1.4). Here we do not see Candrakīrti denying the reality of sentient beings or urging the aspiring moral agent to see them as nonexistent. Instead, we see him emphasizing the discordance between their mode of existence and their mode of appearance. The simile of the moon reflected in water is deployed in different ways in different Buddhist texts. Here the emphasis is on *rippling* water.

There are several aspects to the simile, which, we must remember, is meant to explain how sentient beings are seen by bodhisattvas. First, the basis of the reflection of the moon is the water itself (and we might add, it responds to the light reflected from the moon, although this is not mentioned in canonical commentaries). Second, the reflection of the moon is not itself a moon—it is a mere reflection that appears to be a moon, and it is hence a paradigm of illusion. Third, the reflection is constantly changing as the water ripples. Fourth, the ripples are caused not by the moon, but by the wind agitating the water. Let us unpack each of these aspects in turn to see how rich this second simile is, and how much it reveals about the degree to which Candrakīrti thinks that moral cultivation requires us to take the conventional reality of the world seriously.

First, bodhisattvas see sentient beings' consciousness—not any underlying independent self, but rather the causally connected, constantly changing stream of cognitive and perceptual processes—as the basis of those sentient beings' appearance to themselves. The ocean represents that consciousness as the locus or basis of the appearance. It is caused to represent that appearance by external factors that are different from the appearance themselves, including the moon in the sky and the wind that stirs the surface of the water.

This self-awareness is therefore no different in kind or any less susceptible to illusion than our awareness of external phenomena: in each case, we are caused to have appearances in our minds by sensory stimulation and the activity of our sense faculties and nervous system, generating appearances that we mistake for directly delivered external objects. And so, second, the moon and the light it reflects are the causes, but the rippling image is what we find in the water, just as distal objects or our own minds may be the objects of perception, but what we find in consciousness are constantly changing representations.

Third, bodhisattvas see sentient beings and develop an attitude of care for them not merely as suffering—as in the first verse—but as impermanent, with constantly changing experience. They see these ripples, as well as the difference between that impermanence and the permanence sentient beings take themselves to possess, a disjunction between appearance and reality that causes suffering, and so that inspires an attitude of care.

Finally, those ripples are caused by the wind, by the agitation of extrinsic causes. In the case of sentient beings, the agitation of our minds is the result of karma. How might we understand this? In a canonical reading, this is the effect of past actions in previous lives and in this life, which generate the experiences we are having now. In more modern terms, we might understand this as indicating that our sensory, affective, conative, and cognitive response to what happens around us is determined by our evolutionary history, by our upbringing and experience, and by the way we act and orient ourselves toward the world. Our experience is the result of a massive confluence of causes and conditions—some of which occurred well before we were born, and some of which are more proximate. But experience is never simply the accurate registration of what is in front of us. And since those causes and conditions are constantly changing, so is our experience, hence the appearance of sentient beings to bodhisattvas as impermanent.

Finally, Candrakīrti notes, bodhisattvas see sentient beings as essenceless, and so they develop an attitude of care toward them under that description. To be essenceless is to be dependently originated, to be non-unitary, and to be impermanent, to have no nature of one's own. And this follows directly from the aspects of the simile deployed in this verse. Our existence as sentient beings is determined by a plethora of constantly changing causes and conditions; we are not unitary moons, but sequences of ripples; nothing about us remains constant from moment to moment, and if you were to ask what we are like independent of all of these external influences, there would be no answer to that question. Our identity is entirely dependent. We have no essence of our own.

Nonetheless, despite the fact that we are essenceless, constantly changing beings, whose nature and experience are determined by empirically real, but constantly changing, causes and conditions, we instinctively take ourselves to exist stably, independently, and essentially. This disjunction between reality and appearance constitutes our illusory status, and is a source of suffering, issuing not only in profound self-alienation, but also in the subject-object duality that distorts our moral vision, and in the ego-grasping that leads to the attraction and aversion that generate dissatisfaction.

Bodhisattvas see sentient beings as empty of intrinsic existence, but not therefore as *non-existent*. Tsongkhapa argues that in seeing them this way, they do not have *objectless* care, but rather care toward an *empty object*. And this is what it is to see emptiness as equivalent to dependent origination, an understanding grounded in Nāgārjuna's *Fundamental Verses of the Middle Way* chapter 24. This moderate realism and this understanding of the ontological and epistemological foundations of vice as well as virtue inform all of Candrakīrti's ethical thought, integrating it firmly with his epistemology and ontology.

The second ground on the bodhisattva path is that of purity. On this ground the bodhisattva has been purified of all immoral motivations, and it is on this ground that proper conduct (*śīla*) is cultivated. Here Candrakīrti turns to the root meaning of *śīla* as *cooling*. He writes, "Proper conduct is so called since, when one is not under the sway of the afflictions and misdeeds do not occur, and this has a cooling effect and snuffs out the fires that negatively affect the mind" (2.1; dBu ma, 'a: 231a; 1992: 33).

Once again, though, the two truths are important here. Following the pattern established in verse 1.4, Candrakīrti emphasizes that the precepts of proper conduct are not to be reified and must themselves be treated as only conventionally real: "Even if one attains purity, if one sees things as existing essentially, one's conduct will become impure. Therefore, when practicing any of the three kinds of conduct, one should never stray into dualistic thought" (2.3). In the autocommentary, Candrakīrti quotes from the *Questions of Kāśyapa* in *The Heap of Jewels Sutra* (*Kāśyapaparivartasūtra*):

> Kāśyapa, there are certain ordained monks who uphold moral discipline, abiding scrupulously by the precepts of personal liberation, and are vigilant about even minute transgression of the proper ritual procedures and a proper sphere of conduct. Having adopted this way of life, they follow the foundations of training becoming perfectly pure in body, speech, and mind. But even though they maintain a completely pure way of life, they still speak in terms of selfhood. Kāśyapa. This is the first case of a moral degenerate pretending to have moral discipline . . . Kāśyapa. There are also some ordained monks who adopt the twelve ascetic practices,[2] but they objectify them, maintaining their grasping at "I" and grasping at "mine." Kāśyapa. This is the fourth kind of moral degeneration

[2] They include living on alms, eating in one sitting a day, not eating again in the afternoon, having three robes, wearing felt, wearing refused rags, staying in isolation, living under trees, staying on bare ground, staying in charnel grounds, remaining upright, and let dwelling remain as first prepared (Jayānanda, *Commentary on Introduction to the Middle Way*, dBu ma, ra: 157a; 2021: 428).

> of one assumed to have moral discipline. (Toh 87, Kangyur, dkon brtsegs, cha, 142b2; cited at Jayānanda, dBu ma, ra: 157a; 2021: 427; Candrakīrti, 1992: 37–38)

Jayānanda glosses this passage as following in his Commentary on *Introduction to the Middle Way*:

> The dualistic mind understands morality in terms of subject and object involves two self-graspings: The grasping of "I" reifies the moral subject by presupposing "I am the moral agent." The grasping of "mine" reifies the moral object by presupposing "my moral discipline is what is important." Since one cannot perfect one's morality without relinquishing the clinging to such an objectified view of self, bodhisattvas on the second ground are free from a dualistic mind. They do not objectify. They accept neither the substantialist view nor non-substantialist views of reality and falsity, permanence, and impermanence in relation to the three spheres. (*Commentary on Introduction to the Middle Way* 2.3, dBu ma, ra: 92b; 2021: vol. 1, 429–430)[3]

Once again, Candrakīrti does not deny the existence of the agent, their actions, or other beings, but urges that moral cultivation requires a nondual understanding of the relation among agent, action, and object. This is the heart of the Buddhist approach to ethics as moral phenomenology. Moral cultivation is always understood first and foremost as the development of a more salutary way of seeing the world, a way that leads to a spontaneous responsiveness to others. Instead of a calculative and objectifying attitude toward others and toward oneself, pure proper conduct occurs in what we might call an ethical "flow state."[4]

[3] dmigs par lta ba yin te zhes pa'i bshad pa ni ngar 'dzin pa dang| nga yir 'dzin pa la gnas pa de ni zhes pa'o| |de la ngar 'dzin pa ni kho bo ni tshul khrims dang ldan pa'o| |nga yir 'dzin pa ni tshul khrims 'di kho bo'i 'o| |de'i phyir zhes bya ba ni gang gi phyir tshul khrims kyi ngo bo la mngon par zhen pa yod na tshul khrims 'chal pa yin la| tshul khrims dang ldan pa ma yin pas so| |dngos po dang dngos po med pa la sogs pa zhes bya ba la sogs pa la| sogs pa'i sgras bden pa dang| brdzun pa dang rtag pa dang| mi rtag pa la sogs pa bsdu bar bya'o|

[4] See Garfield 2022d: chs. 2–4 for discussion of Buddhist moral phenomenology.

We can understand this in terms of the kinds of awareness that European phenomenologists have characterized as the foundation of our human embodied experience, and so see this program of ethical progress not as the abandonment of our humanity in favor of something transcendental, but as an achievement of a deeper, more authentic way of being human. Merleau-Ponty points out that an expert football player is not explicitly cognizant of her own position on the field or of the other players, but in the flow of the game simply responds spontaneously to the demands of play; explicit calculative thought would get in the way of fluidity. Heidegger points out that so much of that with which we engage in the world is *ready to hand* (*vorhanden*), but not *present to hand* (*zuhanden*). To be ready to hand is to be available, to guide and to facilitate action, but not to be an object of explicit awareness, in the way that my fingers and keyboard were a moment ago before I directed my attention to them. Now that I direct my attention there, my typing, and my thinking that is so bound up with it, become more labored and less fluent; they are now present to hand as objects distinguished in my experience from my subjectivity.

Candrakīrti is urging that the second-ground bodhisattva finds sentient beings and the means to benefit them as ready, not present to hand, and that the objectification that brings things to presence in this sense inhibits, rather than facilitates, ethical engagement. Once again, though, this is not to *deny*, but to *affirm* the reality of agent, action, and object. It is to say that they exist for us in a way different from that in which they appear to exist when we turn explicit attention to them. This is because it is to superimpose subject-object duality on a reality that is empty of that duality, and intrinsic identity on subjects and objects that exist only conventionally.

In this context, Candrakīrti refers to the discussion in the *Sutra on the Ten Grounds* of the fact that improper conduct leads one to a hellish existence. One can read this cosmologically in terms of literal rebirth, but we can also read this psychologically as reflecting the kind of suffering instituted by improper conduct. The sūtra tells us that theft takes us into one kind of hell, reducing us to the very poverty we try to escape; that sexual misconduct leads to another kind of hell in which our interpersonal relationships are destroyed. Lying and slander make our lives hellish by depriving us of trust, and harsh language by leading us into quarrels, and so on. In each case, we find that by seeing the world as a place in which we relentlessly seek our own individual advantage, we end up living in a world of misery (*Autocommentary to Introduction to the Middle Way* 2.7, dBu ma, 'a: 234a; 1992: 42–44).

Toward the end of the chapter, Candrakīrti reinforces the role of internalizing wisdom transforming mundane proper conduct into a supramundane moral perfection. Candrakīrti gets at this in verse 2.9, another verse that reflects the perspective introduced at 1.4:

> When our conduct objectifies these three:
> The one who abstains from wrongdoing, the action from which they abstain, and the one to whom that action would be directed,
> This action is perfect in the mundane sense;
> But supramundane perfection is free from such objectification.

The moral perfection we are after is not the studied performance of our duty, but rather a way of seeing ourselves and others that affords spontaneous ethical engagement. That may begin with objectification, just as the development of any complex skill begins with careful, explicit thought and attention. But, just as real expertise involves the dropping away of that explicit attention in favor of the direct perception of affordances for attention and action, and for a kind of spontaneity in action, ethical perception requires the dropping away of the objectification of agent action, and beneficiary.

Objectification and the superimposition of subject-object duality animate the mundane, or conventional, world. And this is the world that most inhabit most of the time, however much we might aspire to a more transcendent vision and a more skilled moral engagement. But this does not mean that within the everyday world we cannot distinguish the proper from the improper. Far from it: proper conduct makes sense in the everyday world, and it constitutes the ladder that we climb in order to achieve the expertise that will enable us to stop engaging in the superimposition of duality and intrinsic existence so that we can come to act in the world with the spontaneity of an expert—without deliberation, and without hesitation. And because we can draw the distinction between the proper and improper, there is real content to the ethics in the context of conventional truth, just as the possibility of distinguishing between the warranted and the unwarranted, or between the true and the false, vouchsafes the empirical reality of the world. Not only is Candrakīrti a qualified ethical realist, but he is *justified* in that qualified realism.

Here we see the close parallel between Candrakīrti's treatment of the metaphysical, epistemological, and ethical domains. In each case, our ordinary experience is experience of a world that only exists conventionally and about which we are massively deceived due to the pervasive influence of primal confusion. In each case that deception takes the form of the superimposition of intrinsic reality onto that which is empty of that reality; in each case its true mode of existence—even if we understand it cognitively—typically fails to figure in our ordinary experience.

Nonetheless, in each case there is a real difference between getting it right and wrong; in each case getting the conventionally right is the first step toward direct insight into the ultimate. Moreover, in each case this difference and the soteriological value of getting it right entail that conventional truth is a kind of *truth* and that the beings and entities with which and with whom we interact are *real*, as are we as subjects. If they were unreal, there would be nothing to be empty: as Nāgārjuna reminds us, without the conventional, there can be no ultimate.

This point is already driven home when in the first chapter, Candrakīrti distinguishes two levels of generosity: "The generosity that is empty of giver, gift and recipient is known as the transcendent perfection of generosity. The generosity that involves attachment to these three is known as the mundane perfection of generosity" (1.6). Candrakīrti recognizes two levels of the perfection of generosity, each one of which is ethically commendable. To attain the transcendent perfection, one must first abandon the kind of subject-object duality we discussed above. But even if one has not attained that level of insight and spontaneous engagement, morally beneficial generosity is possible.

Once again, this implicates a commitment to the reality of the conventional. For if giver, gift, and recipient were taken to be entirely nonexistent, mundane generosity would make no sense at all. And since they are not taken to be nonexistent, the emptiness of giver, gift, and recipient cannot be understood as their nonexistence, even from the standpoint of one who has attained transcendent generosity. It can only be understood as their perception as empty of intrinsic identity; otherwise generosity empty of these three would not be *transcendent*, but *deluded* in virtue of failing to see the reality of something that must be understood as real.

On the third bodhisattva ground, the ethical agent cultivates patience (*kṣānti*).[5] The verse that might suggest a nihilistic reading is this: "The bodhisattva who perceives selflessness sees the agent, the object, the time, the action and all phenomena as like reflections in a mirror. Seeing things in this way allows patience to emerge" (3.3). But when properly understood, this verse directly undermines a nihilistic reading. We must first ask, "what is it to see agent, object, etc. as like reflections in a mirror?" One might think that this is to see them as unreal, and that interpretation would support a nihilistic reading. But to interpret this verse that way would be to misread a simile for illusion pretty badly. Reflections in a mirror are illusory precisely because their mode of existence and mode of appearance are different, not because they are nonexistent. When I see myself in the mirror in the morning it appears to me that I am looking at a face staring back at me from behind the wall. But I am not. I am instead staring at a reflection, an aspect of the mirror, not a distinct individual. If I were to jump back and wonder who that strange man is behind my wall, my reaction would be unjustified and unskillful: I would then not only perceive the illusion, but I would fall for it.

When I see my image *as a person behind the mirror* but know that it is just a reflection, I see the delusion, but see through it; only when I see it only *as a reflection* am I no longer subject to delusion. But in each case, the reflection must be taken as a *real reflection*. Just so with agents, objects, times, actions, and so on. Their mode of existence and mode of appearance are distinct. Naïve perception, or the natural attitude, takes them to exist intrinsically, when in fact they exist only interdependently, or conventionally. The goal of practice is to come to see them as interdependent, conventionally real, ultimately empty beings that appear to exist intrinsically.

[5] The semantic range of *kṣānti* also overlaps with that of *serenity*, inasmuch as it consists in not becoming angry or upset in the face of harm, abuse, or other adversity; it is *not* a matter of avoiding boredom, as the English term *patience* sometimes connotes.

When I take other agents to exist intrinsically, I confuse their appearance and their reality, leading in the case of an action or agent to which I react, for instance, with anger or hostility. Such a reaction, though, in virtue of assigning a kind of Augustinian free agency that takes action to originate simply in an uncaused intention to the actor, along with the enriched sense of responsibility it entails, is unjustified and unskillful. When instead I see agents, actions, and the rest as dependently originated, I recognize the indefinite background of causes and conditions that gave rise to them, and this understanding allows me to maintain my serenity in the face of the adversity they entail. This is a point that Śāntideva takes up in chapter 6 of *How to Lead an Awakened Life*, when he argues that anger is unjustified because it ignores all of the causes and conditions external to the agent that lead to the actions that harm us, and so assigns responsibility without justification.[6]

There is another aspect to the mirror simile that is relevant in this context, noted by the third Gungtang Rinpoche (1762–1823; Duckworth et al. 2016: 30–32; Garfield 2021). Gungtang reminds us that when we see a reflection in a mirror, we apprehend it as a duality: a mirror *and* a reflection in that mirror. A reflection may appear to us that way *even when we apprehend it as a reflection*. But to apprehend a reflection this way, he points out, is still to be deluded. It might be a step up from seeing the reflection as a distinct *object* behind the mirror, but it is still illusory: even when I am not fooled into thinking that I am seeing a *person* behind the mirror, I nonetheless think that I am seeing a mirror *and* a reflection in it, taking these to be distinct. But there are not two things there, but one, a mirror reflecting a face. To see *that* is to see the mode of existence of the reflection correctly, and that is to apprehend its nonduality with the mirror. But it is *not* to fail to see the reflection; on the contrary, it is to see the reflection *as it is*. Once again, as Candrakīrti argues in verse 1.4, it is just so with respect to the conventional world: to see correctly is to see nondually; but this is not to *stop* seeing conventional phenomena; it is to see them *as they are*, and that is the first step toward truly skillful ethical engagement.

[6] See especially verses 22–27, 32–47; also see Garfield 2022b: 121–128.

The Bodhisattva Path: Soteriology

The bodhisattva path is not only an ethical path; it is, in virtue of its union of ethical and cognitive cultivation, a comprehensive soteriological path—one to perfection, understood as full awakening so as to become an agent for the liberation of others. We have already discussed Candrakīrti's account of insight into the two truths cultivated on that path in *Introduction to the Middle Way*. Candrakīrti also makes these points explicitly in the context of ethical cultivation and its relation to that insight in his discussion of verse 12.13 of *Commentary on Āryadeva's 400 Stanzas*. "Selflessness is called the door to peace. There is no second: Although it terrifies those with wrong views, It is known by all of the buddhas."[7] Candrakīrti comments as follows:

> Selflessness is terrifying for those with wrong views.... The word *self* refers to the essential nature of things; to have such a nature is to not depend on anything else. The absence of this nature is what is meant by *selflessness*. This is understood in two ways, based on the distinction between phenomena and persons. This is what is called the selflessness of phenomena and the selflessness of persons. *Person* refers to what is imputed in dependence upon the five aggregates. To find a self in a person is impossible when one investigates the aggregates in the fivefold way. *Phenomena* refers to things such as the aggregates, elements, and sources.
>
> This is because all phenomena and persons must depend on causes and conditions. This is because they are produced and because they are imputed dependently: there is therefore no independent self or essence that does not depend on other phenomena. Therefore, persons and phenomena are understood to lack intrinsic nature. And if something does not exist intrinsically, what other essence could ground it? Therefore, things that are known

[7] advitīyaṃ śivadvāraṃ kudṛṣṭīnāṃ bhayaṃkaram | viṣayaḥ sarvabuddhānām iti nairātmyam ucyate ||
zhi sgo gnyis pa med pa dang ||
lta ba ngan rnams 'jigs byed cing ||
sangs rgyas kun gyi yul gyur la ||
bdag med ces ni bya bar brjod ||

to be deceptive in nature because they are entirely nonexistent in terms of their own characteristics, because they are nonetheless appropriated, become the basis for the attachment of those of dull minds. When those who see intrinsic nature as it is meditate on it, they will be led to the complete exhaustion of attachment to both phenomena and persons. This complete exhaustion of attachment is the cause for attaining nirvāṇa. There is nothing other than the view of the absence of intrinsic nature that is like that. Therefore, there is no other cause for the complete exhaustion of attachment.

Therefore, selflessness—the absence of intrinsic existence—is the only gateway to peace. It is the only unrivaled gateway by means of which one can enter the city of nirvāṇa. (*Commentary on Āryadeva's Four Hundred Stanzas* 12.13; dBu ma, ya: 191a; 2019: 333–334)[8]

Here Candrakīrti ties the metaphysics of selflessness to soteriology, and implicitly—in virtue of its context—to ethics. As we have seen,

[8] gang zhig zhi ba'i sgo gnyis pa med pa ni bdag med pa'o || gang zhig lta ba ngan pa rnams 'jigs par byed pa de ni bdag med pa'o || gang zhig sangs rgyas thams cad kyi yul du gyur pa de ni bdag med pa zhes bya'o || de la bdag ces bya ba ni gang zhig dngos po rnams kyi gzhan la rag ma las pa'i ngo bo rang bzhin te de med pa ni bdag med pa'o || de ni chos dang gang zag gi dbye bas gnyis su rtogs te chos kyi bdag med pa pa'o || dang gang zag gi bdag med pa zhes bya'o || de la gang zag ces bya ba ni gang phung po lnga la brten nas brtags pa ste | de ni phung po dag la rnam pa lngas btsal ba ni mi srid do || chos ni phung po dang khams dang skye mched ces bya ba'i dngos po rnams so || de'i phyir chos de rnams dang gang zag la bdag nyid ji lta ba'i rgyu dang rkyen la rag las te; skye ba'i phyir dang brtan nas brtags pa'i phyir bdag gi rang gi ngo bo rang la rag las shing gzhan la rag ma las pa yod pa ma yin pas gang zag dang chos rnams rang bzhin med par rnam par gzhag go || don gang zhig la rang gi ngo bos grub pa yod pa ma yin pa de bdag nyid gzhan gang zhig gis 'grub par 'gyur | de'i phyir dngos po rnam pa thams cad du rang gi mtshan nyid kyis ma grub pa bstan nas sam nye bar blangs nas slu ba'i bdag nyid du 'byung ba rnams ni blo blun pa'i chags pa'i gzhir 'gyur la | rang bzhin ji lta ba bzhin du yang dag par mthong ba rnams kyis bsgoms pa na chos dang gang zag gnyis la chags pa yongs su zad pa 'dren par 'gyur ro || chags pa yongs su zad pa ni mya ngan las 'das pa thob pa'i rgyu yin la | rang bzhin med par lta ba las ma gtogs pa'i chos 'ga' zhig de ltar [191a] || chags pa yongs su zad pa'i rgyu yod pa yang ma yin no || de nyid kyi phyir rang bzhin med pa'i mtshan nyid can gyi bdag med pa 'di ni zhi ba'i sgo gnyis pa med par 'gyur te | mya ngan las 'das pa'i grong khyer du 'jug par bya ba la 'di gcig pu kho na zla med pa'i sgo yin no ||gal te yang stong pa nyid dang mtshan ma med pa dang smon pa med pa zhes bya ba rnam par thar pa'i sgo gsum yod mod kyi | de lta na yang bdag med par lta ba kho na gtso bo yin te | chos ma lus pa bdag med par rig cing dngos po thams cad la chags pa ma lus pa zad pa la 'gar yang 'ga' zhig don du gnyer ba'am mtshan mar dmigs pa ga la yod | de'i phyir bdag med pa 'di ni zhi ba'i sgo gnyis pa med pa kho na zhig go ||

Candrakīrti takes ethical cultivation to entail the rejection of dualistic appearance, which is the reification of the distinction between subject and object. This, he has argued, depends upon an understanding of selflessness and a perception of the world conditioned by that understanding, one that rejects the mode of appearance of self and phenomena to naïve perception in favor of perception in accordance with a recognition of their actual mode of existence.

Candrakīrti emphasizes that this understanding and perception are the entrée into full awakening. In making this point, he is not claiming that upon awakening all appearances vanish, or that we see the world to be nonexistent, or that we become cognitively inert. That is not the soteriology he offers, and it is hard to see why that would be a soteriology to which anyone would aspire. Instead, the awakening Candrakīrti has in mind, one that arises from and supports moral engagement and reflects deep insight into reality, is one that reveals phenomena to us, that shows ourselves as embedded with one another in the world, but that does so without the illusory superimposition of intrinsic identity or subject-object duality. Candrakīrti is no ethical nihilist. The following passage from his *Commentary on Āryadeva's Four Hundred Stanzas* is apposite:

> At this point, someone might object: It is indeed amazing that the sense faculties do not apprehend objects in any way and that visual consciousness nonetheless arises in dependence on the eye and on the material objects it sees.
>
> To this we would respond: Is this really amazing? It makes no sense to say that a sprout to arise from a seed that has ceased or is in the process of ceasing. Nonetheless, a sprout arises in dependence on a seed. Similarly, an action that has been performed and that has become part of one's continuum may have ceased for a very long time, and it never remains. Nonetheless, an effect can actually arise from an action that has ceased long ago. And, when investigated in the fivefold way, such things as pots are found to be neither the same as or different from their causes. Nonetheless, through the force of dependent designation we find that we can use a pot to hold honey or to drink such things as water or milk. What is so amazing about

this? (*Commentary on Āryadeva's Four Hundred Stanzas* 13.23; dBu ma, ya: 207a; 2019: 368–369)[9]

Candrakīrti takes the imagined interlocutor here to be raising a version of Finnigan's charge: the Mādhyamika—even if entitled to a moderate realism about the conventional world—is committed to a version of moral nihilism. The argument seems roundabout: although Candrakīrti is making a point about the moral domain, the objection is framed in terms of the causal structure of visual consciousness. Vision is taken as an example of a causal connection, and the example is to be applied to the causal connections among intentions, actions, and their effects that underlie moral reasoning and assessment. The objector is claiming that the Mādhyamika can make no sense of action, and hence of morality, on the grounds that Madhyamaka philosophy undermines the reality of causation.

The objector poses the objection by asking how a Mādhyamika can say that visual consciousness depends upon the state of the sensory organ and the distal object when there is a temporal lag between the stimulation of the organ by light reflected from the object and the onset of visual consciousness. In that case, the objector suggests, since the object and the cognition never co-occur, there can be no actual relation between them that would enable one to depend on the other: when the cause occurs, the effect is absent; when the effect occurs, the cause is absent. Any relation between them could therefore be at best notional. Since the same would be the case for any supposed causal relation, the implication is that there are no causal relations between agents, actions, and effects, and so no real action, and so no domain of moral assessment.

[9] 'dir smras pa | ci nas kyang dbang po rnams yul 'dzin pa mi srid pa mig dang gzugs la brten nas mig gi rnam par shes pa yang skye'o zhes bya ba 'di ni ngo mtshar ba zhig go || brjod par bya ste | ci 'di kho na ngo mtshar gyi gang 'gags pa dang 'gag bzhin pa'i sa bon las myu gu 'byung bar mi rigs la sa bon la brten nas myu gu skye ba yang yin pa dang | de bzhin du byas shing bsags pa'i las 'gags nas yun shin tu ring por lon pa la 'gar yang gnas pa med mod kyi | 'on kyang 'gags nas bskal pa du mas chod pa'i las las kyang 'bras bu dngos su 'byung ba dang bum pa la sogs pa rnams rang gi rgyu las de nyid dang gzhan du rnam pa lngar dpyad pa na yod pa ma yin mod kyi; de lta na yang brten nas brtags pas sbrang rtsi dang chu dang 'o ma 'dzin pa dang 'chu ba la sogs pa'i bya ba la rung bar 'gyur ba 'di ci ngo mtshar ba zhig gam | de'i phyir de ltar na |

Candrakīrti replies that this objection would only undermine the reality of interdependence if causal interdependence required an intrinsically real causal relation between these episodes, a relation that requires that they be actual at the same time. But ordinary interdependence, as Nāgārjuna argues in chapter 1 of *Fundamental Verses on the Middle Way*, Candrakīrti says, is not like that; it is captured by the stock Buddhist phrase, "when this occurs, that occurs; when this does not occur, that does not occur," placing regularity, not a metaphysical relation, at the heart of causal explanation. He then notes in reply that just as conventionally real phenomena such as pots are useful to us, and hence real, *despite being only conventionally real*, the relations between actions and their effects are important and useful to us in the moral domain despite being only conventionally real.

In making this point, Candrakīrti draws our attention to the homology between on the one hand the relation between perceptual contact and visual consciousness and on the other the relation between action and effect: in each case, conventionally designated phenomena are related to other conventionally designated phenomena in virtue of conventionally designated causal relationships. Just as there is nothing amazing about the fact that a cause with no intrinsic nature at one time can bring about an effect with no intrinsic nature at another, there is nothing amazing about the fact that actions with no intrinsic nature can figure in moral assessments with no intrinsic validity. But in each case, conventional reality is all that is needed to make sense of their reality. His point is then that there is no interesting difference in status between the empirical and the moral domains.

Candrakīrti emphasizes this point nicely in *Clear Words*, in his commentary to verse 24.11 of *Fundamental Verses on the Middle Way*:

> Yogis realize that conventional reality—the product of confusion—lacks intrinsic existence; that is its emptiness. This realization of the characteristic of the ultimate does not fall into the two extremes. . . . Since the conventional reality of the world—which is like a reflection—is not undermined, neither the relation between actions and their effects nor the distinction between virtue and nonvirtue are undermined . . .

> A Mādhyamika does not consider ultimate reality to be substantial reality, as she sees the effects of actions only in things that lack intrinsic reality. Things that do have intrinsic reality do not exist. But an essentialist who asserts that things have intrinsic reality does not see action and its consequences in the context of emptiness, and so does not see anything such as dependent origination. If one cannot see the distinction between the two truths in this way, but sees compounded things as empty, one might believe that compounded things do not exist. Alternatively, by imagining emptiness to be some form of substance, one may imagine that substance to be the basis of things. Both of these views are certainly flawed due to a misunderstanding of emptiness. (24.11; Skt. Vaidya: 1960: B495.9–17; dBu ma, 'a: 164ab; 2003: 442–443)[10]

To say that the conventional world is empty, he emphasizes, is neither to say that it is non-existent, nor to impugn in any way the truth or importance of ethical judgments. Candrakīrti's account of ethical

[10] saṃvṛtisatyaṃ hi ajñānamātrasamutthāpitaṃ niḥsvabhāvaṃ buddhā tasya paramārthalakṣaṇāṃ śūnyatāṃ pratipadyamāno yogī nāntadvaye patati | kiṃ tadāsīdyadidānīṃ nāstītyevaṃ pūrvaṃ bhāvasvabhāvānupalambhāt paścādapi nāstitāṃ na pratipadyate | pratibimbākārāyāśca lokasaṃvṛterabādhanāt karmakarmaphaladharmā dharmādikamapi na bādhate | na cāpi paramārthaṃ bhāvasvabhāvatvena samāropayati | niḥsvabhāvānāmeva padārthānāṃ karmaphalādidarśanāt sasvabhāvanāṃ cādarśanāt || yastu evaṃ satyadvayavibhāgamapaśyan śūnyatāṃ saṃskārāṇāṃ paśyati, sa śūnyatāṃ paśyan mumukṣurnāstitāṃ vā saṃskārāṇāṃ parikalpayed, yadi vā śūnyatāṃ kāṃcidbhāvataḥ satīm, tasyāścāśrayārthaṃ bhāvasvabhāvamapi parikalpayet | ubhayathā cāsya durdṛṣṭā śūnyatā niyataṃ vināśayet |

Tib: rnal 'byor pa kun rdzob kyi bden pa mi shes pa tsam gyis bskyed pa rang bzhin med par rtogs nas de'i stong pa nyid do|| don dam pa'i mtshan nyid rtogs pa ni mtha' gnyis su lhung bar mi 'gyur te| gang zhig da lta med par gyur pa de'i tshe na| ci zhig yod par 'gyur zhes de ltar sngar dngos po'i rang bzhin ma dmigs pas phyis kyang med pa nyid du mi rtogs la| 'jig rten gyi kun rdzob gzugs brnyan dang 'dra ba la gnod pa ma byas pas| las dang las kyi 'bras bu dang chos dang chos ma yin pa la yang gnod pa la ma yin no|| . . . don dam pa dngos po nyid du sgro 'dogs par byed pa yang ma yin te| dngos po rang bzhin dang bcas pa ma yin pa rnams kho na la las kyi 'bras bu la sogs pa mthong b'i phyir dang| dngos po rang bzhin dang bcas pa yod pa ma yin pa'i phyir dang| dngos po rang bzhin dang bcas par smra ba rnams kyi ltar yang| las dang las kyi 'bras bu ma mthong ba dang | rten cing 'brel bar 'byung ba la sogs pa thams cad ma mthong b'i phyir ro|| gang gis de ltar bden pa gnyis kyi rnam bar dbye ba ma mthong bar 'du byed rnams stong pa nyid du mthong ba des ni stong pa nyid mthong bas 'du byed rnams yod pa ma yin pa nyid du rtog par byed la| yang na stong pa nyid 'ga' zhig dngos por brtags nas| de'i rten gyi ched du dngos po'i rang bzhin yang rtog par byed de| de ni gnyi ga ltar yang stong pa nyid la lta nyes pas nges par phung bar byed pa yin no||

cultivation, as articulated in *Introduction to the Middle Way* and in *Commentary on Āryadeva's 400 Stanzas*, proves to be very influential in subsequent Mahāyāna ethical thought in India and in Tibet. His framework—including his use of the bodhisattva stages for moral cultivation, his embrace of the conventional, and his approach to ethics as moral phenomenology—is adopted by Śāntideva in his masterpiece of ethical thought *How to Lead an Awakened Life*, a text that references *Introduction to the Middle Way* many times. *Introduction to the Middle Way* and *How to Lead an Awakened Life* became the principal sources for ethical thought in Tibet.

Tsongkhapa, in particular, relies on Candrakīrti when he develops an understanding of Madhyamaka that takes the reality of the conventional and the possibility of knowledge in the context of massive illusion very seriously, a program that is grounded in the insight that if one does not do so then we can make no sense of the importance of ethics. And it is this anti-foundationalist realism that makes Candrakīrti particularly relevant to contemporary philosophy. In the closing chapter we will address that relevance.

The ethical framework Candrakīrti articulates is deeply tied to his epistemology in another respect. As we have noted, Buddhist ethics is first and foremost a moral phenomenology (Garfield 2022a; Harris 2024; Heim 2020). That is, ethical practice is directed primarily at transforming how we *see* the world, other beings, and ourselves. And we have seen that the same is true of Buddhist epistemology in the Madhyamaka tradition. It is aimed at transforming how we *see* the world and our relationship to it. This is perhaps the deepest and most important connection between these two normative domains to which Candrakīrti's Prāsaṅgika system directs our attention.

The global illusion the natural attitude both induces and reflects is the union of subject-object duality and the givenness of the world to our subjectivity. In the domain of epistemology and metaphysics, that illusion manifests in our taking ourselves as subjects and the objects of experience to exist intrinsically and to exist just as we experience them. Candrakīrti argues that to transcend this is to experience the world as an ensemble of dependently originated, conventionally real phenomena, of which we are part. In the ethical domain it manifests as the illusion that we as subjects and agents stand apart from the world we experience, occupying a unique position outside of the causal order from which free agency can be exercised, and a unique conative status conferring upon our desires and aversions *prima facie* motivating force, and subordinating the interests of others in our decision making. Candrakīrti argues that to transcend this aspect of the illusion is to see ourselves as intimately bound to others, and so our welfare and theirs, and our suffering and theirs as on an equal footing.

It is this vision that grounds the bodhisattva resolution to awaken in order to be a better agent for the welfare of all beings, drawing together in a single aspiration the epistemic and ethical dimensions of the Mahāyāna path. In each dimension, the transformation achieved by insight into emptiness tempered by taking the empty, dependently originated world seriously as a domain of knowledge and action is what makes it possible to engage effectively and sanely with the world we inhabit.

6

Candrakīrti's Legacy

Prāsaṅgika Mādhyamika in Medieval India and Tibet, and in the Contemporary World

Candrakīrti's radical anti-foundationalism and conventionalism appear to have had no impact on orthodox Indian philosophy and only a minimal impact even on subsequent Indian Buddhist philosophy. As Kevin Vose argues, this may well have been due to Candrakīrti's rejection of the epistemology of the Pramāṇavāda school of Dignāga and Dharmakīrti that gained such ascendence in Indian Buddhist philosophy (2009: 8–9). With epistemological foundationalism as the mainstream, Candrakīrti may have appeared to be seriously out of step with the times.

Vose also notes that—as later interpretations of Candrakīrti by his only direct Indian commentator Jayānanda and his close Tibetan colleague Chapa ('Phya pa chos kyi seng ge, 1109–1169) attest—Candrakīrti may have been read even during his own time as implausibly nihilistic regarding the possibility of knowledge. But Candrakīrti was not entirely without influence, even in India. As MacDonald notes (ibid.), his interpretation of Madhyamaka influenced philosophers in the eleventh and twelfth centuries. The fact that his texts were repeatedly copied and studied, and the fact that philosophers such as Jayānanda transmitted his thought to Tibet and encouraged the study of his work, indicates that there was an unbroken lineage of transmission of his work (ibid.).

The earliest Tibetans to mention Candrakīrti, such as Chapa, do so in order to dismiss his position as nihilistic. They interpret him as drawing a sharp distinction between a conventional world regarding which knowledge is impossible in virtue of pervasive ignorance and an ultimate reality that is unknowable to ordinary human beings and directly known only to buddhas. This view, they argue,

By the Light of the Moon. Jay L. Garfield and Sonam Thakchöe, Oxford University Press.
 DOI: 10.1093/oso/9780197830741.003.0007

renders knowledge impossible and so blocks the path to realization. Candrakīrti's version of Madhyamaka was therefore often taken in early Tibetan philosophical history to be a philosophical dead end.

Candrakīrti was effectively reborn in Tibet thanks to the work of scholars such as Patsab Nyima Drak, his student Mabja (rMa bya byang chub brtson 'grus, d. 1185), Rendawa Shönu Lodrö, and a host of their successors, including Rendawa's illustrious student Tsongkhapa. These Tibetan scholars—inspired by Atiśa—followed Śāntideva's and Prajñakaramati's adoption of Candrakīrti's critique of Bhāviveka and of Yogācāra idealism and his model of the path to awakening. Their elevation of Prāsaṅgika Madhyamaka to the apex of the Tibetan doxographic hierarchy led to the celebration of Candrakīrti as the foremost interpreter of the Madhyamaka tradition.[1] This probably reflects both increasing dissatisfaction with Dharmakīrti's foundationalism and the increasing popularity of Śāntideva's *How to Lead an Awakened Life* as a guide to the Bodhisattva path, through the work of Sakya Paṅdita (1182–1251), a scholar of enormous prestige and influence (Vose 2009: 22–23). This elevation may also demonstrate the increased influence of the graduated path model of practice made popular by Atiśa, which gained ascendency during this period and which emphasized the value of engagement with the conventional.

By the fourteenth century, Tibetan Mādhyamikas were almost unanimous in their view that Candrakīrti's exposition of Madhyamaka is correct and in the view that it constitutes the definitive Buddhist epistemological and metaphysical view, even if they disagreed radically with each other regarding the contents of that view. The principal fault line of that disagreement is the question regarding whether conventional truth is actually *true*. Some Tibetan scholars read Candrakīrti as a realist about the conventional; others argue that he denies any reality to the conventional domain and argues that all that really exists is emptiness.

Tsongkhapa read Candrakīrti both as a critic of foundationalism and as a realist about the conventional world, taking seriously the idea that conventional truth is indeed a *truth* and that knowledge

[1] See Vose 2009 and Yakherds 2021: vol. 1, chs. 1–3, for the history of Candrakīrti's later reception in Tibet.

of both the convention and the ultimate is possible. Only thus, he argued, can we make sense of the path to awakening and of the importance of ethics to that path (Yakherds 2021: ch. 2). As we saw in Chapter 1, this position was sharply criticized by those such as Taktsang and the ninth and tenth Karmapas, who followed Chapa and Jayānanda. They emphasized Candrakīrti's affirmation of the pervasion of conventional consciousness by primal confusion, the illusory nature of the conventional world, and the transcendent accounts of a buddha's mind, citing verses in *Introduction to the Middle Way* such as "If ordinary people were epistemically authoritative, then ordinary people would see reality. / In that case, why would we need the noble path? It makes no sense to say that fools are epistemically authoritative!" (6.30). Taking such verses as their hermeneutic anchor, these scholars argued that Candrakīrti denied the possibility of any knowledge of the conventional (Vose 2009: 69–75; Yakherds 2021: ch. 5). And so, in *Freedom from Extremes* Taktsang introduces and defends Prāsaṅgika Illusionism (*Māyopamādvayavāda*), both as the only plausible interpretation of Candrakīrti and as the true understanding of Madhyamaka. He charges Tsongkhapa with an illicit reification of the conventional and with the importation of a Pramāṇavāda understanding of epistemology into the Mādhyamika system, and hence with betraying Candrakīrti's anti-foundationalism. And this is the position in Tibet that is reflected in contemporary nihilistic readings of Candrakīrti.

The debates between those who read Candrakīrti as denying the reality of the conventional world and the possibility of knowledge within the conventional and those who read him as affirming the conventional and our knowledge thereof—whether medieval or contemporary—are not *purely* hermeneutical; they are also substantive, and they concern the very heart of epistemology. For epistemologists and metaphysicians must take seriously the obvious fact that we are not infallible detectors of independently real properties of the world, but rather organisms embedded in a world who respond causally to other mundane phenomena by constructing experience. And we must take seriously the fact that we naïvely confuse that constructed experience with a passively but accurately detected independent reality. This is the inescapable fact of the pervasiveness of illusion in our experience, a fact emphasized in all Buddhist epistemology, familiar in cognitive science, and that should be emphasized in all naturalized epistemology. Debates about interpretation of Candrakīrti are proxies for debates regarding the import of global illusion: does it undermine the very possibility of knowledge and the cogency of any conception of truth or reality, or does it force us to reconceive of knowledge and reality in a way consistent with global illusion?

All Mādhyamikas are *global* illusionists: that is, they agree that all objects of knowledge, and even all subjective states, appear to us to be intrinsically real despite being ultimately empty and existing only conventionally. But there are different kinds of illusionism, and so different ways of taking Candrakīrti to be an illusionist: Taktsang defends a *radical* illusionism in contrast with Tsongkhapa's *moderate* illusionism. While Tsongkhapa takes global illusionism to be consistent with the reality of the conventional world and with the possibility of distinguishing truth from falsity and knowledge from ignorance, Taktsang takes it to entail that apparent phenomena are entirely non-existent and that knowledge of the conventional makes no sense because there is no truth about the conventional. Taktsang illustrates this purely negative account of illusionism with a citation from *Anthology on the Stages of Meditation on the Ultimate Spirit of Awakening* (*Paramārtha-bodhicitta-bhāvanākrama-varṇa-saṃgraha*) attributed to the Indian master Aśvaghoṣa (c. fourth century):

> By imagining that these are mere illusions, they are fooled.
> They also fail to see the ineffable
> Mañjuśrī beyond all fabrications.
> Illusion is not mere illusion.
>
> If it were, it could not be established . . .
> Therefore, when something is of an illusory nature
> It cannot be determined as such. (verses: 18–20, dBu ma, ki:16a, cited, Taktsang 2007: 258)[2]

[2] sgyu ma tsam la brtags pas bslus ||
sems ni sgyu ma'i rnam pa ste ||
byang chub kyang ni sgyu ma 'dra ||

Takstang's radical illusionism is the view that nothing actually exists: illusions, on this view, are not *mere illusions*. That is, they are not things that exist in one way and appear in another; instead, they are complete fabrications, with no underlying reality—more like hallucinations. And, Taktsang concludes, since nothing in fact exists, there can be no difference between being correct and incorrect regarding what appears, and so no claims or perceptions are epistemically warranted.

This is the view Taktsang attributes to Candrakīrti. And as we saw in Chapter 1, contemporary readers such as Tillemans agree with this interpretation when they read Candrakīrti as a "global error theorist." Taktsang and his followers also presume that knowledge makes sense if, and only if, it is grounded in foundations; since human knowledge cannot be so, they conclude that it is impossible. On their view, the only possible knowledge would be that of an omniscient being—one free from all illusion. But that knowledge is inconceivable to us, and it tells us nothing about the world we seem to inhabit.

Tsongkhapa's moderate illusionism, in contrast, takes seriously the gloss of *illusion* in terms of a discordance between mode of existence and mode of appearance. He takes as his hermeneutic anchor passages such as this one from Candrakīrti's *Commentary on Āryadeva's Four Hundred Stanzas*:

> What arises does not come into existence;
> And similarly that which ceases does not go out of existence.
>
> Since this is how things are, how could
> Samsara not all be like a magician's illusion? (15.10)
>
> When the production of dependently originated things is seen this way, they are regarded as like a magician's illusions. But they are

des kyang tshig tu brjod spangs te ||
spros bral 'jam dpal mthong ba min ||
sgyu ma sgyu ma tsam min te ||
gal te yin na de mi grub ||
grub na gzhan gyi gzhung lugs kyang ||
sgyu ma'i chos su thal bar 'gyur ||
de phyir sgyu ma'i rang bzhin ni ||
sgyu bzhin 'di zhes brjod du med ||

> not like the son of a barren woman. If they *were* analyzed like that, the existence of all arisen things would be refuted. And if that were the case, we could not say that the production of compounded phenomena is like a magician's illusion, and we *would* explain using examples such as the son of a barren woman. But since we wish to avoid the absurd consequence that dependently arisen phenomena are nonexistent, we do not use these analogies. Instead, so as not to contradict the existence of dependent origination, we compare the production of things to analogies such as a magician's illusion. (15.10; dBu ma, ya: 225a; 2019: 407–8)[3]

Analogies matter. Here, Candrakīrti distinguishes two different ones often used in Madhyamaka treatises. The son of a barren woman is an analogy for something that does not exist at all—conventionally or ultimately—and that simply makes no sense; something incoherent. The magical illusion, however, is not like that. It exists; if it did not, nobody would attend magic shows; there would be nothing to see. It is dependently originated, brought about by the magician. If it did not depend on a skilled magician, even I could produce the illusion. And finally, while it does exist, it does not exist as it appears; its mode of existence and mode of appearance are discordant. When the magician chants *Abracadabra* over a pile of sticks, he produces a *real illusion* that appears to be, but is not, a *real elephant.* Once again, if the illusion were *not* real, or if the elephant *were*, nobody would pay to see this magic trick.

Candrakīrti is therefore explicitly denying that he (or Āryadeva) rejects the reality of conventional truth: it is *not* like the son of a barren woman. *Instead*, it is like the magical illusion: it exists, but in a way

[3] skyes pa la ni 'ong ba dang ||
de bzhin 'gags la 'gro ba med ||
de lta yin na ji lta bur ||
srid pa sgyu ma 'dra ma yin ||
rten cing 'brel par 'byung ba ni ji lta ba bzhin mthong ba na sgyu ma byas pa lta bur 'gyur gyi mo gsham gyi bu lta bu ni ma yin no || gal te rnam par dpyod pa 'dis
skye ba rnam pa thams cad du bkag pa las 'dus byas skye ba med par bstan par 'dod na ni de'i tshe sgyu ma lta bu nyid du mi 'gyur gyi mo gsham gyi bu la sogs pa dag gis nye bar gzhal bar 'gyur ba zhig na | rten cing 'brel par 'byung ba med par thal bar 'gyur ba'i 'jigs pas de dag dang bstun par mi byed kyi | de dang mi 'gal ba sgyu ma la sogs pa dag dang ni mi byed do ||

that is different from its appearance. Conventional truth is real, but only conventionally real; it appears to us to exist intrinsically, but it does not. Conventional phenomena appear to be independent, but, like the illusion, they are only dependently arisen; they are therefore deceptive, which is, in Sanskrit literature, the definition of *falsity*. Candrakīrti concludes:

> Therefore, when the noble ones see the illusory nature of existence to be essencelesssness, they become liberated by the complete exhaustion of all attachment to this essenceless cyclic existence. So there is nothing incoherent about this. Since this does not deny the reality of the dependently arisen, no account of mundane conventions is undermined. This is because to be liberated is to understand reality as it is. (*Commentary on Āryadeva's Four Hundred Stanzas* 15.10; dBu ma, ya: 225a; 2019: 408)[4]

This is an *affirmation*, not a *denial*, of the reality of the conventional. But, one might wonder, what does this say about the *epistemology* of the conventional? Here we turn to *Clear Words*. In this context, Candrakīrti is responding to one who would argue that to be only conventionally real is to be *unreal* and that only ultimate truth counts as *truth*:

> Since you don't understand ultimate and conventional truth, you don't use appropriate analyses, and so you completely destroy any understanding of the conventional. Since we understand how to think about the conventional, we adhere to mundane ways of thinking about it. So, like experienced participants in mundane practices, we use those practices to dispel the position you defend and to refute your position regarding the conventional. (*Clear Words* 1.3; Skt. Vaidya: 1960: B69.19–22; dBu ma, 'a: 23b; 2003: 50)[5]

[4] de'i phyir 'phags pa ni sgyu ma byas pa lta bu'i srid pa snying po med pa nyid du gzigs pa na snying po med pa'i 'khor ba la chags pa thams cad yongs su zad pas rnam par grol bar 'gyur bas 'di la mi rigs pa ci yang med do || 'di rten cing 'brel par 'byung bar'gyur pa la skur pa ma btab bas 'jig rten pa'i rnam par gzhag pa thams cad mi 'jig la med do ||| yang dag pa ji lta ba bzhin khong du chud par thar pa 'grub pa'i phyir ro ||

[5] bhavāṃstu etāṃ saṃvṛtiparamārthasatyavibhāgadurvidagdhabuddhitayā kkacidupapattimavatārya anyāyato nāśayati | so'haṃ saṃvṛtisatyavyavasthāvaicakṣaṇ

The important point here is not simply that the conventional truth is important and must be understood, but also that mundane epistemic standards can be used to evaluate and to reject *other* standards. This is an appeal to the recursive and self-correcting character of conventional epistemological practices. We use our epistemic instruments not only to determine what our objects of knowledge are like, but also to calibrate and to assess other epistemic standards. Not only do I use the *testimony* of my ophthalmologist to determine whether my vision is good, but I also use my *inferential* understanding of the status of the conventional to compare the *analogies* of the son of a barren woman and a magical illusion. And no extension of any of this knowledge would be possible without *analogy*, since we could never use what we learn about one thing to come to know anything about anything else: our epistemic practices and our ontological commitments form an interdependent web, itself supported by the objects we know and with which we interact, just as Nāgārjuna says it should go in *Replies to Objections* (*Vigrahavyāvartanī*).[6]

Tsongkhapa follows Candrakīrti closely in this regard. In *Great Exposition of the Stages of the Path* he writes: "Candrakīrti repeatedly allows that these conventionalities, such as forms and sounds, do exist. However, they are not in the least established by reasoning that analyzes reality, that is, analyzes whether they have intrinsic nature" (Tsongkhapa 2015: 157). Tsongkhapa here, and throughout his discussion of the epistemology of the conventional in *Great Exposition*, insists that Candrakīrti's analysis of conventional phenomena as empty of any intrinsic identity not only is *consistent* with their

yāllaukika eva pakṣe sthitvā saṃvṛtyekadeśanirākaraṇopakṣiptopapattyantaramupapattyantareṇa vinivartayan lokavṛddha iva lokacārātparibhraśyamānaṃ bhavantameva nivartayāmi na tu saṃvṛtim |

Tib: khyod ni don dam pa dang kun rdzob kyi bden pa la mi mkhas pas la lar 'thad pa bcug nas rigs pa ma yin pa las de 'jig par byed pa yin no || kho bo ni kun rdzob kyi bden pa rnam par 'jog pa la mkhas pa'i phyir | 'jig rten pa'i phyogs nyid la gnas te kun rdzob kyi phyogs gcig bsal ba'i phyir bkod pa'i 'thad pa gzhan 'thad pa gzhan gyis zlog par byed cing 'jig rten gyi rgan rabs ltar | 'jig rten gyi chos lugs las nyams pa khyod kho na zlog par byed pa yin gyi kun rdzob ni ma yin no||

[6] See Garfield 2015: ch. 7 and Westerhoff 2010 for more on Nāgārjuna's epistemology in *Reply to Objections*.

conventional reality, but *presupposes it.* Candrakīrti and Tsongkhapa are in clear agreement that the two truths are two *truths* and that the illusory nature of conventional truth does not undermine its status as a truth. Tsongkhapa's student Khedrup-jé puts this point felicitously in *The Great Digest* (*sTong thun chen mo*):

> It is not contradictory that, on the one hand, it be an object that deceives in so far as, within the consciousness that takes it as its object, the way in which it appears does not accord with the way it exists, and that, on the other hand, this valid cognition is nondeceived in regard to the phenomenon in so far as it establishes that phenomenon as it is in a positive way. (Cabezón 1992: 371)

The sense in which conventional phenomena are deceptive is this: they appear to be more than merely conventional. But just as we may be wrong in believing that a rabbit was conjured from an empty hat while being right that the magician has produced a rabbit and not a wombat, we may be wrong in thinking that a pot is *ultimately* real while being right that the *conventionally* real thing in front of us is a *pot* and that it is blue. And if we are right, that is because our ordinary epistemic instruments are working properly.

This is also to take seriously the normative force of convention and of the proper functioning of perceptual and conceptual faculties. For this reason, Tsongkhapa argues that there are objects about which there is a difference between getting it right and getting it wrong; that while we may not be authoritative with regard to all aspects of an entity, we can nonetheless be authoritative with regard to some; that our epistemic instruments can leverage us on a steady path to greater knowledge and insight. He concludes that since human knowledge can be explained in terms of the coherence of our epistemic instruments with one another and of the body of knowledge they deliver and that their warrant derives from this coherence, so we can distinguish the warranted output of properly functioning faculties from the erroneous output of those that are impaired.

This is the reading of Candrakīrti that we have been defending, not simply because it gets Candrakīrti right, but because it is a compelling vision of the nature of reality and of our experience thereof: it shows us how to make sense of the world we inhabit and our place in it in the context of the emptiness of that world of intrinsic reality, in the absence of any foundations, and in the context of experience constructed by our conventions and our species-specific faculties. And it does so without demoting that world or our values to any second-class status.

Why should we care about this medieval debate regarding how to read Candrakīrti and this outcome? Because the metaphysical, epistemological, and ethical issues raised by this hermeneutical debate are at the center the debates that roil contemporary philosophy, and because if we understand Candrakīrti correctly, we find a plausible position. Candrakīrti shows us a way to think through the choices between foundationalism and coherentism, realism and anti-realism, conventionalism and transcendentalism. The arguments he presents and the disputes in which he and his commentators were involved shed light upon the more contemporary battles between Neurath and Carnap in metaphysics, between Sellars and Chisholm in epistemology, and between O'Neill (2018) or Korsgaard (1996) and Mackie (1977) or Garner (1994) in ethics.

In many of the more contemporary European cases, while it appears that partisans disagree about everything, we find on reflection that they agree about the only thing that really matters—the biconditional presupposed by the debate. In the case of metaphysics, it is the thesis that there is a reality if, and only if, it has an independent, substantial nature. Realists infer from the existence of the real world to the claim that there are essences, or ontological foundations; anti-realists infer from groundlessness that there is no clear sense of reality. In the case of epistemology, it is the thesis that justification is possible if, and only if, there are epistemic foundations. Foundationalists argue that because there is knowledge, there must be foundations; radical skeptics like Unger argue that because there are no foundations, there is no genuine knowledge. And in the case of ethics, it is the claim that there is a difference between right and wrong if, and only if, there are transcendent ethical principles to which we are sensitive. Ethical realists argue that because there are ethical standards, there must be such principles; ethical anti-realists argue that since there are no such transcendent principles, morality is but a fiction.

As Dreyfus (2011), Dreyfus and Garfield (2011), and Garfield (1990) argued, classical Pyrrhonian skeptics in Greece (and their modern heirs such as Hume, Nietzsche, and Wittgenstein) as well as Indian and Tibetan Mādhyamikas saw that the key to resolving these apparently intractable debates was to reject this underlying "dogmatic biconditional" and to turn to the role of convention in constituting the discursive practices whose validity was the subject of those debates. This resolution, they saw, would not take the form of choosing one side or the other, nor would it amount to some kind of compromise position, but rather a suspension (*epochē*) of the debates once the presupposition is rejected and an acceptance of the authority of convention on its own terms.

This is the insight that underlies Candrakīrti's program. In a synoptic vision of the relation between the conventional world and its ultimate emptiness, he sees that we must simply reject the idea that conventions require grounds, and we must recognize that conventions themselves are normative. In doing so, we can become comfortable living in a groundless world. The ontology of the manifest image is irreducible to that of the scientific; but the scientific ontology is also irreducible to the manifest. This is true despite the fact that they are mutually implicative. Justification is possible simply because we have evolved mutually supportive epistemic practices that have pragmatic value and stability, supporting each other, our edifice of knowledge, and supported by that edifice, like sheaves of wheat in the field. And our ethical practices emerge from our concerns as human beings and in return constitute those very concerns, cohering with what we take ourselves to know and what we take our interests to be, without any transcendent ground.

In each case, normativity derives not from a transcendent, absolute source that can only be accessed through mystic intuition, but from our network of everyday practices (*lokavyāvahāra*) and is accepted only conventionally (*lokaprasiddha*), and in each case, the fact that we live our lives for the most part subject to massive cognitive illusion is no obstacle to justification. This is because our *loka* itself demands no ground. It is simply the world into which we are thrown. And this is what Candrakīrti can teach contemporary epistemologists and ethicists.

Candrakīrti is not a nihilist. He is not a transcendentalist. He is instead the champion of the importance of the everyday, and so the champion of the significance of our human life. He does reveal that our life is permeated by illusion. But the principal illusion he urges us to shed is the illusion that there is a higher level of reality beyond that illusion. In the end, we have only the world we inhabit, and that is world enough.

This triple world is not as it appears.
Nor is it otherwise. (*Lankāvatāra-sūtra*)

References

(1) Canonical Sources

(A) Kangyur

Conze, E., ed. (1973). *The Perfection of Wisdom in Eight Thousand Lines and Its Verse Summary.* Wheel Series 1. San Francisco: Four Seasons Foundation.

Conze, E., ed. (1975). *The Large Sutra on Perfect Wisdom, with the Divisions of the Abhisamayālaṅkāra.* Berkeley: University of California Press.

Conze, Ed., ed. (1993). *Perfect Wisdom: The Short Prajñāpāramitā Texts.* Totnes: Buddhist Publishing Group.

Discourse on Samsaric Migration. Bhavasaṃkrāntisūtra. 'Phags pa srid pa 'pho ba zhes bya ba theg pa chen po'i mdo. N 211, Narthang Kangyur vol. 63, mdo sde, tsa, 279b6–282b2. Toh 226, Degé Kangyur, Volume 63, mdo sde, dza, 175a6–177a3.

The Teaching of Akṣayamati. Akṣayamatinirdeśasūtra. Blo gros mi zad pas bstan pa zhes bya ba theg pa chen po'i mdo. H 176, Lhasa Kangyur, Volume 60, mdo sde, pha, 122b5–270b1. Toh 175, Degé Kangyur, Volume 60, mdo sde, ma, 79a–174b. Jens Braarvig and David Welsh (Trans.). (2020). 84000: Translating the Words of the Buddha.

Teaching the Relative and Ultimate Truths. Samvṛtiparamārthasatyanirdeśa. Kun rdzob dang don dam pa'i bden pa bstan pa'i mdo. Toh 179, Degé Kangyur, Volume 60, mdo sde, ma, 244b–266b. Dharmachakra Translation Group (Trans.). (2016). 84000: Translating the Words of the Buddha.

The Ten Bhūmis. Daśabhūmika. Sab cu pa'i mdo. Toh 44–31, Degé Kangyur, Volume 36, phal chen, kha, 166.a–283a. In Peter Alan Roberts (Trans.), *The Ten Bhūmis Chapter from the Mahāvaipulya Sūtra "A Multitude of Buddhas"* (2022). 84000: Translating the Words of the Buddha.

Unraveling the Intent Sūtra. Saṃdhinirmocanasūtra. 'Phags pa dgongs pa nges par 'grel pa. H 109, Lhasa Kangyur, Volume 51, mdo sde, ca, 1b1–87b7. Toh 106, Degé Kangyur, Volume 49, mdo sde, tsha, 1b–55b. Buddhavacana Translation Group (Trans.). (2021). 84000: Translating the Words of the Buddha.

(B) Tengyur

Āryadeva. *Four Hundred Verses. Catuḥśatakaśastrakārikā. Bstan bcos bzhi brgya pa zhes bya ba'i tshig le'ur byas pa.* Toh 3846, Degé Tengyur, dbu ma, tsha, 1b–18a.

Asaṅga (2016). *The Bodhisattva Grounds: The Grounds of the Yogins. Yogācārabhūmaubodhisattvabhūmi. Rnal 'byor spyod pa'i sa las byang chub sems dpa'i sa.* Toh 4037, Degé Tengyur, sems tsam, wi, 1b1–213a7. In A. B. Engle (Ed.). *The Bodhisattva Path to Unsurpassed Enlightenment: A Complete Translation of the Bodhisattvabhūmi.* Ithaca: Snow Lion.

Atiśa Dīpaṃkaraśrījñāna. *Introduction to the Two Truths. Satyadvayāvatāra. Bden pa gnyis la 'jug pa.* Toh 3902, Degé Tengyur, dbu ma, a, 72a–73a.

Bhāviveka (Bhavya). *Blaze of Reasoning: Commentary on the Essence of the Middle Way. Madhyamakahṛdayavṛttitarkajvālā. Dbu ma snying po'i 'grel pa rtog gi 'bar ba.* Toh 3856, Degé Tengyur, dbu ma, dza, 40b–329b.

Bhāviveka (Bhavya). *Jewel Lamp of the Middle Way. Madhyamakaratnapradīpa. Dbu ma rin po che'i sgron ma.* Toh 3854, Degé Tengyur, dbu ma, tsha, 259b–289a.

Candrakīrti. *Clear Words Commentary on the Fundamental Verses of the Middle Way. Mūlamadhyamakavṛttiprasannapadā. Dbu ma rtsa ba'i 'grel pa tshig gsal ba.* Toh 3860, Degé Tengyur, dbu ma, 'a, 1b1–200a.

Candrakīrti. (2003). *Clear Words Commentary on the Fundamental Verses of the Middle Way. Dbu ma rtsa ba'i 'grel pa tshig gsal bzhungs so.* Sarnath: Gelugpa Students' Welfare Committee 32.

Candrakīrti. *Commentary on Introduction to the Middle Way. Madhyamakāvatārabhāṣya. Dbu ma la 'jug pa'i bshad pa.* Toh 3862, Degé Tengyur, dbu ma, 'a, 22b–348a.

Candrakīrti. *Commentary on the Four Hundred Verses. Catuḥśatakaṭīkā. Bzhi brgya pa'i rgya cher 'grel pa.* Toh 3865, Degé Tengyur, dbu ma, ya, 30b6–239a7.

Candrakīrti (2019). *Commentary on the Four Hundred Verses of Bodhisattvas Yogic Practices. Byang chub sems pa'i rnal 'byor spyod pa bzhi brgya pa'i rgya cher 'grel pa zhes by a bzhungs so.* Mundgod: Drepung Loseling Library Society.

Candrakīrti. *Commentary on the Seventy Verses on Emptiness. Śūnyatāsaptativṛtti. Stong nyid bdun cu pa'i 'grel pa.* Toh 3867, Degé Tengyur, dbu ma, ya, 267a1–336b7; Pedurma 60, 2000: 934–1003.

Candrakīrti. *Commentary on the Sixty Verses on Reasoning. Yuktiṣaṣṭikāvṛtti. Rigs pa drug cu pa'i 'grel pa.* Toh 3864, Degé Tengyur, dbu ma, ya, 1b1–30b6; Pedurma 60, 934–1008.

Candrakīrti. *Discussion on the Five Aggregates. Pañcaskandhaprakaraṇa. Phung po lnga'i rab tu byed pa.* Toh 3866, Degé Tengyur, dbu ma, ya, 239b1–266b7; Pedurma 60, 1534–1600.

Candrakīrti. *Introduction to the Middle Way. Madhyamakāvatāra. Dbu ma la 'jug pa.* Toh 3861, Degé Tengyur, dbu ma, 'a, 201b1–219a7.

Candrakīrti (1960). *Madhyamakaśāstravṛtti.* In P. L. Vaidya (Ed.), *Madhyamakaśāstra of Nāgārjuna with the commentary: Prasannapadā by Candrakīrti.* Mithila: The Mithila Institute of Post-Graduate Studies and Research in Sanskrit Learning.

Candrakīrti (1992). *Autocommentary on Introduction to the Middle Way (Madhyamakāvatāra-bhāṣya).* Sarnath: Kagyud Relief and Protection Society.

Candrakīrti (2003). *dBu ma rtsa ba'i 'gral pa tshig gsal ba (Prasannapadā).* Sarnath: Gelug Students Welfare Committee.

Candrakīrti (2005). *Autocommentary on Introduction to the Middle Way (Dbu ma 'jug pa'i rang 'grel).* Sarnath: Varja Vidya Institute Library.

Dignāga. *Commentary on the Compendium of Epistemology. Pramāṇasamuccayavṛtti. Tshad ma kun las btus pa'i 'grel pa.* Toh 4204, Degé Tengyur, tshad ma, ce, 14b1–85b7.

Jayānanda (2012). *Commentary on Introduction to the Middle Way. Madhyamakāvatāraṭīkā. Dbu ma la 'jug pa'i 'grel bshad.* Sarnath: Vajra Vidya Institute.

Jayānanda. *Hammer of Reasoning. Tarkamudgarakārikā. Rtog gi tho ba'i tshig le'ur byas pa.* Toh 3869, Degé Tengyur, dbu ma, ya, 374b–375a; Pedurma 118, 1876–1879.

Nāgārjuna. *Dispeller of the Disputes. Vigrahavyāvartanīkārikā. Rtsod pa bzog pa'i tshig le'ur byas pa.* Toh 3828, Degé Tengyur, dbu ma, tsa, 27a–29a.

Nāgārjuna. *In Praise of The World-transcend. Lokātītastava. 'jig rten las 'das par bstod pa.* Toh 1120, Degé Tengyur, bstod tshogs, ka: 68b4-69b4.

Nāgārjuna. *Stages of Meditation. Bhāvanākrama. Bsgom pa'i rim pa.* Toh 3908, Degé Tengyur, dbu ma, ki, 1b–4a.

Nāgārjuna and Candrakīrti (2024). *The Reason Sixty by Nāgārjuna with the Reason Sixty Commentary by Chandrakīrti.* 2nd edition. J. J. Loizzo, R. A. F. Loizzo, T. F. Yarnall, and P. G. Hackett (Trans.). New York: American Institute of Buddhist Studies at Columbia University, co-published with Columbia University's Center for Buddhist Studies and Tibet House US.

Śāntarakṣita. *Verses on the Ornament of the Middle Way. Madhyamakālaṃkārakārikā. Dbu ma rgyan gyi tshig le'ur bhas pa.* Toh 3884, Degé Tengyur, dbu ma, sa, 56b–84a.

Śāntideva. *Engaging an Awakened Life. Bodhicaryāvatāra. Byang chub sems dpa'i spyod pa la 'jug pa.* Toh 3871, Degé Tengyur, dbu ma, la, 1b1–40a7.

Sthiramati. *Commentary on the Separation of the Middle from the Extremes. Madhyāntavibhāgaṭīkā. Dbus dang mtha' rnam par 'byed pa'i 'grel bshad.* Toh 4032, Degé Tengyur, sems tsam, bi, 189b2–318a7.

Sthiramati. *Commentary on the Thirty Stanzas. Triṃśikābhāṣya. Sum cu pa'i bshad pa.* Toh 4064, Degé Tengyur, sems tsam, shi, 146b2–171b6.

Vasubandhu. *Abhidharmakośabhāṣyam.* Edited by Prahlad Pradana. Patna: K.P. Jayaswal Research Institute.

Vasubandhu. *Commentary on the Twenty Stanzas. Viṃśatikāvṛtti. Nyi shu pa'i 'grel pa.* Toh 4057, Degé Tengyur, sems tsam, shi, 4a3–10a2.

Vasubandhu. *Identifying the Three Natures. Trisvabhāvanirdeśa. Rang bzhin gsum nges par bstan pa.* Toh 4058, Degé Tengyur, sems tsam, shi, 10a3–11b4.

Vasubandhu. *The Thirty Verses. Triṃśikākārikā. Sum cu pa'i tshig le'ur byas pa.* Toh 4055, Degé Tengyur, sems tsam, shi, 1b1–3a3.

Vinītadeva. *Commentary on the Investigation of the Percept. Ālambanaparīkṣāṭīkā. Dmigs pa brtag pa'i 'grel bshad.* Toh 4241, Degé Tengyur, tshad ma, zhe, 175a3–187b5.

Vinītadeva. *Commentary on the Thirty Verses. Triṃśikāṭīkā. Sum cu pa'i 'grel bshad.* Toh 4070, Degé Tengyur, sems tsam, hi, 1b1–63a7.

(C) Tibetan Sources

Taktsang Lotsawa Sherab Rinchen (2007). *Freedom from Extremes Accomplished through Comprehensive Knowledge of Philosophy (Grub mtha' kun shes nas mtha' bral sgrub pa).* In *The Collected Works of Taktsang Lotsawa,* volume 1, 93–121. Peking: Tibetology Press.

Tsong-kha-pa Blo-bzang-grags-pa (2006). *Ocean of Reasoning: A Great Commentary on Nāgrjuna's Mūlamadhyamakārikā.* Jay. L. Garfield and Ngawang Samten (Trans.). New York: Oxford University Press.

Tsong-kha-pa Blo-bzang-grags-pa (2015). *The Great Treatise on the Stages of the Path to Enlightenment: Lam rim chen mo.* Volume 3.W. C. C. Joshua and G. Newland (Eds.). Lamrim Chenmo Translation Committee (Trans.). Ithaca: Snow Lion Publications.

(2) Modern Sources

Atkin, Albert (2023). Peirce's Theory of Signs. In Edward N. Zalta and Uri Nodelman (Ed.), *The Stanford Encyclopedia of Philosophy* (Spring). https://plato.stanford.edu/archives/spr2023/entries/peirce-semiotics/.

Arnold, D. (2008). *Buddhists, Brahmins, and Belief: Epistemology in South Asian Philosophy of Religion*. New York: Columbia University Press.

Arnold, D. (2019). The Sense Madhyamaka Makes as a Buddhist Position: Or, How a "Performativist Account of the Language of Self" Makes Sense of "No-Self." *Journal of Indian Philosophy 47*(4), 697–726. https://doi.org/10.1007/s10781-019-09390-5.

Arnold, D. (2023). The Real According to Madhyamaka, Or: Thoughts on Whether Mark Siderits and I Really Disagree. In C. Coseru (Ed.), *Reasons and Empty Persons: Mind, Metaphysics, and Morality* (pp. 259–279). Cham: Springer Nature.

Arnold, D. (forthoming). Madhyamaka's Recuperation of Conventional Truth. In D. Arnold (Ed.), *A Madhyamaka Reader* (pp. 247–344). New York: Columbia University Press.

Beckwith, C. (2015). *Greek Buddha: Pyrrho's Encounter with Early Buddhism in Central Asia*. Princeton: Princeton University Press.

Bodhi, B. (2000). *The Connected Discourses of the Buddha: A New Translation of the Samyutta Nikaya*. Boston: Wisdom Publications.

Cabezón, J. I. (1992). *A Dose of Emptiness: An Annotated Translation of the sTong thun chen mo of mKhas grub dGe legs dpal bzang*. Albany: SUNY Press.

Cabezón, J. (forthcoming). *Introduction to the Buddha's Path: Buddhaśrī's* Jinamārgāvatāra. Albany: SUNY Press.

Chadha, M. (2019). Two Tables, Images, and Truths. In J. L. Garfield (Ed.), *Wilfrid Sellars and Buddhist Philosophy* (pp. 32–47). New York: Routledge.

Cowherds (2011). *Moonshadows: Conventional Truth in Buddhist Philosophy*. New York: Oxford University Press.

Deguchi, Y., J. L. Garfield, G. Priest, and R. H. Sharf (Eds.) (2022). *What Can't be Said: Paradox and Contradiction in East Asian Thought*. New York: Oxford University Press.

Dreyfus, G. (2011). Can a Madhyamaka be a skeptic? The case of Patsab Nyimadrak. In Cowherds (Ed.), *Moonshadows: Conventional Truth in Buddhist Philosophy* (pp. 89–114). New York: Oxford University Press.

Dreyfus, G., and J. L. Garfield (2011). Madhyamaka and Classical Greek Scepticism. In Cowherds (Ed.), *Moonshadows: Conventional Truth in Buddhist Philosophy* (pp. 115–130). New York: Oxford University Press.

Dreyfus, G., and S. McClintock (Eds.). (2003). *The Svātantrika–Prāsaṅgika Distinction: What Difference Does a Difference Make?* New York: Wisdom Publications.

Duckworth, D. (2019). Sellars and the Steroscopic Vision of Madhyamaka. In J. L. Garfield (Ed.), *Wilfrid Sellars and Buddhist Philosophy* (pp. 67–79). New York: Routledge.

Duckworth, D., et al. (2016). *Dignāga's Investigation of the Percept: A Philosophical Legacy in India and Tibet*. J. L. Garfield, J. Powers, Yeshes Thabkhas, and S. Thakchöe (Trans.). New York: Oxford University Press.

Ferraro, G. (2017). Realistic-Antimetaphysical Reading Vs Any Nihilistic Interpretation of Madhyamaka. *Journal of Indian Philosophy 45*(1), 73–98. https://doi.org/10.1007/s10781-016-9299-6.

Feyerabend, P. (1981). *Realism, Rationalism and Scientific Method*, Volume 1: *Philosophical Papers*. Cambridge: Cambridge University Press.

Finnigan, B. (2015). Madhyamaka Buddhist Meta-ethics: The Justificatory Grounds of Moral Judgments. *Philosophy East and West 65*(3), 765–785.

Forman, J. D. (2020). What Is the World? Neckties, Ghosts, Falling Hairs, and Celestial Cities in a Coherentist Epistemology. *Philosophy East and West 70*(4), 906–931.

Frankfurt, H. (2009). *Demons, Dreamers, and Madmen: The Defense of Reason in Descartes'* Meditations. Princeton: Princeton University Press.

Garfield, J. L. (1990). Epoche and Śūnyatā: Skepticism East and West. *Philosophy East and West, 40*(3), 285–307. https://doi.org/10.2307/1399425.

Garfield, J. L. (1994). Dependent Co-origination and the Emptiness of Emptiness: Why Did Nāgārjuna Begin with Causation? *Philosophy East and West 44*, pp 219–250, reprinted in *Empty Words*, New York: Oxford University Press, 2002, pp 24-45.

Garfield, J. L. (2002). Emptiness and Positionlessness: Do the Mādhyamika Relinquish all Views? In J. Garfield (Ed.), *Empty Words* (pp. 46–68). New York: Oxford University Press.

Garfield, J. L. (2006). The Conventional Status of Reflexive Awareness: What's at Stake in a Tibetan Debate? *Philosophy East and West 56*(2), 201–228. https://doi.org/10.1353/pew.2006.0020.

Garfield, J. L. (2012). *Western Idealism and Its Critics*. Sarnath: Central Institute of Higher Tibetan Studies Press.

Garfield, J. L. (2015). *Engaging Buddhism: Why It Matters to Philosophy*. New York: Oxford University Press.

Garfield, J. L. (2019a). *The Concealed Influence of Custom: Hume's Treatise From the Inside*. New York: Oxford University Press.

Garfield, J. L. (Ed.). (2019b). *Wilfrid Sellars and Buddhist Philosophy*. New York: Routledge.

Garfield, J. L. (2020). Thinking Beyond Thought: Tsongkhapa and Mipham on the Conceptualized Ultimate. *Philosophy East and West 70*(2), 338–353.

Garfield, J. L. (2021). Ten Moons: Consciousness and Intentionality in the Ālambanaparīkṣā and Its Commentaries. *Philosophy East and West 71*(2), 309–325.

Garfield, J. L. (2022a). Candrakīrti and Hume on the Self and the Person. In D. O'Brien (Ed.), *Hume on the Self and Personal Identity* (pp. 225–249). Springer International Publishing. https://doi.org/10.1007/978-3-031-04275-1_10.

Garfield, J. L. (2022b). Cognitive Illusion and the Immediacy of Experience: Perspectives from Buddhist Philosophy. In I. Shani and S. Beiweis (Eds.), *Cross-Cultural Approaches to Consciousness* (pp. 245–266). Bloomsbury.

Garfield, J. L. (2022c). *Losing Ourselves: Learning to Live without a Self*. New York: Oxford University Press.

Garfield, J. L. (2022d). *Buddhist Ethics: A Philosophical Exploration*. New York: Oxford University Press.

Garfield, J. L. (2023). Knowing Knowledge: Geluk and Sellarsian Epistemology and the Emergence of Tibetan Modernity. In H. Gayley and A. Quintman (Eds.), *Living Treasure: Tibetan and Buddhist Studies in Honor of Janet Gyatso* (pp. 445–467). Boston: Wisdom Publications.

Garfield, J. L. (2024). Tibetan Buddhist Accounts of the Epistemology of Awakening: Omniscience and Epistemic Authority. In Y. Nagasawa and M. S. Zarepour (Eds.), *Global Dialogues in the Philosophy of Religion: From Religious Experience to the Afterlife* (pp. 7–21). New York: Oxford University Press.

Garfield, J. L., and G. Priest (2003). Nāgārjuna and the Limits of Thought. *Philosophy East and West 53*(1), 1–21.

Garfield, J. L., and G. Priest (2009). Mountains are Just Mountains. In M. D'Amato, J. Garfield, and T. Tillemans (Eds.), *Pointing at the Moon: Buddhism, Logic, Analysis* (pp. 71–82). New York: Oxford University Press.

Garfield, J. L., and G. Priest (2021). Dining on Painted Rice Cakes. In Deguchi, Garfield, Priest, and Sharf (Eds.), *What Can't Be Said: Paradox and Contradiction in East Asian Philosophy* (pp. 104–121). New York: Oxford University Press.

Garfield, J. L., and S. Thakchöe (2011). Identifying the Object of Negation and the Status of Conventional Truth: Why the dGag Bya Matters So Much to Tibetan Mādhyamikas. In Cowherds (Ed.), *Moonshadows: Conventional Truth in Buddhist Philosophy* (pp. 73–87). New York: Oxford University Press.

Garfield, J. L., and S. Thakchöe (2015). *The Two Truths Debate: Tsongkhapa and Gorampa on the Middle Way.* Wisdom Publications.

Garner, R. (1994). *Beyond Morality.* Philadelphia: Temple University Press.

Gold, J. C. (2015). *Paving the Great Way: Vasubandhu's Unifying Buddhist Philosophy.* New York: Columbia University Press.

Goodman, N. (1978). *Ways of Worldmaking.* Brighton: Harvester Press.

Harris, S. (2024). *Bodhisattva Ethics and the Bodhisattva Path: Śāntideva on Virtue and Well-Being.* London: Bloomsbury.

Haugeland, J. (2013). *Dasein Disclosed:: John Haugeland's Heidegger.* J. Rouse (Ed.). Cambridge: Harvard University Press.

Heidegger, M. (1962). *Being and Time.* J. Macquarrie and E. Robinson (Trans.). New York: Harper & Row.

Heim, M. (2020). *Buddhist Ethics.* Cambridge: Cambridge University Press.

Jenkins, S. (2015). Waking into Compassion: The three *Ālambana* of *Karuṇā*. In Cowherds (Ed.), *Moonpaths: Ethics and Emptiness* (pp. 97–118). New York: Oxford University Press.

Korsgaard, C. (1996). *The Sources of Normativity.* Cambridge: Cambridge University Press.

Kriegel, U. (2009). *Subjective Consciousness: A Self-Representational Theory.* New York: Oxford University Press.

Kriegel, U. (2011). *The Sources of Intentionality.* New York: Oxford University Press.

Kuzminski, A. (2008). *Pyrrhonism: How the Ancient Greeks Re-invented Buddhism.* New York: Lexington Books.

Lang, K. (2003). *Four Illusions: Candrakīrti's Advice for Travelers on the Bodhisattva Path.* New York: Oxford University Press.

Li, S. (2019). Dimensions of Candrakīti's Conventional Reality. *Journal of Indian Philosophy 47*, 49–72.

Loizzo, J. (2001). Candrakīrti and the Moon-Flower of Nālandā: Objectivity and Self-Correction in India's Central Therapeutic Philosophy of Language [PhD dissertation, New York: Columbia University].

MacDonald, A. (2009). Knowing Nothing: Candrakīrti and Yogic Perception. In E. Franco and E. Eigner (Eds.), *Yogic Perception, Meditation, and Altered States of Consciousness* (pp. 133–167). Vienna: Australian Academy of Sciences.

MacDonald, A. (2015a). *In Clear Words: The Prasannapadā, Chapter One: Introduction, Manuscript Description and Sanskrit Text*, Volume 1: *Beiträge Zur Kultur- Und Geistesgeschichte Asiens, Nr. 86.* Vienna: Verlag der Österreichischen Akademie der Wissenschaften.

MacDonald, A. (2015b). *In Clear Words: The Prasannapadā, Chapter One*, Volume 2: *Annotated Translation, Tibetan Text.* Vienna: VÖAW.

McNamara, D. (2019). Nihilists and Noble Ones: Ranākaraśānti's Engagement with Nāgārjuna, Mādhyamikas and Mahayāna in Madhyamakālaṃkāra- vṛtti. [PhD dissertation, University of Wisconsin].

Mackie, J. L. (1977). *Ethics: Inventing Right and Wrong.* London: Penguin Books.

Mathur, A. (2024). Jayāndanda's and Tsongkhapa's Views on *Pramāṇa.* Paper presented to the International Madhyamaka Conference. Vienna: Austrian Academy of Sciences.

McEvilley. T. (2012). *The Shape of Ancient Thought.* New York: Allworth Press.

Mukerji, A. C. (1938). *The Nature of Self.* Allahabad: The Indian Press, Ltd.

Nagel, T. (1974). *What Is It Like to Be a Bat? The Philosophical Review 83*(4), 435–450. https://doi.org/10.2307/2183914.

Newland, G. (2011). Weighing the Butter Levels of Explanation, and Falsification: Models of the Conventional in Tsongkhapa's Account of the Conventional. In Cowherds (Ed.), *Moonshadows: Conventional Truth in Buddhist Philosophy* (pp. 57–72). New York: Oxford University Press.

Newland, G., and T. J. F. Tillemans (2011). An Introduction to Conventional Truth. In Cowherds (Ed.), *Moonshadows: Conventional Truth in Buddhist Philosophy* (pp. 3–22). New York: Oxford University Press.

Newman, J. (2024). Candrakīrti on lokaprasiddhi: A Bad Hand, or an Ace in the Hole? *Journal of Indian Philosophy 52*(1), 73–99. https://doi.org/10.1007/s10781-024-09557-9.

Nurboo, T. (2023). Candrakīrti's Epistemology: A Re-examination of Jamyang Zhepa's Interpretation. *Journal of Indian Philosophy 51*(4), 515–537. https://doi.org/10.1007/s10781-023-09547-3.

O'Neil, O. (2018). Linking Trust to Trustworthiness. *International Journal of Philosophical Studies 26*(2), 293–300.

Powers, J. (2021). The Disputed Middle Ground: Tibetan Mādhyamikas on How to Interpret Nāgārjuna and Candrakīrti. *Religions 12*(11), Article 11. https://doi.org/10.3390/rel12110991.

Priest, G., M. Siderits, and T. J. F. Tillemans (2011). The (Two) Truths about Truth. In Cowherds (Ed.), *Moonshadows: Conventional Truth in Buddhist Philosophy* (pp. 131–150). New York: Oxford University Press.

Putnam, H. (1981). *Reason, Truth and History.* Cambridge University Press.

Quine, W. V. (1968). Ontological Relativity. *The Journal of Philosophy 65*(7), 185–212. https://doi.org/10.2307/2024305.

Ruegg, D. (1981). *The Literature of the Madhyamaka School.* Wiesbaden: Harassowitz.

Salvini, M. (2014). Dependent Arising, Non-arising, and the Mind: MMK1 and the Abhidharma. *Journal of Indian Philosophy 42*(4), 471–497.

Salvini, M. (2019). Etymologies of What Can(not) be Said: Candrakīrti on Conventions and Elaborations. *Journal of Indian Philosophy 47*(4), 661–695. https://doi.org/10.1007/s10781-019-09402-4.

Salvini, M. (2022). Gardener of Skyflowers. In W. Edelglass, P.-J. Harter, and S. McClintock (Eds.), *The Routledge Handbook of Indian Philosophy* (pp. 404–420). London: Routledge.

Sellars, W. (1963). Philosophy and the Scientific Image of Man. In W. Sellars (Ed.), *Science, Perception and Reality* (pp. 1–40). Atascadero, CA: Ridgeview Publishing Company.

Sellars, W. (2007). *In the Space of Reasons: Selected Essays of Wilfrid Sellars.* S. Kevin and R. Brandom (Eds.). Cambridge: Harvard University Press.

Siderits, M. (2007). *Buddhism as Philosophy.* Indianapolis: Hackett Publishing.

Siderits, M. (2015). *Personal Identity and Buddhist Philosophy.* 2nd edition. Abingdon, UK: Ashgate Publishing Company.

Siderits, M. (2016). *Studies in Buddhist Philosophy.* J. Westerhoff (Ed.). New York: Oxford University Press.

Silk, J. (2018). *Materials Toward the Study of Vasubandhu's* Viṁśikā: *Sanskrit and Tibetan Critical Editions of the Verses and Autocommentary, an English Translation and Annotations.* Cambridge: Harvard University Press.

Suzuki, K. (1994). *Sanskrit Fragments and Tibetan Translation of Candrakīrti's* Bodhisattvayogācāracatuḥśatakaṭīkā. Tokyo: Sankibo Press.

Thakchöe, S. (2011). Prāsaṅgika Epistemology in Context. In Cowherds (Ed.), *Moonshadows: Conventional Truth in Buddhist Philosophy* (pp. 39–55). New York: Oxford University Press.

Thakchöe, S. (2012). Candrakīrti's Theory of Perception: A Case for Non-Foundationalist Epistemology in Madhyamaka. *Acta Orientalia Vilnensia 11*(1), 93–124.

Thakchöe, S. (2013). Prāsaṅgika Epistemology: A Reply to Stag tsang's Charge Against Tsongkhapa's Uses of Pramāṇa in Candrakīrti's Philosophy. *Journal of Indian Philosophy 41*(5), 535–561. https://doi.org/10.1007/s10781-013-9186-3.

Thakchöe, S. (2015). Reification and Nihilism: The Three Nature Theory and Its Implications. In J. Westerhoff and J. L. Garfield (Eds.), *Madhyamaka and Yogācāra: Allies or Rivals?* (pp. 72–110). New York: Oxford University Press.

Thakchöe, S. (2021). Two Truths in Buddhism. In C. Taliaferro and S. Goetz (Eds.), *The Encyclopedia of Philosophy of Religion.* https://doi.org/10.1002/9781119009924.eopr0396.

Thakchöe, S. (2023). *The Two Truths in Indian Buddhism: Reality, Knowledge, and Freedom.* Boston: Wisdom Publications.

Thakchöe, S. (forthcoming). Candrakīrti's Tripartite Theory of Conventional Truths: A Case against Typical-Atypical Readings. In S. L. McClintock (Ed.), *Essays in Conversation with Tom Tillemans.* Boston: Wisdom Publications.

Thakchoe, S., and J. T. Wiltshire. (2019). Madhyamaka Philosophy of No-Mind: Taktsang Lotsāwa's On Prāsaṅgika, Pramāṇa, Buddhahood and a

Defense of No-Mind Thesis. *Journal of Indian Philosophy* 47(3): 453–487. https://doi.org/10.1007/s10781-019-09388-z.

Thompson, E. (2007). *Mind in Life: Biology, Phenomenology, and the Sciences of Mind*. Cambridge: Harvard University Press.

Thompson, E. (2017). *Waking, Dreaming, Being: Self and Consciousness in Neuroscience, Meditation, and Philosophy*. New York: Columbia University Press.

Thurman, R. A. F. (1980). Philosophical Nonegocentrism in Wittgenstein and Candrakīrti in Their Treatment of the Private Language Problem. *Philosophy East and West* 30(3), 321–337. https://doi.org/10.2307/1399191.

Tillemans, T. J. F. (1990). *Materials for the study of Āryadeva, Dharmapāla and Candrakīrti: The Catuḥśataka of Āryadeva, chapters XII and XIII, with the commentaries of Dharmapāla and Candrakīrti: Introduction, translation, Sanskrit, Tibetan and Chinese texts, notes*. Vienna: Arbeitskreis für Tibetische und Buddhistische Studien, Universität Wien.

Tillemans, T. J. F. (2003). Metaphysics for Mādhyamikas. In G. B. J. Dreyfus and S. L. McClintock (Eds.), *The Svātantrika-Prāsaṅgika Distinction: What Difference Does a Difference Make?* (pp. 93–123). Boston: Wisdom Publications.

Tillemans, T. J. F. (2009). How do Mādhyamikas Think? Remarks on Jay Garfield, Graham Priest and Paraconsistent Logic. In J. L. Garfield, M. D'Amato, and T. J. F. Tillemans (Eds.), *Pointing at the Moon: Buddhism, Logic, Analytic Philosophy* (pp. 83–100). New York: Oxford University Press.

Tillemans, T. J. F. (2011). How Far Can a Mādhyamika Buddhist Reform Conventional Truth? Dismal Relativism, Fictionalism, Easy-Easy Truth, and the Alternatives. In Cowherds (Ed.), *Moonshadows: Conventional Truth in Buddhist Philosophy* (pp. 152–165). New York: Oxford University Press.

Tillemans, T. J. F. (2016). *How Do Madhyamikas Think?: And Other Essays on the Buddhist Philosophy of the Middle*. Boston: Wisdom Publications.

Tillemans, T. J. F. (2019). Mādhyamikas Playing Bad Hands: The Case of Customary Truth. *Journal of Indian Philosophy* 47(4), 635–644.

Tuck, A. (1990). *Comparative Philosophy and the Philosophy of Scholarship*. New York: Oxford University Press.

Tzohar, R. (2017). Does Early Yogācāra Have a Theory of Meaning? Sthiramati's Arguments on Metaphor in the Triṃśikā-bhāṣya. *Journal of Indian Philosophy* 45(1), 99–120. https://doi.org/10.1007/s10781-016-9300-4.

Vose, I. (2024). What in the World Does a Mādhyamika Rely On? Candrakīrti and the Prāsaṅgikas on the Value of the Conventional. Unpublished ms of key-note address to International Conference on Madhyamaka in India, Tibet, and Beyond, Austrian Academy of Sciences, Vienna, August 2024.

Vose, K. (2009). *Resurrecting Candrakirti: Disputes in the Tibetan Creation of Prasangika*. Boston: Wisdom Publications.

Waldron, W. (2003). *The Buddhist Unconscious: The Alaya-Vijñnāna in the Context of Buddhist Thought*. London: Routledge.

Waldron, W. (2023). *Making Sense of Mind Only: Why Yogācāra Matters*. Boston: Wisdom Publications.

Walsh, E. (2015). Relativism in Buddhist)hilosophy: Candrakīrti on Mutual Dependence and the Basis of Convention. In K. Tanaka, Y. Deguchi, J. L. Garfield, and G. Priest (Eds.), *The Moon Points Back* (pp. 220–244). New York: Oxford University Press.

Westerhoff, J. (2010). *Twelve Examples of Illusion.* New York: Oxford University Press.

Westerhoff, J. (2016). On the Nihilist Interpretation of Madhyamaka. *Journal of Indian Philosophy* 44(2), 337–376.

Wittgenstein, L. (1922). *Tractatus Logico-Philosophicus.* New York: Harcourt, Brace, & Company, Inc.

Wittgenstein, L. (1969). *On Certainty.* G. E. M. Anscombe and G. H. von Wright (Eds.). New York: Harper's & Row.

Wood, T. (1995). *Nāgārjunian Disputations: Through an Indian Looking-Glass.* Honolulu: University of Hawai'i Press.

Yakherds. (2021). *Knowing Illusion: Bringing a Tibetan Debate into Contemporary Discourse.* Volumes 1–2. New York: Oxford University Press.

Zahavi, D. (2005). *Subjectivity and Selfhood: Investigating the First-Person Perspective.* Cambridge: The MIT Press.

Index

For the benefit of digital users, indexed terms that span two pages (e.g., 52–53) may, on occasion, appear on only one of those pages.